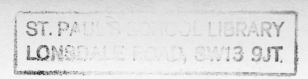
# PIMLICO

## 554

# 'HELL WITH A CAPITAL H'

Katherine Lambert has worked for many years as a
magazine and book editor and producer. She was
assistant editor of *The Bankers' Magazine*, editor of
*Expedition*, the house magazine of the World
Expeditionary Association, and is currently managing editor of the annual *Good Gardens Guide*. She
was co-editor, with Rosemary Verey, of *The
American Man's Garden* and *Secret Gardens*, and
assisted Peter King with *Scott's Last Journey*.

# 'HELL WITH A CAPITAL H'

An Epic Story of Antarctic Survival

---

## KATHERINE LAMBERT

*With an Introduction by Peter King*

Published by Pimlico 2002

2 4 6 8 10 9 7 5 3 1

First published in Great Britain by
Pimlico 2002

Pimlico
Random House, 20 Vauxhall Bridge Road,
London SW1V 2SA

Random House Australia (Pty) Limited
20 Alfred Street, Milsons Point, Sydney,
New South Wales 2061, Australia

Random House New Zealand Limited
18 Poland Road, Glenfield,
Auckland 10, New Zealand

Random House (Pty) Limited
Endulini, 5A Jubilee Road, Parktown 2193, South Africa

The Random House Group Limited Reg. No. 954009
www.randomhouse.co.uk

A CIP catalogue record for this book
is available from the British Library

ISBN 0-7126-7995-2

Papers used by Random House are natural,
recyclable products made from wood grown in sustainable forests;
the manufacturing processes conform to the environmental
regulations of the country of origin

Typeset by Deltatype Ltd, Birkenhead, Merseyside
Printed and bound in Great Britain by
Clays Ltd, St Ives PLC

To my father,
magician with words,
who told me about Ananias
and the strange physiognomy
of the snowy petrel

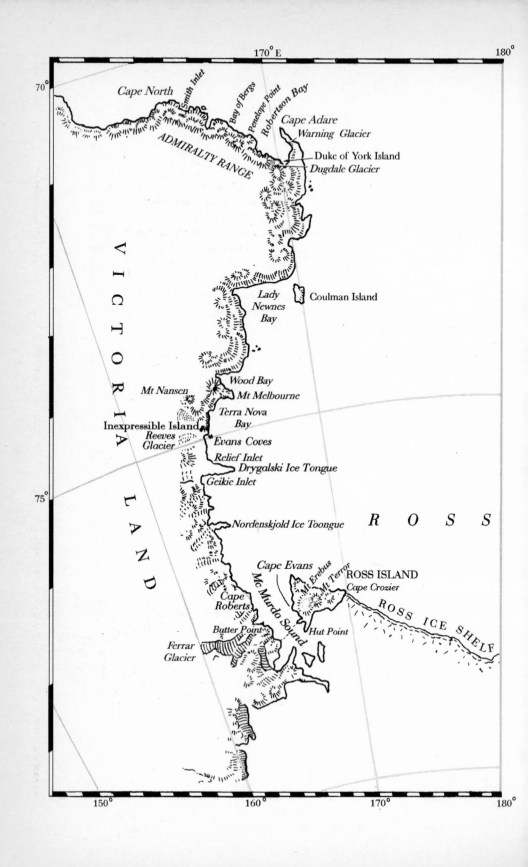

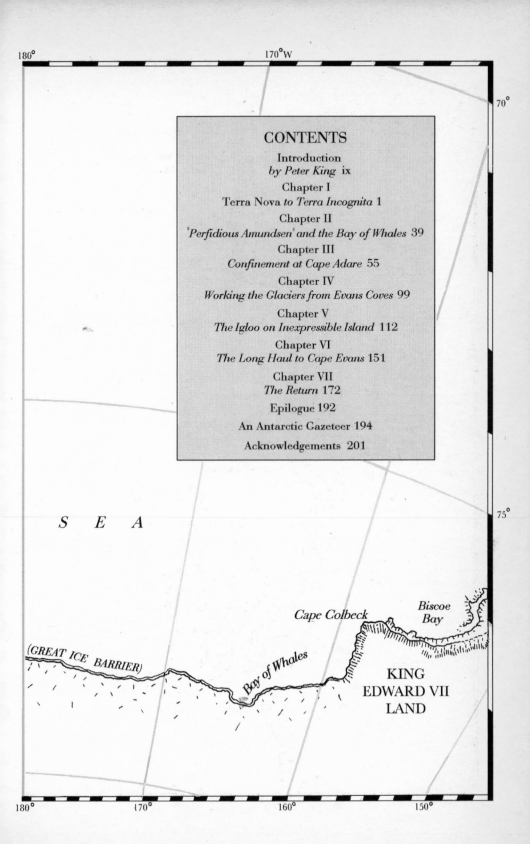

# CONTENTS

Introduction
*by Peter King* ix

# Introduction

## *by Peter King*

This is not an account of polar tragedy; it does not tell of mortal remains perfectly preserved in ice. Instead it chronicles a struggle for survival by a small group of men who passed through 'Hell with a capital H'* and who, against all the odds, came out the other side.

The six members of the Northern Party, led by Lieutenant Victor Campbell, had been specially chosen by Scott to concentrate on scientific research and exploration. Their remarkable story is retold here largely in their own words, from their diaries and notes. The diaries of four of the men have never been published before. What emerges is on the one hand a straightforward account of polar adventure, and on the other a chilling saga of misadventure, during which they endured near-starvation, physical exhaustion and acute or debilitating illness, and experienced extremities of emotion that would have felled men of lesser resilience.

For the reader today it is difficult to imagine how primitive Antarctic exploration was at the beginning of the twentieth century. The scientist Raymond Priestley – the sole civilian member of the Northern Party, and the only one of the six to return later in life to the polar continent – made two further visits to Antarctica, in 1957 and 1959. On the second occasion he realised that he had seen more of the coastline in those two months than he had seen in three years, half a century earlier, and recalled: 'We were in the old days the prisoners of our limitations.'

Those limitations were legion. No aeroplanes to drop off team members, lift off casualties, bring in supplies. A vast land with no communications – no wireless, no telegraph system, no mobile telephones, no satellite technology. When Scott and his companions died in March 1912, the world knew nothing of the disaster until their ship, *Terra Nova*, reached New Zealand almost a year afterwards.

---

* A remark made by their leader to another number of the party.

At the beginning of the twenty-first century – in the year that this book is published – *The Times* of 18 May 2002 reported on a lone English explorer, Dave Mill, whose ambition had been to conquer the North Pole solo, by walking some 500 miles from Resolute Bay in Canada. He had been stopped in his tracks 200 miles after he had set out, as the pack ice broke up all around him unseasonably early. Immediately a rescue operation swung into action. His back-up emergency team pinpointed his position by satellite. He e-mailed them a digital image of the 400-metre landing strip he had created with the aid of his sledge-boat. A light aircraft set off from Resolute Bay on the evening of 19 May and landed safely on his makeshift runway at 2 a.m. the following morning. By 8 a.m. that day he had been rescued. With an eye to history, his comment to *The Times* by satellite telephone was: 'As I walk, I can feel what Shackleton felt and what Scott must have experienced. They had no rescue aircraft and no mobile phones. They were the first adventurers.'

Historically, of course, Mill was mentally wiping out nearly two and a half thousand years of exploration since Pytheas in 325 BC had embarked on one of the most remarkable voyages of discovery ever made. His journey had expanded the limits of the known world northward as far as the Arctic Circle. Yet it was not until 1773, almost two thousand years later, that the Antarctic Circle was crossed for the first time by James Cook, the first explorer of the heroic age. A hundred years later, Sir James Clark Ross sailed along hundreds of miles of Antarctic coastline, penetrated the continent as far as 78° 11'S, and fixed the position of the South Magnetic Pole with relative accuracy – an extraordinary tally of achievements. Ross was followed by Scott aboard *Discovery* in 1901–04 and Shackleton aboard *Nimrod* in 1907–09. All broke scientific and territorial barriers, yet Apsley Cherry-Garrard, a member of Scott's last expedition, was still able to write at its conclusion: 'the interior of this supposed continent is entirely unknown and uncharted except in the Ross Sea area, while the fringes of the land are only discovered in perhaps half a dozen places on a circumference of about eleven thousand miles.' Cook, Ross, Shackleton and Scott – and other great names before and in between – had still barely scratched the surface of Antarctica.

This book recreates the world in which Scott and his contemporaries operated – a world of sailing ships and sledges, of animal-driving and man-hauling, in which diaries, photographs and letters were the only reliable records of scientific achievement, daily life and private thoughts. From these, the six members of the Northern Party emerge as men of very different personalities. They became also a disciplined and positive force for good, with all – and one man in particular – working hard to make the team function, to prevent strife and to anticipate and deal with physical and mental stress. The outstanding member of the team was the naval surgeon Dr Murray Levick. He emerges from these pages as an unsung hero of the heroic age of polar exploration.

Those officers of Royal Navy status who took part in Scott's expeditions were obliged as a condition of service to keep diaries which might later be written up to form part of the official record rushed into print by Smith, Elder & Co in 1913, and of the body of scientific reports published over several years by the British Museum. Campbell and Levick both kept diaries, and so did Priestley, who, as one of the expedition's three geologists was anyway accustomed to writing comprehensive and accurate notes as part of the scientific discipline. The three 'men' of the party, Abbott, Dickason and Browning, who were carefully chosen from the most experienced seamen of the Royal Navy, were unusual in also choosing to keep written records.

Two types of diary were issued to members of the expedition – a 100-page book for daily use when in camp or aboard ship, and the so-called sledging diaries. The latter were small red-bound books that would slip easily into a pocket, and were written up in pencil (ink would run) in tents during breaks in daily travels. Those preserved today at the Scott Polar Research Institute in Cambridge show signs of hard wear and tear. When the sledgers returned to their base, the rough notes scrawled in the pages of the sledging diaries were worked up and added to the narrative of the 'fair copy' journals. These were rather splendid black, cloth-bound volumes, supplied as standard to the expedition by a City of London stationer. Levick broke his only stylographic pen during the voyage out to Antarctica, so he swopped his 12-bore double-barrelled shotgun for a crew member's fountain pen: 'This will give some idea of how the relative value of articles out here changes as their owner require them or not.'

Priestley alone of the Northern Party typed out his comprehensive diaries, on the machine allocated to Apsley Cherry-Garrard as editor of the 'in-house' magazine, *The South Polar Times*, and in 1914 polished them up in narrative form for publication as a book under the title *Antarctic Adventure*. There can be little doubt that he intended his notes for publication the moment he began them, otherwise he would have been unable to meet the rigorous timetable imposed by his publishers.

Levick was also racing to meet the keen publishing deadline of March 1914 set by Heinemann, publishers of his classic book *Antarctic Penguins*. This, a popular version of the careful zoological report he wrote for the British Museum Natural History series, was the outcome of copious observations taken when the Northern Party were living in the middle of a penguin rookery, and was graphically illustrated with his own photographs. Levick also supplied photographs for the reports on glaciology and physiography, and others for Priestley's book. The majority of the photographs for the second volume of the official account, *Scott's Last*

1. The keeping of diaries was regarded as an essential tool of polar expeditions. According to taste, they ranged from mere lists of facts and data to full-blown autobiography. Dr Murray Levick, who tended towards the latter, illustrated his fair-copy journal with photographs, usually his own.

*Expedition*, published by Smith, Elder in 1913, are his too. This was a remarkable effort, as he knew nothing about photography until he set out. Herbert Ponting, the expedition's 'camera artist', gave him lessons, and, in Priestley's view, 'some very peculiar things happened while he was learning, but he finished up second only to the master himself, with this advantage over [Ponting] – he would take anything he was asked'.

Like his photographs, Levick's diaries reveal an ability to observe both the natural world and his fellows. He writes simply and directly, with touches of humour and introspection. Unlike Campbell, he was under no obligation to use his diaries as the basis of an official publication; unlike Priestley, his ambition was not to produce a narrative of the Northern Party but a book of popular zoology, and there is some evidence that he also had ambitions to become a novelist and travel writer. His journals display a freshness uninhibited by ulterior motives or 'political correctness', and it is upon them that this book is principally based.

George Murray Levick, born in 1877 in Newcastle-upon-Tyne, was the only child of a civil engineer who must have been reasonably well off. He was sent to St Paul's School in London, where he was a scholar. His last school report does not record any particular academic brilliance, although he was said to be a keen rugby player, a good oar and a magnificent gymnast. His friend Priestley wrote that it was at St Paul's that Levick developed the concern for physical fitness and enthusiasm for outdoor activities which remained with him always and which, combined with a very real interest in his fellow men, 'became the dominant factor in his life'. Levick's aim was to be a surgeon, so after leaving school he went, not to university, but to one of London's great teaching hospitals, St Bartholomew's. He qualified as a surgeon in 1902, and in the same year was commissioned as a surgeon/doctor in the Royal Navy. This allowed him to continue his athletic and sporting activities in a milieu similar to that he had previously enjoyed, meeting many of his old friends on the field of play.

When he joined the Royal Navy, Levick, twenty-six years old, was at the height of his physical powers. After nearly a year of service on shore, he earned a commission aboard HMS *Bulwark*, flag ship of the Mediterranean Fleet, following which he served on HMS *Queen* and at the Royal Hospital, Chatham. A new challenge came in 1908. He was appointed to the battleship HMS *Essex*, commanded by Scott, who was drawing together his crew for the polar expedition of 1910. The following year he went to HMS *Ganges*, a boys' training ship, as medical officer with special responsibility for physical training, before being selected by Scott.

Levick's duties had not, as far as we know, been spelled out in detail by Scott, but no doubt he expected to deal with routine accidents and would have hoped to pursue his new interest in diet and fitness. In fact, as expedition doctor his medical duties were few – although on two occasions he was literally responsible for saving life and limb. Instead, he acted primarily as photographer and zoologist, and became increasingly skilled at both. His journals show that he was also fully alert to the psychological problems facing a small group of men forced to rely on themselves and each other for extended periods. He used a variety of methods to ease difficulties – jokes, lectures, physical exercises and medicinal tots of brandy – but we are also able to read in his journals comments of a critical nature on other members of the party (a rare experience in Antarctic literature, since they are edited out of most 'fair copies'). As their situation worsened, Levick's criticisms diminished.

This is the background to the unknown man who emerges as the star of this book at the point where he joined Scott's expedition. It was at one and the same time a select and a motley group. The scientists had been chosen by Dr Edward Wilson, Chief of Scientific Staff. Lieutenant Edward Evans as second-in-command of the expedition and Campbell as First Mate of *Terra Nova* were largely responsible for picking the ratings. Scott naturally took a keen interest in interviewing the officers himself. (Some 8,000 had volunteered for the 60-odd places.) Most of the recruits were strangers to one another, and strangers to the Antarctic. They had volunteered for many reasons: for adventure, for love of the icy wastes, to advance careers, to escape from wives. The senior members certainly were not in it for the money – Scott had found it so difficult to meet the budget that many of the officers had been required to forego their salaries if the expedition ran into a third year, while a major consideration in accepting two of their number was that they brought with them the substantial sum of £1,000 each.

From very early on, Campbell's small group was set apart from the rest of the expedition. The six men were scheduled to operate independently of both the Polar Party and the rest of the shore party (scientists and others) whose base was Cape Evans. As a roving satellite group, the Northern Party were therefore detached physically from the other members of the expedition and cut off from the momentous events in train. They gathered snatches of news from time to time from the crew of *Terra Nova* as they were embarked and disembarked at different destinations, but they would not be able to grasp the whole picture until the very end of the expedition. They knew nothing of the drama unfolding at Cape Crozier – which forms the heart of Cherry-Garrard's polar classic, *The Worst Journey in the World* – nor of the acute attack of scurvy which nearly killed Scott's second-in-command, nor of the growing anxiety about the fate of the Polar Party and the final news of their deaths. They were in effect confined within their own small bubble, seeing the wider picture through a limited and distorted lens.

In London and the wider world, the focus was all on Scott – his personality and his strategy. When it became clear that he and Amundsen would be racing to the Pole, opinions were divided largely along national lines. But nobody – not those eagerly awaiting the outcome of Scott's expedition, nor those encamped in Antarctica – expected Scott, Wilson, Oates, Bowers and Petty Officer Evans to perish. Far less did they envisage that the Northern Party would be the main focus of concern for seven long months. However, once Campbell and his five companions were beyond recall, this was very much the case. The leader of one of Scott's other scientific groups, Griffith Taylor, wrote: 'I had never anticipated any serious accident to the Pole party . . . But I should not have been surprised to hear of disaster in Campbell's northern party, for no one had lived through a winter in such a fashion before.'

1

# *Terra Nova* to *Terra Incognita*

## 1 June 1910–25 January 1911

For centuries London's great artery, the Thames, has hosted events of national mourning or rejoicing. The Lord Mayor's Show was held on the river annually from the fifteenth century until the City of London reluctantly ceded control of the capital's waterway in 1857. In the winter of 1564–5 a great freeze enabled archery, dancing and the roasting of an ox to take place, and 130 years later crowds walked across the ice to mourn the death of Mary II, William III's queen, at Westminster Abbey. On 15 May 1749 the Duke of Richmond staged a famous fireworks display from his town house in Whitehall. In 1806, draped in black, Nelson's coffin was borne silently upstream from Greenwich for his funeral at St Paul's Cathedral; in 1965 Churchill's was the next to be accorded this sombre honour.

Further east the buildings which line the banks of the Thames are (fewer and fewer now) wharves and warehouses, the river craft ocean-going liners or dirty great instruments of commerce. This mercantile stretch has seen its displays of pageantry too: Henry VIII launched his flagship 'Great Harry', built at Deptford, with a spectacular ceremony at Greenwich in 1514; 335 years later a royal procession sailed down the river to mark the opening of the Coal Exchange in the City of London. Still further east, as it winds towards the sea, the Thames transcribes a perfect 'U', which since the early nineteenth century has enclosed and protected the Isle of Dogs and the West India Docks.

Here, on 1 June 1910, all eyes were on an old terrier of a ship – the *Terra Nova*, a 3-masted, 747-ton Dundee whaler with massive oak timbers and a bow sheathed in iron plates. Veteran of many seasons' hard labour among the ice floes, the paint and patches applied during her latest refit could not disguise her age.* On one of her journeys she had

---

* *Discovery* had been custom-built for Scott's first Antarctic expedition, and *Fram* was sixteen when she sailed under Amundsen. *Terra Nova* was now twenty-six.

1

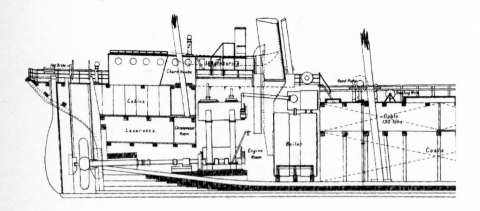

TERRA

Scale, ⅛"

been crushed in pack ice to the point where her hatches had popped out of line.

*Terra Nova* had not been Scott's first choice for his second Antarctic venture. He had hoped to sail again aboard *Discovery*, the ship which, having survived two winters in the pack in 1902 and 1903, had brought his first National Antarctic Expedition safely home. She too was a Dundee whaler, but had been designed by no less a person than the Chief Contractor of the Admiralty, and had been disposed of by the Admiralty in the sour aftermath of the expedition for £10,000 (well over £500,000 today). The price for *Terra Nova* was £5,000 down and £7,500 to pay. She had also played a small part in Scott's first Antarctic expedition, backing up *Morning* as an extra, unexpected and unwelcome relief ship. Now she was the bride; by an irony of fate her bridesmaid *Discovery* was also moored in the West India Docks on that day in June, looking rather tatty and weather-beaten.

Scott's last enterprise must be viewed in the wider context of Arctic and Antarctic exploration. His was just the latest in a long line of expeditions inspired by curiosity, patriotism or greed to make sense of the blank canvases at opposite ends of the globe. The fantastical maps devised by

2

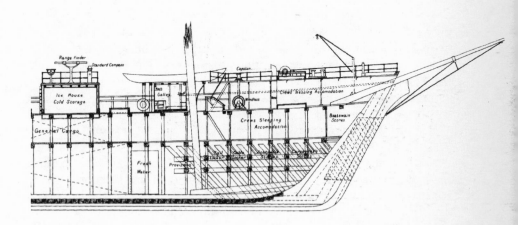

2. The expedition ship, *Terra Nova*, was a sturdy 747-ton Dundee whaler, three-masted and barque-rigged and carrying auxiliary steam and screw.

early cartographers had been progressively corrected, unexplored land masses claimed, lucrative whale and seal fishing grounds identified. By 1910 Antarctica had taken shape as a large continent (but by no means as large as originally envisaged) protected by a broad ice-belt. The exploration of this inner core was a genuine scientific enterprise, the race to the South Pole a purely human conceit.

Most of the eighteenth- and nineteenth-century naval ships and whalers had approached Antarctica from Australia, South America or South Africa via Cape Horn. It was the British explorers, Ross, Shackleton and Scott himself, who had established a tradition of using New Zealand as their terminus. For Scott this pinpointed Ross Island as his landing point in Antarctica, gave him a direct route to the Pole, and dictated the number and extent of scientific researches his team would be able to undertake. The *Terra Nova* expedition's brief was to make a thorough geographical

3

and scientific survey of the territory spreading out eastwards, westwards and possibly also northwards from their anticipated base on Ross Island. To the south lay the Pole, and data would be collected along that route also.

Scott's ambitions were sharply defined by the weather – anticipated and actual. By setting out in June, he expected to arrive in Antarctica in plenty of time to establish his main base and to lay the essential depots on the route to the Pole before the onset of winter. This interlude would also allow substantial scientific journeys to be made before all work closed down for the dead months of darkness, which lasted from the middle of May until the end of July. Towards the end of spring – August to October – the five-month push for the Pole would take place, while the rest of the expedition would fulfil other scientific programmes. The Pole reached and the Polar Party safely back at base, the expedition would reassemble to await the return of the ship. A contingency plan allowed for a further winter on the continent.

For many of the men assembled at the dockside, it was an unknown and unquantifiable challenge, but a few had accompanied Scott to Antarctica nine years earlier – the present expedition's Chief of Scientific Staff, Dr Edward Wilson, Petty Officers Evans, Crean, Williamson and Heald, Chief Stoker Lashly, and Lieutenant Edward Evans, who had been second-in-command of *Morning*. The bo'sun Alf Cheetham and the motor engineer Bernard Day were old 'Shackleton men', members of the 1907–09 *Nimrod* expedition, and Cheetham was unique in having served both with Scott aboard *Discovery* and with Shackleton.

The peripatetic nature of naval and scientific life – the twin poaching grounds for British polar expeditions of the period – meant that men were arbitrarily thrown together, then as cavalierly split up. Although some remained fast friends (Scott and Wilson, for example), most philosophically shed the companions with whom they had shared hilarious, horrendous, tedious and embarrassing experiences for months and years, and prepared to go through the same thing again with a fresh set.

Raymond Priestley had been studying geology at Bristol University College when he was picked for Shackleton's *Nimrod* team, and had noted then one of the draws (or drawbacks in the case of a man as introverted as Scott*) of being an explorer on a high-profile expedition: 'Before they had had a chance to justify themselves the men were fêted, wined and dined, exposed to flattery and special attention, listened to with respect as authorities on subjects of which they often knew little enough . . . It

---

* Although Scott did gain a wife, Kathleen Bruce, as a result of his lionising by London hostesses.

requires the nerves and temperament of a test match cricketer of the better sort to withstand the strain.'*

For many months Lieutenant Edward ('Teddy') Evans and the acting First Mate, Lieutenant Victor Campbell, had been in the forefront of the action at the West India Docks. Evans had been given the job of supervising the refitting, refurbishing and customising of the ship in her painful transition from whaler to polar explorer. This included fitting bunks for the officers and some of the men (the rest slept in hammocks), an ice house, rooms to house instruments and chronometers, laboratories and clothing stores. Campbell and the two other senior officers, Harry Pennell and Henry Rennick, plus Henry Bowers as stores officer, had joined six weeks before the sailing date of 1 June. In order to achieve the impossible, Evans used cajolery, Campbell intimidation. They made a powerful duo. Scott, who had been pressurised by Sir Clements Markham, President of the Royal Geographical Society, into accepting Evans as his second-in-command, was mollified.† He was also impressed by Campbell's quiet efficiency and Bowers' infinite capacity for hard work.

Amazingly, the ship was ready on time. The razzmatazz started up as she cast off and slipped slowly down to the mouth of the Thames – attended by the travellers' families and friends, assorted bigwigs and 'gold lace and cocked hats and dignitaries enough to run a Navy', according to one American guest. Almost every craft on the river was dressed overall for the occasion, and *Terra Nova* herself sported both the White Ensign of the British Navy and the esteemed burgee of the Royal Yacht Squadron.‡ Dockers, seamen and East Enders in their thousands cheered from the banks, accompanied by a chorus of shrill blasts and mournful hoots from the assembled shipping.

In what had become a polar tradition, this populist and patriotic send-off was repeated on a grand scale as *Terra Nova* steamed through the lines of battleships and cruisers of the Home Fleet massed in Portland Bay.§ 'They clapped us heartily as we passed each ship, the good old British cheer not being allowed', wrote one of the Petty Officers, George Abbott, in his diary. Letting themselves out through the 'hole in the wall' (a gap in

---

* From a lecture to the Australian Institute of Philosophy and Psychology in 1935. Priestley's audience no doubt appreciated the cricketing analogy.

† Evans had announced his own Antarctic ambitions before Scott put his bid in, but agreed to abandon them and add the funds he had raised to Scott's kitty, in return for his appointment as deputy leader.

‡ Scott's membership of the RYS, which cost the expedition £100, carried with it the tangible advantage that his ship would not be bound by normal Board of Trade loading regulations, so *Terra Nova* sank guiltlessly lower into the water as her stores were packed in.

§ *Discovery* had been honoured by a visit from members of the Royal Family during the Cowes Regatta of 1901, and *Nimrod* likewise in 1907, when the carefully stage-managed occasion was the Naval Review of the Fleet.

ın-made breakwater), they rounded Portland Bill at sunset and
ed their way westward past Land's End and along the coasts of
ɾnwall and north Devon to Wales, where they were greeted with
genuine enthusiasm by the people and dignitaries of the City of Cardiff, a
notably generous donor to the expedition's depleted coffers.* Visitors were
given guided tours of the ship at 2s. 6d. a head, with proceeds going to the
Cardiff Infirmary; the Lord Mayor hosted a party at City Hall, complete
with all-male choir, and PO 'Taff' Evans disgraced his Welsh patrimony
by a drunken binge in front of his home crowd. After a fortnight's
junketing – a long fortnight for Scott, who instinctively shrank from the
national limelight – the ship at last made it down the Bristol Channel and
out into the Atlantic on 15 June.

Scott himself was not on board. He stayed behind to drum up additional
funds before making all speed to South Africa for the same purpose. He
was finding money-grubbing as distasteful as ever. On the eve of *Terra
Nova*'s departure, Teddy Evans wrote lightheartedly: 'While we go on a
yachting cruise, visiting various parts of the Empire, Captain Scott has the
unpleasant duty of going round with the hat in his hand, beseeching people
for money to pay his staff.' It was uphill work, partly due to 'expedition
fatigue' generated by his own and Shackleton's earlier journeys, and
compounded by competition from Shackleton's own projected trans-
Antarctic venture. It did not help that Edward VII had died on 6 May, and
that the country was limping between inconclusive elections.

Scott was determined, however, that the naval contingent, and as many
scientists as possible, would sail together to the Antarctic, so that they
would arrive physically hardened and psychologically bonded. Only nine
men would join the ship at her last country of call, New Zealand – the
three geologists, the four animal handlers and the motor expert, none of
whose services were required at that stage. (Lawrence 'Titus' Oates, the
horse expert, had also been due to join in New Zealand, but Scott had been
so taken with him that he had enrolled him as a midshipman for the
journey out.) The final absentee was the photographer, Herbert Ponting,
who had failed to assemble all his equipment in time to sail from London.

In Scott's absence, life on board *Terra Nova* was regulated by a
triumvirate of very different characters. In temporary command was the
affable and gregarious Teddy Evans. He was to prove a popular leader
(although Scott's brother-in-law Wilfrid Bruce, a member of the ship's
crew who had been sent to Russia to help collect the dogs and ponies, later
described him disparagingly as 'a sort of Peter Pan'). He had already
revealed himself an inspired fundraiser (far better than Scott), and now
showed talent as an emollient, smoothing over differences and welding

---

* Cardiff contributed some £2,500, plus an equivalent amount in coal, oil, scientific
equipment, etc.

together the rag-bag of civilians, officers, ratings, navy and merchant navy men. Although the way he had insinuated himself into the expedition had raised a question mark in some minds, and others came later to regard him as slippery and self-serving, at this stage his tact and bonhomie were invaluable. He fostered a holiday atmosphere, and the voyage out remained, for those who survived, a memorably enjoyable part of the expedition.

Having played a key role in bringing the ship up to scratch, Victor Campbell turned his attention to her human cargo. He was one of the 'hungry hundred' – officers of the merchant marine who were allowed to cross over to the Royal Navy during a period of expansion at the turn of the twentieth century. Although he had retired in 1907 at the early age of thirty-four, marital problems had prompted him to return to sea; he was now on the navy's Emergency List. He set a high standard of routine and discipline and maintained it rigorously throughout the seven-month voyage. Generally mild of manner and soft-spoken, his voice could rise to a penetrating rasp, 'audible', according to one of the geologists, Frank Debenham, in a *Polar Record* article, 'in a gale of wind from the poop all over the ship's deck' – and woe betide anyone who 'dropped some tar on his lily white decks, or failed to recognize the correct halliard'.

Although 'The Wicked Mate', as Campbell was soon known, joined in the horseplay which became an integral part of shipboard life and could take a joke against himself with the best, he was apt to lose his temper with awesome speed – according to Debenham, 'on deck you learned to jump to his bidding as if he had a rope's end in his hand'. 'I was very frightened of Campbell', wrote Apsley Cherry-Garrard, a junior member of the expedition. But one less easily cowed, 'Uncle Bill' Wilson, felt this was a bit of a front: 'Campbell as the "President of the Purity Brigade" wears a halo, but it has been broken so often that it hardly holds together and has a permanent cant.' Charles Wright, the expedition's physicist, observed that he was 'supposed to be a martinet and tries to live up to it'.

The third of the ship's officers, Lieutenant Harry Pennell, had no need of such tactics. Wilson considered him 'by far the most capable man on the whole expedition', and Scott and Evans had nothing but praise for his attitude and his seamanship. He slept, or rather cat-napped, under the chart table, and spent any spare moment pursuing magnetic and ornithological studies. He also found time to watch over the men on the messdeck, listening to their complaints, settling quarrels and keeping an eye on their alcohol intake. Although on the voyage out he was merely the navigator, he would take over command of *Terra Nova* once the shore party, including Evans and Campbell, had been disembarked. Pennell's job was as onerous as any. Not only did he act as chauffeur, retrieving or depositing various members of the party at preordained points, but in all he made three arduous journeys from and to New Zealand in order to prevent the ship being frozen into the pack. The zig-zag trail of *Terra Nova*'s journeys mapped in *Scott's Last Expedition*\* testifies to his industry. Pennell carried another burden of responsibility. Because it had been decided after the bruising *Discovery* experience not to overwinter the ship in Antarctica, no relief ship had been laid on. If *Terra Nova* were to be lost, the whole shore party would be in limbo, their fate uncertain.

Cherry-Garrard, who apart from being one of the youngest of the group had signed on as a complete neophyte,† described the routine on board with a rather charming assumption of seafaring knowledge: 'Watches were of course consigned immediately to the executive officers. The crew was divided into a port and starboard watch, and the ordinary routine of a sailing ship with auxiliary steam was followed.' Officers and scientists alike pitched in to help the lower ranks, and much of the heavy-duty work, such as heaving coal, shifting cargo or pumping (from the start the ship had leaked persistently), was done by calling for volunteers. This may have made these sweaty and exhausting chores seem less like drudgery but placed an unfair burden on life's suckers, of whom Cherry-Garrard, good-natured to a fault and anxious to prove himself, was a prime example. If Abbott were a typical seaman, however, pumping out the bilges was not unenjoyable: 'this is rather fine exercise & is done in the fresh air . . . Many an hour we spent pumping'.

Despite this convivial team atmosphere, traditional naval barriers were not dismantled. On 15 July the ceremony of 'crossing the line', during which the polar novices of all ranks were treated to a good ducking, was to bring the usual reversal of roles: PO Evans was cast as Father Neptune and PO Browning as his queen, 'the spotted Amphitrite', while Captain Oates and Lieutenant Atkinson were given walk-on parts as bears. Taff Evans seized the opportunity to make sly digs at his superiors, much enjoyed by the messdeck: 'Is your good ship towing a sea anchor, or is it those ariel [sic] observation wires that so often bring the Officer of the Watch up with a jerk; or else perhaps your rudder is athwartships with carrying too much weather helm which checks your way, as your ship seems remarkably slow; but I presume that she will go a long way in a long time. I think also that a few more steadies from your worthy Navigator would be beneficial to you.' Neptune's speech and the aquatics which followed were recorded *verbatim* by several of the ratings (here by Abbott).

But there was little relaxation of service etiquette. Officers continued to address ratings by their surnames, and to be addressed in their turn as 'Sir'

---

\* The official two-volume account, published by Smith, Elder in 1913.

† He and Oates, who had paid £1,000 apiece to join the expedition, were classed vaguely as 'adaptable helpers'.

or 'Mr'.* Naval routines were rigorously observed. The Sunday service was followed by 'rounds', on which the captain, the two senior doctors, Wilson and Levick, and the other officers filed solemnly round inspecting the ship, including the men's quarters and the engine room, for hygiene and orderliness. When the ship's carpenter left a lamp alight in the hold, setting off a small fire, he was immediately 'logged' and fined, *pour encourager les autres.*†

Gerard Fiennes wrote in the *Pall Mall Gazette* in 1912: 'We expect our bluejackets to take part of their wages in the coin of flattery.' They took the other part in the coin of maltreatment. Basic rates of pay had changed little since the 1850s, and it was almost impossible for ratings to cross over from messdeck to wardroom. When *Terra Nova* set sail, a naval commander could still mete out the following punishments without trial: reduction to the ranks, solitary confinement for up to two weeks, imprisonment for up to three months, dismissal with disgrace. Crimes included swearing, gambling, drunkenness and negligence.

Times were changing, however. Although Scott had used his powers on the *Discovery* expedition briefly to clap the lazy and insubordinate cook in irons, the crew of *Terra Nova* did not expect – or receive – draconian treatment. Ratings volunteered for such expeditions in order to improve their career prospects and to escape from the mindless and arbitrary discipline of ordinary naval life. From men such as Lashly and Evans, Scott would have acquired a reputation for treating the messdeck reasonably and rewarding loyal service. Elspeth Huxley, in her perceptive book *Scott of the Antarctic*, analysed the polar *status quo* thus:

> In outward forms, there was no equality. Wardroom, warrant officers' mess, messdeck; officers to order, men to obey. But in essentials there was an equality seldom realised, at that time, in British society, and never in the Royal Navy. When men trudge together in their harness, share a sleeping bag, starve together, fall down the same crevasse . . . when every man's life depends on the fidelity of his companions; then class distinctions vanish, not by a conscious effort but in the natural order of things. That they could reappear, without objection on either side, in the more normal conditions of shipboard life, was a phenomenon that nobody questioned; that, too, was in the natural order of things.

---

* Apsley Cherry-Garrard was thus 'Cherry/Chewwy/Cheery/Cheery Blackguard' to his peers and 'Mr Gerard' to the ratings.

† 'Logging' was described by Wilson as 'a very serious offence in the Navy . . . for it means that [the culprit] is brought up before the Captain and the First Lieutenant on the bridge, and generally reprimanded and then the offence is written down in ink in the official log book and signed by the offender himself on the spot'.

The trudging, starving and dying were yet to come, but already aboard *Terra Nova* the polarisation of wardroom and messdeck was noticeably less distinct.

Still, some of the scientists found the system difficult to adjust to. The physicist Charles Wright commented in an interview, apropos of Scott: 'I'd never had any experience with British naval captains, how much they were alone, how much like God almighty they had to be. He lived in his own quarters and got in touch with his sailors through his officers – he'd give an order and it'd be done at once, no questions at all. How different from the scientific approach where you're *expected* to argue!'*

Scott was not one to discuss his plans with all and sundry, so few were aware of the way his strategy for the expedition was maturing and refining itself in his mind. The Polar Party was not yet finalised, but a few individuals were already beginning to surface as dominant personalities. It seemed certain to their comrades that four at least would shape the course – perhaps even the outcome – of the expedition. Ponting voiced the opinion of many on board: 'the party selected by Captain Scott to accompany him on the last stage of the Pole journey were the four men who possessed the most striking personalities in our community'.

Of these four, Taff Evans was already a big man in the messdeck. During the epic 725-mile, 59-day trek that he, Lashly and Scott had made to the Ferrar Glacier in *Discovery* days, he had displayed commendable coolness when he and Scott had fallen into a seemingly bottomless crevasse. Evans was now PO First Class and had capitalised on his good fortune by specialising as a naval gunnery instructor. Impressively muscled, he was also adept with saw and needle, giving new life to sails, sleeping bags and sledges. Unfortunately, as had been revealed at Cardiff, he was also something of a boozer.

Lieutenant 'Birdie' Bowers of the Royal Indian Marine was physically decidedly unimpressive, being small and squat (5 feet, 4 inches and 12 stone), red-haired and beaky-nosed. At their first meeting Scott had more or less written him off, saying to Wilson, 'Well, we're landed with him now and must make the best of it.' But his Quasimodo exterior concealed awesome physical strength and endurance, a fierce will and an engaging personality. He was also a fine seaman and a first-rate stores manager. His social superiors freely acknowledged his power and charisma, while the messdeck, unsentimental judges of those set above them, were equally captivated.

Captain 'Titus' Oates (described after his death by Lord Curzon as 'the Eton boy, the cavalry officer, the South African hero, the English gentleman') also possessed the common touch which made him popular

---

* *The Canadian Magazine*, 1974: 'With Scott in Antarctica – Reminiscences by Charles Wright'.

with the 'men'. He stood out among the crowd of young recruits, isolated by a detachment bordering on misanthropy. Although he and his cabin-mate, Dr Edward ('Atch') Atkinson, struck up an almost wordless alliance, to the amusement of their more voluble companions, he much preferred animals to men (let alone, God forbid, women*). When he joined in shipboard pranks it was with gusto, but otherwise he pored silently over Napier's *History of the Peninsular War*, and his substitute for conversation was a series of muttered asides – waspish, acute and often amusing. Complicated, difficult and occasionally truculent, 'Soldier' came to be regarded with affectionate respect by his peers, and with admiration by the lower ranks. He treated both alike, often inviting favoured ratings to lunch or dine with him during interludes on shore.

It is impossible to find a single person with anything negative to say about Dr Edward Wilson. In Bowers' view, 'There is no qualifying *but* about "our Bill". He is without any *buts* – from any point of view.' Although godly through and through, no nauseating aura of sanctity clung to him. He more than held his own in the quips, arguments and wardroom tussles, and on one memorable occasion the unlikely trio of 'Uncle Bill', 'Cherry' and 'the Wicked Mate' were busily engaged in holding the largest cabin against all comers: 'It has lasted an hour or so, and half of us were nearly naked towards the finish, having had our clothes torn off our backs – all is excellent fun and splendid exercise.' Everyone sought Wilson's advice. Bowers described him as 'always the balancing point in the mess', and Scott relied on him utterly, as adviser, channel of communication, morale-booster and confidante. Only Kathleen, Scott's free-thinking wife, seems to have found his unshakeable integrity hard to take. For the rest: 'we all loved him', one of the young scientists stated simply.

The question of who would make up the party for the final assault on the Pole was at the back of everyone's mind, but the subsidiary scientific and exploration teams were now actively being lined up. None was more important to Scott than the so-called Eastern Party, the group Victor Campbell was chosen early on to lead. The six men were expected to play an important scientific role as well as undertaking the only pioneering piece of exploration of the entire expedition.

The Eastern Party's destination was King Edward VII Land, one of the outer edges of a wedge of Antarctica regarded by the British at that time as their particular fiefdom, the other side of the wedge being Victoria Land. As the skua flies, it is some 400 miles east of Cape Evans, at the other end of the Ross Ice Shelf, along which in 1841 James Clark Ross had been the first to sail, and which he had named the Great Ice Barrier. Ross had also

---

* A ditty composed by Teddy Evans ran: 'Who doesn't like women? / I, said Captain Oates, / I prefer goats.'

glimpsed King Edward VII Land, as had Scott in 1902, and Shackleton had made desperate attempts to land there in 1908. In the words of Roland Huntford, author of the thought-provoking *Scott and Amundsen*, '*Terra Nova* was not carrying one expedition, but two; Scott's main party for McMurdo Sound, and Campbell's group for King Edward VII Land.' Teddy Evans recorded that they were envied by many on board.

Apart from Campbell, five other men had to be chosen, and Raymond Priestley seemed a likely bet as scientist. Still only twenty-four years old, he had won his polar spurs on the *Nimrod* expedition, where he had served under T. Edgeworth David, the eminent Professor of Geology at Sydney University; after the expedition's dissolution, Priestley had continued to study under David and to write up the geological findings. He would now be the only scientist in an important group, an enviable position.

For such an extensive journey – nearly a year in the field – a doctor was required. Murray Levick was a practising naval surgeon and therefore qualified to deal with any medical crises that might arise. He had served under Scott in HMS *Essex*; like Dr Atkinson, he had been released by the Admiralty for his present assignment at Scott's own request. The Director-General of the Admiralty's Medical Department had endorsed both transfers on the grounds that they were two outstanding officers who would add lustre to a (then-ailing) branch of the service. In pecking order Levick stood above Atkinson. While Atkinson's special interests were bacteriology and parasitology, Levick had begun to make a name for himself in the spheres of diet and physical fitness. These were subjects that would require all his knowledge and ingenuity in the time to come.

Levick shared the cabin opposite Scott's with Atkinson and Oates, but this propinquity does not seem initially to have done him much good. Scott may have remembered Levick's name from *Essex* days, but not the man himself, writing in his unpublished diary: 'I am told that he has some knowledge of his profession, but there it ends. He seems quite incapable of learning anything fresh. Left alone, I verily believe he would do nothing from sheer lack of initiative.' Scott's snap judgements of Levick and Bowers were thus equally negative – and equally wrong. He dismissed Levick in a sentence – 'I am afraid there is little to be expected of him' – and clearly considered him little better than a half-wit, referring rudely to his 'vacant smile'. Even the fact that he 'takes any amount of chaff' was probably to Scott further proof of idiocy.

A later assessment of Levick by Frank Debenham in a *Polar Record* article presents a more balanced picture: 'His comparative slowness in taking in a situation, and his imperturbable good temper, ensured that he came in for more teasing than most, while his strength – he had been a notable rugger man – made him an excellent man in the sledge-races.' Levick himself was to write about 'chewing the mental cud', and this phrase summons up a vivid picture of his cheerful, slightly bovine countenance and leisurely mental digestive processes. Scott later admitted that 'Levick has a really charming nature', and 'The Old Sport' or 'Tofferino'* became a large and amiable foil for the quicker and more articulate members of the wardroom. Atkinson, his cabin-mate, was to write an affectionate character study in *The South Polar Times*:

> The Eastern Party. His Doctor and Storekeeper was a famous man. Rubicund of countenance and renowned in the world of sport; slow to move and act, but wise at bottom, he had a magnificent fund of anecdote. His aptitude for photography was marvellous as the Court records will show. His habits were secretive. Like a jackdaw he acquired articles and hid them, and then forgot all about them. There are few of the Southern Party who have not benefited from this forgetfulness.

The scientists also poked gentle fun at him. Wright recorded: 'Dr. Levick . . . has been trying since leaving England to get into his head the elements of Navigation. Has not succeeded and will not – is learning to bake bread for the Eastern Party. Is great at "attempts at" photography. On being asked to photo some of the chaps who had been down coal trimming he kept them shivering in their light (and black) clothes for a full half hour, while he got the instrument ready for use.' The geologist Griffith Taylor, who joined the ship in New Zealand, recorded an unusual experiment as they neared Antarctica: 'Members of the party were soon seized by Dr Levick in the interests of science. He was armed with a wonderful array of strips of coloured glass, and with a simple telescope, across which the glasses could be inserted. With these he examined the colour of all our eyes, for it is maintained that there is a perceptible change in the iris effect after a sojourn in polar regions.'

Although he was well liked, Levick appears to have been one of those men who, when thrown into a group, simply do not stand out. His name crops up only briefly in the diaries and books of his contemporaries and in the narratives of later polar biographers. The sharp wit of the young scientists, the irony of Oates, the boyish charm of Cherry-Garrard, the social skills of Priestley and Teddy Evans, the radiant mental energy of Bowers, Pennell and Wilson – Levick had none of these. But his

---

* Levick acquired his nicknames early on. Priestley recorded the circumstances in his diary: 'It seems that at Cardiff a certain well-known citizen invited two of the members of the Expedition to stay with him . . . Levick was one of the favoured ones & legend has it that on being introduced Dan [Ratcliffe] smote Levick on the chest with the classic remark "Hello! Tofferino me old sport, come along & have a drink." The name stuck & the only alternative name he is ever known by is "Mother" the reason for which latter is obvious when you have known him a few weeks.'

3. Biologist Denis Lillie examining the fruits of a trawl with Murray Levick (sporting his favourite rabbit's wool helmet worn as a cap) on the deck of *Terra Nova*. The scientific goals of the expedition were pursued throughout by all hands. The specimens landed ranged from microscopic organisms to giant sponges, and were carefully sifted before being bottled up to await dissection in British laboratories.

kindliness, compassion and total lack of ego helped him to increase in stature when later he and his five companions were faced with unimaginable hardships.

That left the three 'men' of the Eastern Party, who were chosen by Campbell after he had assessed their strength, stamina and team spirit during the journey out. Wilson had taken PO George Abbott under his capacious wing as assistant taxidermist, describing him as 'an exceedingly nice gentlemanly fellow and a tower of strength'. An amateur wrestler in the pink of condition (he kept up his 'Swedish exercises'* throughout the

---

\* Swedish exercises, designed to work on key muscles in rotation, formed part of the fitness regime of both Army and Navy. Levick was a great enthusiast, and Priestley considered they should be made compulsory in schools.

voyage, and even instructed Anton Omelchenko, the Russian pony-handler, in the art), he was also dextrous at sewing and carpentry.* In many ways he was cast in the same mould as Taff Evans. Able Seaman Harry Dickason had useful cooking skills, currently being enhanced by lessons from the ship's cook, and general resourcefulness (in Priestley's phrase, he 'would create a respectable fire out of a block of ice'). Petty Officer Frank Browning, the cheerful and adaptable all-rounder who was to act the part of Neptune's wife, would complete the party. In a rather Victorian turn of phrase, Priestley described all three men in a magazine article as 'physically hard, mentally alert and morally sound'.

Once the Eastern Party had been named, Campbell, Levick and Priestley began, naturally enough, to consolidate their position. 'In the port after-cabin', recorded Taylor, 'are held the mysterious consultations of the officers of the Eastern Party. It is rumoured that there is a capacious private store in which all unclaimed articles are deposited for their future benefit. But this is only a base libel, aroused by the orderly character of Lieutenant Campbell.' Levick, however, confirmed their thievery, revealing that they were squirrelling away secret stores around the ship: 'The others say they daren't leave anything lying about when any of the Eastern Party are around, and it is becoming a standard joke on the ship.' Teddy Evans's recollection was that the rot started at the top:

> Campbell had the face of an angel and the heart of a hornet. With the most refined and innocent smile he would come up to me and ask whether the Eastern Party could have a small amount of this or that luxury. Of course I would agree, and sure enough Bowers would tell me that Campbell had already appropriated a far greater share than he was ever entitled to of the commodity in question. This happened again and again, but the refined smile was irresistible.

On her journey to Antarctica, *Terra Nova* touched at three continents – Africa, South America and Australasia. The travellers stopped off at one paradisal island, Madeira, and one uninhabited one, South Trinidad. During their 150 days at sea they studied at first hand birds, fish, mammals and insects which few of their countrymen had ever seen. They sunbathed on deck or ran naked beneath rainstorm skies. They ate and drank their way steadily and convivially through the mountains of provisions that had initially caused the ship to sink alarmingly low in the water, including such

---

* Abbott was also something of a barber, giving both Teddy Evans and Scott a trim on deck. With the latter he had an interesting chat about 'sailing ships dying out in the Navy. I told him I once served in H.M.S. Raleigh (a full rigged ship). He of course knew her & admired her sailing powers.'

essential articles of the British diet as Oxo, Bovril, Colman's mustard, Lyle's golden syrup, Cooper's Oxford marmalade and 'King's Ale' (named for King Edward VII in 1902). They pooled their books, talked of home and Antarctica, argued, teased one another and laughed a lot. Even shovelling coal into the greedy innards of the ship's furnace was satisfying, hard, man's work. The journey was in essence what Scott had hoped it would be – a bonding and toughening Outward Bound course. Thoughts of the future were suspended in enjoyment of the present.

At this early stage of the expedition, morale was noticeably better than it had been aboard *Discovery*. Wilson, who had observed both, wrote to Scott from Madeira, their first port of call: 'You have got a crew of pirates that it would be exceedingly difficult to beat – or equal. I have never been with such a persistently cheery lot before.' Harmony had partly been arrived at, schoolboy fashion, through noisy horseplay. Frank Debenham, who joined the ship in New Zealand, described one 'grand scrap' in his vivid and light-hearted little book of the expedition:*

> The general principle was that no one must be left standing so if, when under a pile of struggling humanity, you caught sight of a leg in an upright position you grabbed it and tugged, regardless of whether it belonged to friend or foe. It raged up and down between the solid wardroom table and the cabins for a long time and great was the damage to shins and elbows. Everyone achieved great glory; it was a noble battle.

In Lillie's accompanying cartoon, 'Toffer' Levick is shown photographing the *mêlée* from the sidelines.

Following Scott's precepts, the naval officers and scientists were by and large a young bunch. Scott himself was the oldest at forty-two, followed by Ponting at forty. Wilson, Oates, Bowers, Campbell and Levick were in their thirties, Teddy Evans, Pennell, Cherry-Garrard and most of the scientists in their twenties. Tryggve Gran, the sole Norwegian, was just twenty-one. Among the scientists, Charles ('Silas'†) Wright, a 'lusty' and 'sturdy' physicist with a great capacity for work and an infectious sense of humour, was universally popular. Initially rejected for the expedition, he and another live wire, his friend the Australian geologist Griffith ('Griff') Taylor, had walked the fifty miles from Cambridge to London to persuade Wilson to change his mind. Wilson was duly persuaded. The marine biologist Denis Lillie was nothing like as straightforward. He was a deep

---

* *In the Antarctic: Stories of Scott's 'Last Expedition'*, John Murray, 1952.

† The nickname was bestowed on the grounds that it was the best Yankee name anyone could come up with. Wright was in fact Canadian.

thinker and a believer in reincarnation – he had been a Persian and a Roman in previous existences. He was an odd, tormented and interesting man, and a talented cartoonist. It was somehow symbolic that of the sixty-odd people on board he alone should have succumbed to an attack of measles; he was isolated in Ponting's darkroom until it wore off. Otherwise he shared a cabin with the other biologist, Edward Nelson, stigmatised early on by Scott as failing to pull his weight.

The baby of the expedition, the recently qualified naval cadet Tryggve Gran, shared the 'nursery' (which also housed the pianola) with the other children, Wright and Cherry-Garrard. In Norway he moved in the same exalted circles as Nansen, Borchgrevink and Amundsen, and his wealth (his father owned a shipyard), self-confidence bordering on arrogance, and skiing prowess were initially resented by some. Scott, who had persuaded him to join the expedition more or less sight unseen, after meeting him with Nansen, took one of his frequent dislikes to him. To his credit, Gran adapted himself quickly and well to the strange *mores* of his new companions. In addition to his primary job as ski instructor, he found himself at various times rescuing Cherry-Garrard from his sleep-walking trips, making a speech at the Christmas Day banquet and playing nine-a-side football on the ice. He even managed to defuse a row with Oates, who combined patriotism and xenophobia to an advanced degree, by confirming that in case of a war he would unhesitatingly side with Britain. He was to remain to the end of his very long life unswervingly loyal to Scott.

A question mark raises itself in the prurient twentieth-first-century mind – did any of these friendships have homosexual overtones? It is a point worth raising only because of the way such sentiments might affect the nature of life on board and on shore. The pointers are few and faint indeed – Oates' dislike of women and attachment to Atkinson; Lillie's revelation (uncorroborated) to Gran that he was a woman trapped in a man's body; the strenuous horseplay, much of which involved stripping each other naked; the girlish nicknames ('Penny' or 'Penelope' Pennell, 'Marie' Nelson, 'Jane' Atkinson); Teddy Evans's rallying call for a 'grand scrap' ('Hello girls, what's doing?'). But many of those involved were little more than the 'grown-up schoolboys' Debenham called them. Some were married; Pennell was shortly to father a child. It remains just that – a question mark.

*Terra Nova*, under sail and steam, took just over 200 days to reach Antarctica, of which about fifty were spent on shore. The first two short stop-offs increased the adventure-holiday atmosphere. On 23 June most of the officers were treated to three clean-clad and clean-shaven days in Madeira, like every other visitor enjoying the lush vegetation and breathtaking mountain views; more than most, they appreciated the local cuisine. (Abbott, however, was not impressed: 'Very badly drained town.

Should not like to live here.') The ratings were also given shore leave. Abbott, Browning and Dickason joined in a football match against the island's Eastern Telegraph Company ('Very pleasant game, but very hot, great merriment among the Natives when any of the players fell, the ground was awful pebbles'). The score was a diplomatic 1–1 draw.

One month later they were anchored off the rocky outcrop of South Trinidad Island, in Brazilian waters that teamed with shark, bream, rockfish, cod and mullet; fish was on the breakfast and supper menu for days. When they were not painting the ship and scraping the weed off her hull, ratings took cautious dips over the side. As described by Bowers in a letter to his mother, this stop-off was a somewhat surreal experience: 'Campbell and I sighted S. Trinidad from the fore yardarm on 25th [July], and on 26th, at first thing in the morning, we crept up to an anchorage in a sea of glass.' Eleven men set off to explore the island, their footsteps dogged 'with a sickly deliberation' by an army of cannibalistic land-crabs. 'Their dead staring eyes', shuddered the arachnaphobic Bowers, 'follow your every step as if to say, "If only you will drop down we will do the rest." To lie down and sleep on any part of the island would be suicidal.'

The shore party was soon groaning with booty – plants, birds and insects – but, alerted by a rocket fired from *Terra Nova*, hurried down to the shore, by then being assaulted by breakers of monstrous size. As their two small boats would have been pounded to bits close in, they hauled themselves across the 'awe-inspiring cauldron' hanging on to a rope – 'it meant a tough swim for all of us'. One of the stewards, Hooper, was lucky to escape with his life. Wilson remarked later to Cherry-Garrard that 'it was a curious thing that a number of men, knowing that there was nothing they could do, could quietly watch a man fighting for his life, and he did not think that any but the British temperament could do so'.

Dr Atkinson remained behind with a sick seaman, Brewster, before being picked up the following day, the two men having huddled together all night under the unnerving gaze of a circle of crabs and white terns. ('Birdie' Bowers would have been tested to his considerable limits). Rescuing the two Crusoes plus waterlogged 'clothes, watches and ancient guns, rifles, ammunition, birds (dead) and all specimens' was a hair-raising battle against 40-foot rollers. But, Bowers recounted reassuringly, 'we arrived aboard after eight hours' wash and wetness, and none the worse, except for a few scratches, and yours truly in high spirits'. It was classic *Boys' Own* stuff, and all the more enjoyable for that.

Alfred James Brewster was a most interesting member of the expedition – the seaman who never was. He is mentioned by name in Teddy Evans's *South with Scott* and as an anonymous 'sick man' in Abbott's diary and Bowers's letter to his mother, but he does not appear in the official list of expedition members. In fact, like Bowers, he fell down one of the ship's hatches, but unlike Bowers, he did not bounce; he damaged his knee so badly that he was taken off at Simonstown, in South Africa, rejoining her later. Brewster was evidently a remarkable man, breaking through the navy's glass ceiling and rising through the ranks. His wedding photograph shows him in the garb of a Warrant Officer, and having served in submarines during the First World War and on a supply ship during the Second, he retired as Commander. After his death his dress uniform was given to the Paignton Amateur Dramatic and Operatic Society, where it featured in a production of *HMS Pinafore*.

Simonstown, just south of Cape Town, they reached on 15 August after hitching an exhilarating ride on the westerlies, monitored by giant albatrosses wheeling about the ship and beautiful snowy petrels darting silently like bats in the night.* The rough weather caused a certain commotion on board. Browning described on 1 August 'having lively time in galley, getting washed out occasionally followed by pots and pans'; the 'nautical lingo' was freely used on several occasions. The Sunday service was cancelled that week, but in his diary Campbell wrote, lyrically for him: 'We had our hardest breeze two days before making Cape of Good Hope. Being down to lower topsails and foresail, we carried the breeze with us right in to False Bay.'

Visitors came on board (after Abbott had showed a party round, 'one Gentleman & Lady wrote to me & sent me a Pipe. I put the Gentleman first because it was he wrote to me, not the Lady') and the expedition cat was the focus of attention. Having started life as a pub kitten, Nigger had been adopted by Browning: 'at first was rather disliked as he was kicking up a row all day. No one seemed to look after him, so I took on the job myself, and as he grew older and learnt a few tricks as jumping, climbing a rope, and going up aloft he became quite a favourite with all hands'.

As usual, the expedition was fêted at every level. Abbott's diary gives an interesting insight into the shore life of a popular and gregarious member of the messdeck. He dined and played billards with Oates and Atkinson, attended church, and was invited to a 'smoker' at the Masonic Club: 'We had a jolly good time here; some of the fair sex were present & dancing was indulged in.' But there was some serious business too. On 22 August, 'Capt. Evans asked me if I was keen on landing in the Antarctic. I said yes & thought every one on board was. He said I should probably land with the Eastern Party as Lieut. Campbell wanted me, so I was mightily pleased, but had to keep it a secret.'

---

* These fascinating birds, which breed in large colonies on bare rock 200 miles inland, have a prominent tube on their beak which ornithologists now think operates as an in-built desalination plant. Like other scavengers, such as Manx shearwaters, they seem able to smell their underwater prey from the air.

In fact Simonstown marked the start of a new and less carefree stage. Apart from anything else, 'The Owner' was back. Scott, who had sailed from England on 16 July, had only succeeded in raising £1,000 or so from the diamond- and gold-rich South Africans. The expedition was still £7,000 short of funds, and things were looking serious.* Wilson, much to his chagrin, was dispatched to Melbourne by liner to continue the distasteful job of money-raising, and to act as escort to Kathleen Scott, Hilda Evans and his own wife Oriana.† Having refitted and restocked, *Terra Nova* set off for Melbourne in her turn. It would take forty days.

Scott's main purpose in joining the South Africa–Australia leg of the journey was to assess in greater depth the strengths and weaknesses of his team, both individually and in groups, and to draw up a framework of overlapping assignments. A certain amount of canvassing and jockeying for position had already taken place among his juniors. Bowers revealed nonchalantly to his mother: 'By the bye, Evans and Wilson are very keen on my being in the Western Party‡ while Campbell wants me with him in the Eastern Party. I have not asked to go ashore, but am keen on anything and am ready to do anything. In fact there is so much going on that I feel I should like to be in all three places at once – East, West and Ship.' Wilson would also have liked to poach Campbell, having earmarked him as 'a delightful man, pleasant and sensible, and rather quieter than most of the others. I should have liked to have him.'

30 September was an important day for the messdeck, as Browning recorded: 'Capt Scott had ships company aft and made known his selection for landing party, was very pleased to hear my name among them. I was to form one of the Eastern Party under Lieu V Campbell and try to get to King Edward VII Land.' The thoughts of all began to turn to the job ahead; sledges and sleeping bags were inspected and improved. As they rounded the south coast of Australia the prolonged summer holiday was relegated to its proper status as a transitory idyll.

The nine-word telegram lurking innocently among the parcel of mail awaiting collection in Melbourne on the evening of 12 October read: 'Beg leave to inform you *Fram* proceeding Antarctic. AMUNDSEN.' Scott's streak of pessimism in a way helped to insulate him against the shock of the news. It was just the latest of a series of unwelcome surprises that had popped up like targets in a shooting gallery from the moment his expedition had coughed into life. Even Peary's achievement at the opposite end of the

---

* The total estimated cost was set at £50,000, some £2½ million today.

† This left Cherry-Garrard as the only zoologist. He performed well – the 'helper' was proving himself extremely adaptable.

‡ Bowers means here the main shore party, from which the selection would later be made of the men laying depots for the party trying for the Pole, and the Polar Party itself.

globe had conspired against him, indeed was largely responsible for this disastrous new turn of events. If Peary had not bagged the North Pole, Amundsen would never have switched his sights south. If Peary's news had been announced much later than April 1909, Amundsen would not have been able to mount his own expedition in time to meet Scott head on.

Scott refused to discuss the implications of Amundsen's move. His official line was to wish his rival well and to continue his plans exactly as before. Media questions were deflected and his team mates not consulted. It took some time for the news to filter down to them, but then, as is the way with human nature, they enjoyed their righteous indignation to the full, although there were a few dissenting voices. The naturally tight-lipped Oates wrote to his mother: 'They say Amundsen has been underhand in the way he has gone about it but personally I don't see it is underhand to keep your mouth shut.'

The official British position was set out in Admiral Markham's biography of his kinsman, Sir Clements Markham. Then President of the Royal Geographical Society, Sir Clements was the enabler, fundraiser, mouthpiece, in fact the embodiment of British exploration for over fifty years. The Admiral's view reflected the sentiments being aired in gentlemen's clubs, pubs and omnibuses the length and breadth of the kingdom. He worked himself into a furious lather:

> Amundsen's expedition was in no way initiated in the interests of science; his intention was to make a dash for the Pole, so as to be able to claim priority of discovery for Norway, and nothing more . . . Scott, on the other hand, intended making a thorough scientific exploration, and was not to be inveigled into taking part with another competitor in a senseless race to the Pole. It will be noted that Amundsen concealed his intention of going to the South until *after* Scott had sailed, which certainly did not evince a kindly disposition towards the English enterprise.

In a magazine article Priestley was later to describe Amundsen's coup as 'the greatest geographical impertinence ever committed'.

Although comments made off the record indicate that Scott was beside himself with rage on reading the fateful telegram, his public reaction was typical of his character, class, generation and nationality: to retreat into himself. He may, as Roland Huntford suggests, have been acting with 'wilful complacency'; he may alternatively have been in denial, or behaving like a rabbit paralysed by a stoat. Certainly he failed to capitalise on the sympathy (and cash) he might have been expected to garner from the Australian fraternity by bad-mouthing Amundsen. But in fact, thanks to Teddy Evans' golden touch, the Government of New South Wales and a single private benefactor disgorged a further £5,000, which took care of the bulk of the shortfall. Scott could not undo what had been done; anyway, all the insiders thought that Amundsen would almost certainly make his attempt from a base in the Weddell Sea, on the other side of Antarctica from the Ross Sea, Scott's own destination.

Scott also had the morale of his team to consider. Speculation about the outcome of a 'race' could only erode the confidence and enthusiasm that had built up over the past four months. The four days that *Terra Nova* lay in Melbourne were quite long enough as far as Scott was concerned; better for the men to be back under sail and steam than putting together rumours and half-truths. And indeed for many, including Cherry-Garrard, it was all a bit of a nine-day wonder. He dwelt hardly at all on the telegram, and continued cheerfully, as Wilson rejoined the ship and Scott left her: 'I think he had seen enough of the personnel of the expedition to be able to pass a fair judgement upon them. I cannot but think that he was pleased.' Scott was pleased, but preoccupied. The others were probably not sorry to lose the faintly repressive shadow cast by his presence on board.

Although the mood of camaraderie did not falter, they were all feeling a bit jaded after so long at sea. Twelve days later, on 28 October, after crossing the Tasman Sea and rounding the southern tip of New Zealand's South Island, they steamed into Lyttelton Bay, just south of Christchurch. A month spent ashore among its famously hospitable families seemed all at once compellingly attractive. Abbott wrote after a memorable round of parties, excursions and amateur wrestling bouts: 'I shall always look back on it as one of the finest times I ever had,' adding poignantly that he was looking forward to seeing the 'fine and patriotic' people of New Zealand again. Work and play were both energetically pursued. Work meant unloading the ship in order to trace the leak which had plagued them since leaving England, reloading her and then cramming in a massive amount of extra cargo, including fresh dairy products and cured meats. All the provisions had already been packed into light and immensely strong three-ply colour-coded boxes – red for the main party, green for the Eastern. The bulkiest items were the motor sledges and two huts in kit form; the most delicate the array of state-of-the-art scientific instruments and photographic paraphernalia; the noisiest and most troublesome the ponies and dogs, which had been awaiting their arrival at nearby Quail Island.* Play meant for some agreeable flirtations, and for others official engagements to local girls. For Taff Evans, it meant another bout

---

* Abbott and two others sailed over to the island on a pleasure trip, and after visiting the Governor, went to inspect the animals: 'The ponies were mostly white & looked a handy lot; but the dogs appealed to me the most, they were a fine fierce lot . . . A few weeks later I saw the poor beasts in quite a subjected mood.' Later he went back several times to exercise the two ponies allocated to the Eastern Party.

of heavy drinking. He was sent in disgrace to Port Chalmers, their last port of call, to await his reinstatement by Scott.

Into this scene of chaos were catapulted the nine late arrivals. Four were already attuned to mayhem. These were the animal handlers: the exotic and much-travelled Cecil Meares, Wilfrid Bruce, and the two Russian helpers, Dimitri Gerof and Anton Omelchenko. Then came the motor handler, Bernard Day, and the three geologists, who fortunately were all outgoing and adaptable. The Englishman Raymond Priestley, recruited by Wilson in Sydney, had already witnessed a similar scene (minus the motor sledges) during *Nimrod*'s departure on 1 January 1908, and the two Australians, Frank Debenham and Griffith Taylor (the latter British-born but largely living and working in Sydney), were both engagingly extrovert. By his charm and irreverence, the voluble 'Griff' escaped being labelled a gasbag (as Shackleton had been on the *Discovery* expedition).

The person to whom this *galère* was most alien was Herbert Ponting, the official expedition photographer or, as he preferred to be called, 'camera artist'. He was disarmingly honest about the world into which he was pitchforked, writing in his book, *The Great White South*: 'I soon found that life on the *Terra Nova* was a very different matter to travelling on comfortable ocean liners.' But although his dapper moustache and fussy mannerisms became a source of mirth (his nickname was 'Ponco' and a new verb 'to pont' entered the language, defined by Taylor as 'to spend a deuce of a time posing in an uncomfortable position'),* his comical appearance belied an adventurous and often dangerous career. This he summarised airily as 'six years' ranching and mining in Western America; a couple of voyages round the world; three years of travel in Japan; some months as war correspondent with the First Japanese Army during the war with Russia; and in the Philippines during the American war with Spain . . . and several years of travel in a score of other lands'. He was also a first-class photographer, very highly valued – in every sense of the word – to this day.

Cherry-Garrard described the chaos on board:

The scene on the morning of Saturday, November 26, baffles description. There is no deck visible; in addition to 30 tons of coal in sacks on deck there are $2\frac{1}{2}$ tons of petrol, stowed in drums which in turn are cased in wood. On the top of sacks and cases, and on the roof of the ice-house, are thirty-three dogs, chained far enough apart to keep them from following their first instinct – to fight the nearest animal they can see; the ship is a hubbub of howls. In the forecastle and in the four stalls

---

* Levick and Meares were his main models. 'I have not yet discovered', wrote Wright, 'whether they like it or are merely more obliging than the rest of us.'

on deck are the nineteen ponies, wedged tightly in their wooden stalls, and dwarfing everything are the three motor sledges in their huge crates.

The motor-crates encroached badly on the men's quarters, as did the ponies. Abbott wrote cheerfully: 'The Ponies were berthed under the Focs'le on the Seamans Mess Deck, so we had to shift down below between decks & camp out al fresco.' The others were not immune from discomfort. In the wardroom, it was such a tight fit for the twenty-four officers and scientists that at meals four of them had to find a perch on floor or stove.

The by-now-familiar hullabaloo attended their departure from Lyttelton, but two events – one before and one after their departure – threatened to scupper the expedition before they had so much as sighted their first iceberg. The first of these was a row between Scott and Lieutenant Evans, mainly and ostensibly about Scott's decision to reprieve the disgraced Taff Evans. Although Teddy Evans was minded to resign and several other officers contemplated joining the mutiny, this storm in a teacup was averted thanks to a truce brokered by Wilson, and Taff was allowed to creep back on board at Port Chalmers when they stopped to ship coal.

Most of those on board were also relieved to be quit of the three senior wives, whose public quarrels and private schemings seemed to be proof positive that women had no place on a polar expedition. Bowers' view of Kathleen Scott was that 'Nobody likes her on the expedition, and the painful silence when she arrives is the only jarring note of the whole thing,' while the running feud between her and Hilda Evans exacerbated the natural lack of sympathy between their two husbands. Even Wilson was relieved when, having waved off his beloved Oriana on 29 November, he could pick up his paints and skinning tools once more, and retreat for silent vigils to his private chapel in the crow's nest.

The near-disaster which befell them two days out from New Zealand, on 1 December, was another sort of storm entirely. Starting at Force 10 (55–63 mph winds), it worked itself into a Force 11 frenzy, whipping up 35-foot-high waves. Ponting wrote: 'The ship rolled and plunged and squirmed as she wallowed in the tremendous seas which boomed and crashed all that night against the weather side, sending tons of water aboard every minute. Screaming gusts would strike her with hurricane force, and sometimes she would lay over to an angle of 40° – nearly half a right angle from an even keel.'

That was the layman's impression. Scott in a private letter outlined the sailor's view: 'We knew that normally the ship was not making much water, but we also knew that a considerable part of the water washing over the upper deck must be finding its way below; the decks were leaking in

4. *Terra Nova* leaked from the start of the voyage, but manning the pumps – already a regular pursuit – became a matter of life or death during the ferocious storm of 1 December 1911. Two ponies and a dog died, and the grossly overladen ship was saved from foundering with all hands by one bold leadership decision and a concerted show of strength and stamina by most of those on board. The unmistakable features of Lt 'Birdie' Bowers appear on the left of the photograph.

streams. The ship was very deeply laden; it did not need the addition of much water to get her waterlogged, in which condition anything might have happened.' In fact the 'landsmen' were not told how dire the situation was. Scott took Bowers aside and said quietly, 'I am afraid it's a bad business for us.' The others were not fooled, however. Debenham's recollection was that 'the chief feeling was not so much of the inevitable doom as of the tremendous pity that a great expedition should perish at its very start'.

As the storm struck, there were two priorities. One was to lash and relash the loads on the upper deck. Motor sledges could kill, animals be killed. The most lethal weapons were the bags of coal and cans of petrol crashing round the deck like things possessed. Then, if the ship were not to be dismasted, the sails had to be speedily reduced to a minimum. Campbell summarised the tricky and hazardous operation, carried out at speed and under pressure:

2.30. Wind and sea rising. Took in t'gallant [top gallant] sails.
4.0. Furled mainsail and outer jib.
5.0. Furled fore and main upper topsails and foresail.
6.5. Eased to 45 revs.

It must be realised what this entailed – a swarm of sailors climbing up the rigging while the ship 'plunged and squirmed' through the mountainous waves, then wrestling the sodden, flapping canvases into submission before lashing them to the masts. It took five men just to furl the jib. Cherry-Garrard recorded how 'Bowers and four others went out on the bowsprit, being buried deep in the enormous seas every time the ship plunged her nose into them with great force. It was an education to see him lead those men out into that roaring inferno.'

Once cargo and sails had been rendered impotent, the ship had to be kept bodily afloat. If she could continue to plough her way through the deluge, she might yet be pumped out of trouble. Levick was one of a party given the job of keeping the engine room dry enough to fuel the boilers. As the waters continued to rise, the coal bunkers became inaccessible, so coal had to be passed down in buckets from the upper deck. At the root of the problem was the build-up of coal balls (a mixture of coal and oil), which progressively choked the suction pumps in the bilges. The admirable Lashly cleaned these out, diving again and again into the filthy water until it rose too high. It was a losing battle. By 8 a.m. on 2 December, wrote Levick, 'the water had risen so high in the stokehold that the fires were extinguished. The ship was so low in the water, & so heavy that she made no attempt at rising to the seas which swept continuously over her.' She was, in fact, slowly sinking.

Browning was one of the ratings pumping in water up to his waist, and

at times when the ship rolled heavily it would be up to our armpits; it was almost impossible to keep on our feet, and as the water rushed across the deck we had to hang on to the pump handle to prevent our been [sic] swept overboard . . . a good number of cases of petrol were washed overboard, occasionally one of these cases being swept across the [deck] by the heavy seas would knock you off your feet, we started now to throw some of our cargo overboard bags of coal and trusses of hay.

Since it was impossible to open the hatchway to get at the pumps

26

from above, the bold decision was taken for the chief engineer, Williams, and the carpenter, Davies, to cut two holes through the engine-room bulkhead and the pump shaft; someone would then have to squeeze through to try and free the blockage that way. The two men reckoned it would take them twelve hours. They started work at dawn on 2 December.

While this radical and exhausting surgery was under way, it was all other hands to the buckets, filled with water now, not coal. Every man who could be spared bailed in an unceasing rota – two hours on, two hours off – for twenty-four hours, in a human chain that stretched from the boiler room to the upper deck. Scott's wry aside was: 'What a measure to count as the sole safeguard of the ship from sinking, practically to bale her out!' Wilson's diary depicts an unearthly scene: 'It was a weird night's work with the howling gale and the darkness and the immense sea running over the ship every few minutes, and no engines and no sail, and we all in the engine-room black as ink, singing chanties as we passed slopping buckets full of bilge, each man above slopping a little over the heads of all of us below him; wet through to the skin, so much so that some of the party worked altogether naked like Chinese coolies.'

The darkest moment came when a shout of 'Smoke!' came up from the bowels of the ship. A fire in the engine room could only have been extinguished by opening the hatches. In such mountainous seas that would have sounded the death knell for the ship. Luckily the smoke turned out to be steam.

While Scott, Campbell, Bowers and Pennell were taking life-and-death decisions from the bridge, Priestley, positioned at the top of the ladder, was being half-drowned by icy spray. Levick the rugger player, Atkinson the boxer, Abbott the wrestler and Taff Evans the physical instructor used their strong arms and shoulders to good effect on the progressively more stifling rungs below. Fortified by hot food and cocoa provided by the two boy-stewards, those not bailing simply sat and waited in sopping silence to bail again. Bowers, writing to his mother and scratching around for ways to soften his harrowing account, injected an unintentional note of comedy: 'My dressing gown was my great comfort as it was not very wet, and it is a lovely warm thing.'

Four men were excused bailing duty; they were fully occupied with the animals, whose circumstances were truly pitiable. Horses were Oates's one true love, and with his friend Atkinson he worked tirelessly to keep his charges on their feet, while Meares and Dimitri battled to save the dogs from drowning or strangulation. Two ponies and one dog were lost. Another dog, Osman, was washed overboard, then washed back again – he went on to become leader of the pack.

The 'camera artist' was also absent from the human chain. He had previously bruised his shin and lamented: 'I was quite unable to get on to the bridge to witness the grandeur of the storm, as I could not risk further injury to my leg.' He obviously had no idea of the apocalyptic scenes going on all around him. The images of 'Birdie' swathed in his mother's parting gift and 'Ponco' hobbling around his lab trying to salvage his precious photographic equipment are priceless flashes of light relief in a vision of hell.

Once the pump shaft had finally been breached, Bowers and Teddy Evans squeezed through and managed, diving repeatedly underwater, to clear twenty bucketfuls of coal balls from the pump, until water began to emerge from it in a blessed stream. It took them two hours. 'From this moment', wrote Scott with characteristic understatement, 'it was evident we should get over the difficulty.' The flood gradually diminished and at 9 a.m. on 3 December they raised steam again.

Judging by the lengthy descriptions written by many of the participants (except the phlegmatic Campbell), the Great Storm was an exceptionally vivid experience. For Scott it was seminal, and temporarily served to drive all thoughts of Amundsen from his mind. The past two days had thrown up many heroes. Bowers, Teddy Evans, Lashly and Oates had conclusively proved their worth in terms of strength, ingenuity, endurance and courage, and the whole team had showed astonishing reserves of stamina. Scott singled out the ratings for special praise. Water, plus manure and litter from the stable directly above their quarters, had filled their hammocks and bedding; their only source of light (artificial) was faulty at best, and they had very little air. 'All things considered, their cheerful fortitude is little short of wonderful.' The inhabitants of the nursery – the thoroughfare between the engine room and the wardroom – had fared no better, finding their books, diaries and other precious possessions trodden into an unrecognisable black pulp.

Scott himself had not been found wanting. Bowers noted approvingly: 'Captain Scott was simply splendid, he might have been at Cowes . . . he is one of the best, and behaved up to our best traditions at a time when his own outlook must have been the blackness of darkness'.

Losses were bad, but not catastrophic, summarised by Campbell as '2 ponies dead, 1 dog washed overboard, nearly all our port bulwarks, 4 cases of petrol, several bales of fodder, 10 bags of coal'. The resulting shortage of coal, however, was to have profound implications for his own Eastern Party.

The animals were slow to recover from their ordeal as the ship continued to pitch and roll her way southwards. So were some of the men – Priestley was pole-axed by seasickness, as was Ponting, who continued

5. The expedition was trapped in the pack for 27 days. The officer on watch in the crow's nest would scour the horizon to chart any hopeful 'leads' opening up in the ice-field; it was as frustrating and time-consuming as following the contortions of a maze. The ship then charged its way through before, inevitably, the briefly opened door slammed shut again.

his photographic routine holding a developing dish in one hand and a sick-basin in the other. Both species gradually dried out; Wilson transferred himself to the top bunk in Campbell's cabin, 'which is seldom wet, though mouldy'.

On 7 December the first icebergs were sighted in the distance. Two days later they became commonplace, and then 'Bump!' wrote Cherry-Garrard excitedly. The helmsman – probably Bowers, always the boldest at tackling the enemy head on – charged the first big floe and they were in the pack. Those new to Antarctica gazed with awed delight at the icescape stretching to the horizon. On cloudy days the scene could look drab and bleak (and impossible to photograph), but under a clear sky the sun, sparkling on floes and bergs, transformed it into a land of astonishingly strong and varied light.

Wright, Priestley and Debenham were set to work compiling an ice log, and Ponting was in seventh heaven:

Innumerable ice-floes, with edges upturned from constant contact with each other, lay upon the now unruffled surface of the sea, looking like huge Victoria Regia lily-leaves on the placid surface of some tropical lake. When at midnight the great red orb dipped almost to the southern horizon, the blazing heavens turned the sea to molten gold; the lily-leaves took on autumn tints of orange with russet shadows, and their upturned edges were topaz; whilst the distant icebergs slowly changed into blocks of mother-o'-pearl and jasper.

Less exalted activities included the resumption of bridge evenings by the established foursome of Scott, Teddy Evans, Nelson and Levick, although the latter complained that it was not much fun playing with no money involved.

On 9 December they entered the loose ice fields on the outer limits of the pack. All were entranced by the beauty and grandeur of the scene – the dense carpet of white shimmering in the sunlight, cut through by wide lanes of black water and populated with icebergs of every shape and size. Levick marvelled:

Their walls are clean cut greenish blue, clear ice, in which can be seen the layers of which they are formed . . . Each of these bergs represents a year in their history . . . As the sunlight falls on top of these bergs, it is reflected out of the glassy walls forming the sides in every shade of gleaming cobalt and there are generally a lot of caves, the mouths of which appear a deep cobalt, and some of these are guarded by long hanging icicles that bar the entrance. When the sun is shining brightly the whole scene is dazzling beyond description, but when it is clouded over, it becomes a cold and dreadful waste.

On 10 December the ship pushed her way into the Antarctic Circle. Making fast to a floe, a dozen men landed to 'water ship', a procedure which meant taking on several tons of ice. 'Unfortunately', noted Levick, 'the water when it is drawn from the tanks tastes very oily.' They also shot four crab-eater seals, a protracted killing and 'not a pleasant sight'. That evening they had seal liver for dinner, an unfamiliar delicacy, almost black in colour.

Scott was beginning to fret. The pack was on them much sooner than they had expected. His diary entries are fractured with concern. On 13 December he noted: 'Heavy hummocked bay ice, the floes standing 7 or 8 feet out of the water, and very deep below . . . I have never seen anything more formidable.' Five days later: 'What an exasperating game this is! – one cannot tell what is going to happen in the next half or even quarter of an hour. At one moment everything looks flourishing, the next one begins to doubt if it is possible to get through.' If they raised steam and then got locked into the pack they wasted precious coal, but if the ship stood idle and failed to take advantage of leads suddenly opening up in the ice, they wasted precious opportunities. He started to worry that they were drifting too far east, 'and so away to regions of permanent pack'.

While Scott tried to conceal his anxiety, those under him were making the most of their enforced immobility. In a strange assortment of garments, the men surged onto the ice. On 19 December Priestley's diary recorded:

> We are a funny-looking lot. My own costume at present consists of a pair of dress boots, the same ones belonging to Shackleton that I wore in London, a pair of thin socks, a pair of cricket trousers . . . one thin singlet, one black shirt (originally black), one gaudy silk neckerchief & one scarlet tasselled cap. Finally I am braced together by one ferocious belt two inches broad & containing one sheath & sheath knife. I fancy I am supposed by the rest of the company to look more like a half-mad pirate than anything else.

Levick's dress code was rather more conservative: 'My clothing at present consists of a rather thin summer vest, then a thick Jaeger vest, then a blue jersey, with a sweater over that, and I wear a thick "Lambey" coat, made of a kind of fur, when on deck, with a woollen scarf and rabbits wool helmet worn simply as a cap. On my legs are a pair of fairly thin woollen socks, thin woollen drawers down to my knees, & thick sea boots which come up to the top of my thighs.'

When the ship was held fast in the pack for three days, Meares and Dimitri harnessed some of the wildly excited dogs to the sledges for a much-needed run, and Gran set up a ski school for those humans in need of exercise – a thankless task, as most of his pupils imagined that skiing was essentially skating with planks.* A natural athlete, Levick took to it quickly: 'I am getting on famously. It is a grand way of getting along.' He also suffered his first dose of an affliction that was to become all too common – snow blindness. 'Early in the afternoon the glare on the snow was very great, and after a while I began to see patches of dark purple & then half the field of vision became the same colour, & as we have not yet had our snow goggles served out, I came back to the ship.' Later he made

---

* Ponting's laborious description of skis (or 'ski', as they were then known), shows how utterly unfamiliar he expected them to be to his readers: 'Ski have of recent years become very popular among winter-sporters in Switzerland. They are narrow strips of wood, about seven or eight feet long, which are strapped to the boots.'

himself a rather sophisticated pair of leather snow goggles with amber glass. Meanwhile, Campbell (who was an expert skier), Scott and Teddy Evans practised hauling 320-pound loads over the floes – 'what a puzzle this pulling of loads is!' remarked Scott.

For most it was their first acquaintance with the delightfully tame and characterful Adélie penguins and the liquid-eyed seals, and with alarming predators such as the fearsomely toothed sea leopard* – the Adélies' bane – and the blue whale. Wilson and Ponting busied themselves with pencil and camera, and Wilson affirmed with deep contentment: 'We have now broad daylight night and day, but the beauty of the day with its lovely blues and greens amongst the bergs and ice-floes is eclipsed altogether by the marvellous beauty of the midnight when white ice becomes deepest purple and golden rose and the sky is lemon green without a cloud. No scene in the whole world was ever more beautiful than a clear midnight in the pack.'

The ship's galloping consumption of coal during her entrapment in the ice affected the Eastern Party most immediately. If supplies (already fine-tuned to a degree that did not allow for many emergencies) ran low, their landing miles along the Ross Ice Shelf would be the first casualty. Gran noted in his diary as early as 22 December: 'We are already beginning to discuss the possibility that we shall not be in a position to put the eastern party ashore. This will be a hard blow for Campbell.' Ten days later Levick outlined the broader picture, but omitted its ramifications for his own group: 'These continuous delays are very disappointing. Not only are the ponies beginning to knock up, but all the skipper's arrangements for depot laying this year are being upset, and the scientific cruise which the ship was to have made after landing us all, will be an impossibility, as she will have to go Northward at once to avoid being frozen in for the winter.'

On Christmas Day, Scott's private opinion was that 'The scene is altogether too Christmassy'. The festivities were in the well-established polar tradition of conspicuous consumption and revelry. 'It is rather a surprising circumstance', he noted drily, 'that such an unmusical party should be so keen on singing.' The wardroom tucked into their feast – which included asparagus, a sirloin of beef, plum pudding and mince pies, champagne, port and liqueurs – in the evening. The messdeck consumed their mutton (rejecting penguin out of hand) at lunchtime, and were able to raise their bottles of stout to toast a birth, or rather seventeen – a litter produced by Crean's pet rabbit, bedded down on a heap of fodder in the fo'c'sle.

The three weeks spent in the pack were by and large agreeable, especially for those seeing the continent for the first time. Levick spent

---

* The leopard seal, *Hydrurga leptonyx*.

much of his time acquiring new skills – skiing, skinning and printing photographs – although he grumbled to his diary: 'I find I can't get any information out of Ponting. He won't give anything away as to his methods of exposure, developing etc. Though I should not think he can lose much by teaching me.' He added, in an uncharacteristically grumpy outburst: 'I am getting thoroughly fed up with ship life – six months out of eight is too much, even for anyone that likes the sea & I hate it.' Levick was not alone in feeling the strain, but overall the homogeneity was miraculously unaffected. He wrote on 28 December: 'The marvellous thing is that in spite of the inactivity of these days, we are all on such perfect terms with each other. It goes on month after month. The discipline on board is perfect as a man o war, and yet it seems to come quite naturally, and no doubt is the result of having the ship run by naval officers of the first order.'* In the light of this spontaneous observation, Scott's persistent daubing of every event and character with a rosy hue seems rather less untrustworthy.

For Scott himself, this idle waiting was far more of a test than the recent storm; he found it 'the worst of conditions'. His polar strategy depended on establishing a major depot on the Great Ice Barrier before the onset of winter; instead, as he wrote desolately on Christmas Day, 'We are captured.'

Five days later, the pack released its grip, and *Terra Nova* steamed into the open water of the Ross Sea. It had taken them 27 days to force a passage through 400 miles of ice, compared with 5 days for *Discovery*. *Nimrod* had encountered no pack at all; *Fram* was to make it in 4.

They steered first for Cape Crozier, on the eastern side of Ross Island – chosen because it was relatively sheltered, protected by Mount Terror, and also led directly onto the Ross Ice Shelf, which the Polar Party would have to cross before negotiating the mountains leading up to the polar plateau. If they made their base on a piece of land abutting the Barrier, they would not have to take into account the uncertain nature of the sea ice in McMurdo Sound on the western side of the island. Scott summarised its other attractions as if he were composing a travel agent's brochure: 'Comfortable quarters for the hut, ice for water, snow for the animals, good slopes for skiing, vast tracks of rock for walks.' It was especially favoured by Ponting and Wilson because, among a mass of other wildlife, it housed a substantial rookery of Adélies and was also a breeding ground for emperor penguins, about whose habits virtually nothing was known.

---

* Levick did, however, have two specific complaints: severe headaches, self-diagnosed as being gouty in nature due to lack of exercise, and inadequate bathing facilities. ('Our allowance is a teacupful of water daily. I dip my tooth brush in this, & clean my teeth; then pour half the water on my tooth brush and rinse my teeth, then dip a towel into what remains & rub over my face & neck.')

A boat was lowered to investigate on 3 January, but Scott decided that landing in the heavy swell, crashing with icebergs, was impossible.* They tracked westwards along the inhospitable coast to Cape Bird (at the entrance of McMurdo Sound), then southwards, heading towards Shackleton's old camp at Hut Point on the southern extremity of Ross Island. Thickening ice made Scott reluctant to push on further, so he fixed, *force majeure*, on a rocky outcrop with a gently sloping beach already known to him and to Wilson as 'The Skuary'. Scott renamed it Cape Evans after his second-in-command; it would become the sanctuary to which the various parties would return with relief at intervals during the coming months. Hut Point, 16 miles from Cape Evans, would function as an essential second home for those laying depots for the Polar Party.

It was a beautiful spot. Scott described it in a glowing passage:

Cape Evans is one of the many spurs of [Mount] Erebus and the one that stands closest under the mountain, so that always towering above us we have the grand snowy peak with its smoking summit. North and south of us are deep bays, beyond which great glaciers come rippling over the lower slopes to thrust high blue-walled snouts into the sea . . . whilst far over the Sound, yet so bold and magnificent as to appear near, stand the beautiful Western Mountains.

Disembarkation started at once – only twelve weeks of daylight remained to the depot parties. Cape Evans put Gran in mind of an Indian encampment, swarming with men and beasts, and littered with packing cases. Campbell was put in charge of transport; he and Levick were station masters, while Priestley, Gran and assorted navvies steered the loads. It was 1½ miles ship to shore, and Browning estimated that he had made 32 miles to and from the ship in a single day. Meanwhile Teddy Evans and Bowers organised the erection of the hut, Oates the stabling of the horses, Meares the kennelling of the dogs, and just about everybody else the stashing of the supplies.

Two incidents disturbed the orderly disorder of the scene. On 5 January Ponting had a close encounter with a pack of killer whales, which attacked the floes on which he was photographing. 'What irony', wrote Campbell,

* Ponting was also denied the carrot promised to him at his recruitment, that he would be given time to photograph the Barrier; this was the only section available to him. Lack of time and coal – equally precious commodities – meant that Scott had to renege on his promise. Ponting wrote disconsolately: 'with a heavy heart I then impotently watched the bastioned rampart slowly disappear astern – one of the most remarkable features of the earth, to see which, and in the hope of illustrating it, so that others might see it too, I had come over more than a third of the circumference of the globe.'

6. Scott pioneered the significant use of motor sledges in Antarctica, but his best vehicle was shortly to be lost in 100 fathoms of water, nearly carrying the geologist Raymond Priestley down with it. Lt Victor Campbell, shortly by then nominated leader of the Eastern (then Northern) Party, was in charge of the disembarkation.

'to be eaten for a seal and spat out because one was a man.' Ponting himself reckoned that 'if they did get me, how very unpleasant the first bite would feel, but that it would not matter much about the second'.

Three days later their best motor sledge disappeared when it sank through a patch of rotten ice, pulling several men in after it. Although Campbell was in charge, the order had been given by Scott, and a brave face was put on it. To many its loss did not seem much of a calamity. On the ice the remaining two motors were to prove brutes to manoeuvre and a permanent headache to Bernard Day. Some heretics were even heard to regret that they had not sunk as well.

Ponting photographed the scene moments before the disaster, and continued indefatigably to record every aspect of life at Cape Evans. On 12 January Levick had intimations of immortality: 'As we took our load up the little hill approaching the hut this afternoon, we saw Ponting cinematographing us, so I suppose the Eastern Party will in a few months be performing nightly at the London music halls, as the ship is to take back a lot of films with her after she leaves us.'

Fuelled by irrepressible high spirits, hard labour was turned into a winter sporting event. Campbell, Priestley and Levick, as representatives of the Eastern Party, took on all comers, including a team led by Griffith Taylor. The rivalry was so intense that after a ten-load hauling competition, Browning (who had temporarily joined the enemy) was on the sick list the following day with blistered feet, and Taylor himself, 'whose pluck is far beyond his physique', retired to his bunk completely broken up, 'whilst we', boasted Levick, 'went merrily on'.

On 15 January, Bruce and Levick embarked on a rather ambitious trip.* Climbing up the Southern Plank of Mount Erebus was easy, if warm, work. Bruce recorded an enjoyable halt: 'We then sat down, lit our pipes, and tried to pick out and name all the peaks we could see in the mountain ranges of Victoria Land from memory, for both of us had studied the maps pretty thoroughly.† It was a very clear day, and the view in all directions was magnificent.' Coming down, the novices' airy self-confidence was swiftly punctured as they tackled the precipitous slopes lying between them and the safety of hut and ship, 2,000 feet below. 'Without any grip at all, we found that, whatever we did, the skis turned straight down the hill. Our only course was to fall at once, which we had to do on so many occasions, that we were both pretty well knocked about by the time we got on to negotiable snow. I had started with a pipe in my mouth, and had several loose teeth for a long time after.'

On the 18th the shore party were able to start moving into the capacious and already comfortable hut. Officers and men were segregated, as they had been on board, this time by a wall of crates and cases; it was a tradition Campbell was to adopt throughout the Eastern Party's peregrinations. 'Grand scraps' were banned, because of the danger to the scientific instruments, but verbal battles and practical jokes abounded. The base at Cape Evans was also provided with a bicameral ice house carved into a snow drift, one as a store for frozen carcasses, the other for magnetic instruments. It was slow and arduous work, but became a precedent the Eastern Party would also turn to their advantage.

Two days earlier Campbell, Levick and Priestley had left the scenes of frenzied activity for a brief expedition to Cape Royds, eight miles away. They were extending their 'borrowing' activities to Shackleton's old hut, hoping to find a paraffin stove for their future home. Although it was

---

* Related by Bruce in *The Blue Peter*, 'Reminiscences of the "Terra Nova" in the Antarctic'.

† Levick does not divulge whether his geography lesson stood him in any stead during their later journeys, made with the help of an inadequate and outdated Admiralty map.

billed as a combined seal-killing* and geological field trip, it seems also to have been something of a bonding exercise. If so, it worked – Levick called it a 'grand little holiday'.

They found the hut doorless but undamaged. As described by Levick, they were greeted by a scene typical of the Victorian era, entitled perhaps 'The Last Supper'. 'A tray of bread scones stood on a box, and tins of every description of food stood in piles and on shelves round the walls . . . All the little personal belongings of the late expedition lay about, as they had left them in their hurried departure.' Priestley, who knew the place of old, found the experience decidedly unsettling: 'Nothing is changed at all except the company. It is almost dismal. I expect to see people come in through the door after a walk over the surrounding hills . . . The whole place is very eerie, there is such a feeling of life about it. Not only do I feel it but the others also.' Campbell, more prosaically, noted that the biscuit and butter were still 'quite good'.

Shaking off the *Nimrod* ghosts, they visited the penguin rookery and travelled to Cape Barne and the foothills of Mount Erebus. As they encountered a series of crevasses, Priestley noted: 'It was quite good exercise getting Levick over, for he required a strong yank with the rope delivered just at the right moment.' Levick himself did not much enjoy this, his first encounter. Some of the crevasses had been exposed by the wind, '& their thin lids lay gleaming green like the eyes of wicked beasts waiting for an unwary prey'. At other times they had collapsed in places, or were dislodged by their crossing, 'in which case you could look down on apparently unfathomable depth of blue space. They varied in width from a mere crack to eight or ten feet or more. It was a relief when we were over them.'

The three senior members of the Eastern Party returned to Cape Evans on 21 January, less than a week before the start of their own big adventure. They had missed an exciting moment when *Terra Nova* ran aground. Pennell kept his nerve and ordered the cargo shifted. 'Then', recounted Gran, 'we executed a rather unusual drill in which officers and men were paraded on the main hatch and on the word of command ran together from side to side.' Dickason was one of those 'rolling' or 'sallying', while Abbott manned the whaler which took Teddy Evans out to inspect the damage and help direct the ship into deeper waters.

The officers of the Eastern Party discovered that work had been

---

* They were not yet accustomed to slaughtering the appealing creatures and even Levick, used to piercing flesh with scalpel, found his first kill distasteful: 'The old bull lay sound asleep, grunting a little as if he was dreaming. I heard him give a sigh of contentment as I stole up to him. Raising the iron bar high over my head, I brought it down across his nose, and as he lay stunned, ran in with a grand hunting knife about 10 inches long which I bought in Christchurch, and lifting up his flipper, ran it right into his heart. The blood spurted out by the gallon, & I had killed my first seal.'

continuing unabated in their absence, and Cherry-Garrard was in a mood to complain: 'Scott seems very cheery about things. And well he might be. A man could hardly be better served. We slaved until we were nearly dead-beat and then we found something else to do until we were quite dead-beat.' A diary entry of Priestley's showed more of an edge. 'We seem at present to be doing a lot of work without any actual advantage accruing to ourselves . . . I shall be glad to get away in search of our new home.'

# 2

# 'Perfidious Amundsen' and the Bay of Whales

## 26 January–8 February 1911

On 26 January 1911, the members of the expedition gathered in force on a tongue of ice beneath the slopes of mighty Erebus. The day had been declared a holiday in honour of the thirteen men of the Southern Depot Party, who, divided into three teams leading dogs and ponies, were to lay down a series of provisions on the route to the Pole; they returned to Hut Point on 5 March.

Three other groups were to head off in different directions the following day. The First Western Party's brief was to reconnoitre a trio of great glaciers west of Cape Evans. The two geologists, Taylor and Debenham, the physicist Wright and PO Forde were in the field from 27 January to 14 March; Taff Evans went along to teach them sledging techniques. Ponting, Nelson, Day and Lashly set out at the same time for a ten-day photographic trip to Cape Royds. The third group was the Eastern Party, bound for King Edward VII Land.

Scott ended his short but moving speech with the words: 'I do most heartily trust that all will be successful in their ventures, for indeed their unselfishness and their generous high spirit deserves reward. God bless them.' Present-day Tolkien fans may be reminded here of the sending forth of the Nine Walkers of the Fellowship of the Ring,* and Priestley's account of Scott's farewell was even more Tolkienesque:

---

* 'Elrond came out with Gandalf, and he called the Company to him. "This is my last word," he said in a low voice. "The Ring-bearer is setting out on the Quest of Mount Doom. On him alone is any charge laid . . . The others go with him as free companions, to help him on his way. You may tarry, or come back, or turn aside into other paths, as chance allows. The further you go, the less easy will it be to withdraw; yet no oath or bond is laid on you to go further than you will. For you do not yet know the strength of your hearts, and you cannot foresee what each may meet upon the road." '

Six, at any rate, of those who are alive to-day are destined to have that scene engraved on their memories for the remainder of their lives, for it was there that we . . . said farewell to our companions who were to make the final successful attack on the South Pole; and though no forebodings disturbed the serenity of the parting, it was ordained that we should never set eyes again on five of the men whom we were proud to number among our friends.

A successful 'conquest' by the Eastern Party of King Edward VII Land, an unexplored region of considerable importance, would be a fine feather in Scott's cap, not least as a pleasingly neat counter-coup in Scott's ongoing rivalry with Shackleton. During the *Nimrod* expedition of 1907–09, Shackleton (through no fault of his own) had been forced to give up the idea of landing there, retreating instead to the territory at McMurdo Sound that Scott considered his own patch. During Shackleton's tenancy the South Magnetic Pole had been reached and many valuable scientific results obtained.* Now Scott intended to storm the bastion that Shackleton had tried so hard to breach. Campbell was fully aware of the honour and responsibility of his appointment as their leader. He wrote to his cousin Vera on 30 January 1911, 'I'm awfully pleased with this command.'

Scott's own leadership qualities, especially by comparison with Amundsen and Shackleton, have been roundly criticised ever since his death, and rather less robustly defended. Indeed to admire Shackleton it is now apparently necessary to denigrate Scott. It is a subject that will no doubt be debated with relish for generations to come, but some of Scott's less controversial qualities are often overlooked in the process. Whatever individual expedition members' private opinions of Scott as a leader and a man might have been, his genuine and profound attachment to the pursuit of knowledge was referred to time and again by the scientists present, all of whom were or would become eminent in their chosen fields. The meteorologist George Simpson went so far as to declare: 'I do not think that I have ever met a man who had the true scientific spirit so utterly unalloyed . . . To most of us who have given our lives to science our investigations are frequently tinged with an unscientific desire to increase our scientific reputations, but with him it was the added knowledge alone which gave pleasure.' The geologist and geographer Debenham agreed: 'Scott was really a scientist very successfully disguised as a naval captain.' Wilson had always known Scott to be a genuine ally: 'We want the

---

* The North and South Magnetic Poles are the two points on the earth's surface where the terrestrial magnetic field has only a vertical component and a zero horizontal component. At these points a dip needle points vertically downwards. Thus a magnetic compass is useless for navigation in the vicinity of the Magnetic Poles, which are continuously in competition.

scientific work to make the bagging of the Pole merely an item in the results.'

Scott had been stung by criticism from the scientific establishment in Britain, especially the Physical Society of London, concerning the amateurish nature of the meteorological results collected on his *Discovery* expedition, and had written harshly to Major Darwin of the Royal Geographical Society in 1909: 'We must have a considered programme of work and must not be the dumping ground of scientific freaks as the *Discovery* was.' Admiral Markham (admittedly partisan) later declared that there was no doubt about the value of the scientific results achieved on the *Terra Nova* expedition. The scientists had, he said,

> brought back with them a rich store of information both geographical and geological, with elaborate plans and surveys of the surrounding country, with complete climatic and other observations, extending over a period of nearly two years, all of which were absolutely new to science. They had set themselves to endeavour to determine the nature and extent of the Antarctic Continent; to ascertain the character and depth of the ice cap; to take pendulum observations in the highest latitude possible, as well as regular magnetic and meteorological observations; to give an account of the mammals, birds, and fishes, and otherwise to report on the scientific aspect of the new discoveries. All of this was satisfactorily accomplished. In short, the results achieved by the English expedition far surpassed any that had ever been obtained by previous Polar expeditions.

Of the two other leaders with their eyes on the polar prize in 1911, Amundsen, whose scientific results have been described as 'negligible', freely admitted that his sole aim was to pip the Englishmen to the Pole: 'On this little détour science would have to look after itself.' Waiting impatiently in the wings back home to learn the outcome of the race, Shackleton, according to two of his biographers, 'for all the quickness and orderliness of his mind, was not the kind of man ever to make a pure scientist . . . [indeed] he regarded scientists with a certain respect tempered with scorn'.* Amundsen, in a carefully crafted (and partially convincing) apologia for his secret switch of venue from North Pole to South and his subsequent actions, included the line: 'The British expedition was designed entirely for scientific research. The Pole was only a side-issue.' This was both disingenuous and untrue, but Scott would not have disagreed with the underlying sentiment. For him, the Pole came first in the scheme of things – but only just. It was a duality of purpose that

---

* James and Margery Fisher, in *Shackleton* (1957).

Priestley recognised and for which he was grateful: 'Our leader was, before everything, a scientist, and it is to this fact that the [Eastern] Party owes its existence as a separate entity; for although from the first he made no secret of the fact that the conquest of the South Pole was to be his main object, yet he intended to make his expedition as efficient as possible for scientific purposes.'

The Eastern Party was only *primus inter pares* as far as the pursuit of science was concerned, for Scott had by now set in train an intricate and overlapping network of sub-groups thrusting out from the main base at Cape Evans to explore and document as wide a geographical area as possible. These would be amended as circumstances changed. Members of the Polar Party were themselves involved in these and other journeys during the early stages of the expedition. Thus PO Evans was a member of the First Western Party, and four months later, in July 1911, two others, Wilson and Bowers (plus Cherry-Garrard, who immortalised their terrible ordeal in *The Worst Journey in the World*), left to explore the emperor penguin colony at Cape Crozier – a project especially dear to Wilson's heart.* Poignantly, Scott arranged for the Second Western Party to set out on 15 November 1911, ten days after he himself had left for the Pole. He was never to know how much of scientific value Taylor, Debenham, Gran and Forde managed to amass during their nine-week trip.

That the six members of the Eastern Party were alone in being selected for a single substantial foray indicates the importance Scott attached to their efforts. His instructions to Campbell were contained in a lengthy letter written at Cape Evans on 23 January. They began with the following:

> Whilst I hope that you may be able to land in King Edward's Land, I fully realise the possibility of the conditions being unfavourable and the difficulty of the task which has been set you.
>
> I do not think you should attempt a landing unless the Ship can remain in security near you for at least three days, unless all your stores can be placed in a position of safety in a shorter time.
>
> The Ship will give you all possible help in erecting your hut, &tc., but I hope you will not find it necessary to keep her by you for any length of time.
>
> Should you succeed in landing, the object you will hold in view is to discover the nature and extent of King Edward's Land. The possibilities of your situation are so various that it must be left to you entirely to determine how this object may best be achieved.
>
> In this connexion it remains only to say that you should be at your winter station and ready to embark on February 1, 1912.

---

* He had spent seven weeks at Cape Crozier studying their habits during Scott's *Discovery* expedition, and was longing to renew the acquaintance.

Admirably clear instructions, issuing the minimum of advice, promising back-up where needed, and giving *carte blanche* once the party had arrived at their destination. A team leader's dream – providing that all went according to plan.

After Scott had bidden them farewell on 26 January, the two parties assembled on *Terra Nova*. They were still under Campbell's command; Pennell would only take over as captain of the ship once the Eastern Party had been deposited on King Edward VII Land. First they dropped off the five men of the Western Party at Butter Point. Campbell, Priestley and Debenham climbed a short way up the Ferrar Glacier to find the depot left there during the *Nimrod* expedition for Professor David's South Magnetic Pole Party, and Levick volunteered to give a group of seamen a lesson in killing seals the humane way. Griff Taylor revealed the truth: 'He described the method to us on his return, but the effect was spoilt by the butcher declaring that the seal had travelled a hundred yards after Levick had officially killed it!'*

Returning briefly to Cape Evans to land Ponting, Nelson and Dimitri, Campbell and Priestley took the opportunity to visit the ice cave, now completed by anyone who could be spared, working in pairs. The latter was impressed: 'They have lined it with rough felt & protected it by a low passage several yards long with a porch & blanket hangings at either end of the porch & it is very comfortable & quite equable in temperature.' Much later, they would remember their tour of inspection and hark back to its fittings.

A final halt in familiar territory was at Cape Royds in the early hours of 29 January. The three senior men of the Eastern Party bagged twenty penguins to swell the larder of those remaining at Cape Evans, and also managed to liberate a few final items from Shackleton's hut for themselves; not much, lamented Levick, 'as we had orders not to take away many of his stores'. Then, rounding Cape Bird, *Terra Nova* turned south-east in order to reach Cape Crozier and start the long cruise along the Ross Ice Shelf. Expectations were running high. Levick made no entries in his diary for the next few days, except to note: 'We are undoubtedly now reaching the most interesting stage of the Expedition. Whereas the main party have landed on a land which has been partially explored before, we are now entering an entirely new arena, and do not know what we shall find. May it be land!'

The majesty of the extraordinary natural feature that is the Great Ice Barrier, stretching unbroken into the distance, must have been familiar to many of those on board *Terra Nova* from Ross's description of 1841. He had called it 'an extraordinary barrier of ice, of probably more than a

_____

* Levick did not allude to this (obvious calumny) in his diary, recording merely: 'I killed six fine seals . . .'

7. Twin caves in which to house meteorological instruments and frozen carcasses were dug out at Cape Evans. Here Scott's second-in-command, Teddy Evans, and the biologist Edward Nelson are the master masons. Campbell and Priestley paid a visit to the completed caverns on the day their small party's peregrinations began – their own troglodyte existence lay fourteen months in the future.

thousand feet in thickness, [which] crushed the undulations of the waves, and disregards the violence: it is a mighty and wonderful object, far beyond any thing we could have thought or conceived.' The next sightseers had been members of the 1898-1900 *Southern Cross* expedition led by the Norwegian Carsten Borchgrevink. He had rated it the eighth wonder of the world, comparable with the Pyramids, the hanging gardens of Babylon and the Colossus of Rhodes. 'Imagine a perpendicular wall of ice, from 100 to 200 ft. high, suddenly rising up before you out of the ocean, where the depth of that ocean is measured by hundreds of fathoms, and hundreds of miles distant from any visible land.'

For Wilson, aboard *Discovery* with Scott in 1902, it had been the colour and intricate beauty of the Barrier's physical features that had appealed to his artistic soul: 'In these cliffs were the most wonderful bright blue caves, and the whole face was hung with long thin icicles which made the most fantastic grottoes, with pure blue depths in the caves and cracks.' For Scott himself, the Barrier was inextricably bound up with his quest for the Pole:

> Now for the first time this extraordinary ice-formation was seen from above [he had climbed a high volcanic cone to get a better view]. The sea to the north lay clear and blue, save where it was dotted by snowy-white bergs; the barrier edge, in shadow, looked like a long narrowing black ribbon as it ran with slight windings to the eastern horizon. South of this line, to the S.E. of our position a vast plain extended indefinitely, whilst faint shadows on its blue-grey surface seemed to indicate some slight inequality in level; further yet to the south the sun faced us, and the plain was lost in the glitter of its reflection. It was an impressive sight, and the very vastness of what lay at our feet seemed to add to our sense of its mystery.

The Barrier never failed to arouse awe in those seeing it for the first time, but in the Eastern Party this was tempered by an urgent desire to pursue that 'long narrowing black ribbon' until they touched base at its far end. The early part of the journey was to be devoted to assessing physical changes that had taken place since Scott's brief visit. The *Southern Cross* expedition had found that the coastline had retreated considerably since Ross's day, and the Eastern Party were witness in their turn that the Barrier was in a constant state of change – on 30 and 31 January two large chunks of cliff broke away, accompanied by a thunderous noise and a cloud of spray.

Then, facing a south-easterly wind whipping down from the great ice shelf, and with the currents also against them, they changed course and headed out into the Ross Sea. Dickason gave a seaman's view of their progress: 'Head wind and sea, doing about one and an onion. Good old tub, shall never be caught exceeding the speed limit.' But Cape Colbeck, which they hoped would be their gateway to the huge dome of ice that was King Edward VII Land, proved as bleakly unwelcoming as it had been to Shackleton before them. From the crow's nest – since the dawn of the age of tall-masted ships the best way of viewing the wide horizon – as far as eyesight and telescope extended they could see only solid ice stretching in an unbroken field, with enormous bergs frozen fast into it. There was no question of landing there, nor further to the east.

They had no choice but to sail back along the Barrier. Levick charted their movements on 3 February as the options started to run out. 'We looked everywhere for a place to land, and were quite prepared to do so on this desolate spot, but could find no possible place where we could take the ship alongside the ice, so reluctantly turned and started back Westward.'

The weather was atrocious. They found themselves in the midst of a fearful south-easterly blizzard so thick that at times they could see no more than 50 yards ahead, with a bitterly cold wind which iced up the rigging. (Levick had been trying to develop some photographic plates, but found them frozen solid in the tank; when he thawed them out later, they shattered.)

As King Edward VII Land receded behind them, there was a difference of opinion between the three officers of the Eastern Party. Priestley, thought Levick, 'seems rather to kick at landing on the Barrier', understandably so since his geological work demanded a sufficiency of rocks, and they would be faced by mile upon mile of snow and ice. Campbell took Levick aside on 2 February and asked him if he would be prepared to land somewhere on the Barrier. 'Of course I said I didn't care twopence where we went.' For Campbell, anxious not to be forced northwards to Robertson Bay, this was a clincher.

Their attempt to land the following day was no more successful: on the eastern shore the cliff seemed promisingly firm and chiselled, but the western side was cracked and crumbling, seamed with caves. A few deep inlets ran inwards, but these were too narrow and the cliffs on either side too high and overhanging to venture into with the ship. One of the places they now had in their sights was Balloon Bight, from which Scott and Shackleton had made their foolhardy, and mercifully singular, balloon ascent in January 1902. They found that the inlet had vanished.

Next along, the Bay of Whales was a spot familiar to polar enthusiasts from Shackleton's *Nimrod* expedition. He had described his arrival there in a letter dashed off to his wife Emily on 26 January 1908:

> It was not till nearly midnight that we turned a sharp corner and there in front of us lay a long range of peaks and undulations which certainly looked like land though even now I will not call it so as I did not see any bare rock and facing this Place which I call the Bay of Whales because of the hundreds of whales blowing there: was a plain of flat long ice about 4 feet thick on which were several seals and some Emperor penguins we came up against the ice and saw that it would be impossible to journey over it with safety to reach the cliffs in the distance as the ice was rapidly breaking up long cracks were visible in it which meant that it was liable to go out any moment.

Three years almost to the day after Shackleton's *Nimrod* visit, *Terra Nova* rounded the same headland shortly after midnight. Campbell must have been experiencing feelings of frustration and despair as great as those poured out by Shackleton to Emily: 'Child o' mine I have been through a sort of Hell since the 23rd and I cannot even now realize that I am on my way back to McMurdo Sound and that all idea of wintering on the Barrier or at King Edward VII Land is at an end that I have had to break my word to Scott and go back to the old base, and that all my plans and ideas have now to be changed and changed by the overwhelming forces of Nature.'

Dismally, history seemed to be repeating itself – but events then took an extraordinary turn. Killer whales were still blowing in the bay, and seals and penguins carpeted the ice as before, but this time, moored in the south-eastern corner, was a ship. 'We dressed & tore on deck at learning this tremendous news . . . None of us needed to be told it was *Fram*.' The veteran three-masted schooner made famous by Nansen's epic Arctic journey of 1893-6* had a revolutionary and distinctively rounded outline, which lifted her above the pack. Roald Amundsen had taken possession of the bay.

Tactically, the Norwegians had the advantage over the British in more ways than one. In his diary Gjertsen, the second mate of *Fram*, makes it clear that Scott's plans for the Eastern Party were known to them, and that the sight of *Terra Nova* came as no surprise: 'We had long been waiting for its arrival in the bay when it went east with the party that was going to land on King Edward VII Land.' Even so, the ship crept up on them unawares: 'When "Terra Nova" arrived our guard was below in the galley so he did not hear anything until "Terra Nova" lay to in the ice right in front of us, but as you can imagine he ran up to find out what all the noise was about. He imagined that half the barrier had calved [broken off the mass] and was bearing down on us. – Well, thank goodness it was only "Terra Nova", lying calmly over there, working on getting her ice anchors on land.'†

The Norwegian guard, who clearly was not overburdened with brains, was the sole witness of their approach. Gjertsen described with relish how, shortly after the intrepid watchman spotted the ship, 'he saw 2 men land, put on their skis and wander quickly, for foreigners, up towards the barrier, following the dog tracks. "Well", the guard thought, "if they are planning something bad (we were constantly asking ourselves in what light the Englishmen would view our competition), the dogs will manage to make them turn back; it will be worse when they sail free of 'Fram',

---

* Fridtjof Nansen, who was appointed Norway's first Ambassador to Britain in 1907, had achieved with a sole companion a farthest-north record of 86° 14' N. His traumatic return journey and rescue bear comparison with Shackleton's yet more famous *Endurance* expedition, still in the future.

† In fact Amundsen had entirely misunderstood the composition and stability of the Bay of Whales. Susan Solomon, in her book *The Coldest March*, makes the point that 'The Barrier near the Bay of Whales continually flows at an average rate of about a quarter-mile per year, and it is also subject to occasional abrupt calving . . . If the ice of the Barrier underlying Amundsen's hut had broken off during 1911, as it has on some other occasions, the Norwegian party likely would have survived because the breaking off of a large berg is a slow process. But surely their story would have been profoundly different.'

where I am the only one on watch. I had better be armed for all eventualities." ' Relying on the dual protection offered by an ancient gun and equally venerable English grammar, he bravely stood his ground as the enemy approached. The enemy in question materialised in the person of Campbell, the only Norwegian speaker of the party, with Levick and Priestley hard on his heels. They discovered that Amundsen and the four other expedition members* were at Framheim, the hut they had built three miles inland, and that they had been in the bay since 11 January.

Priestley recorded in his diary the arrival of the great man himself on 4 February. Woken by Levick demanding the use of his camera,† he discovered that Amundsen had already boarded *Terra Nova* to talk to Campbell and Pennell. The famous Norwegian, dressed from head to foot in sealskins, had evidently arrived *con brio*: 'His dogs were running well, and he did not check them until he was right alongside the ship. He then gave a whistle, and the whole team stopped as one dog. With a word of command he inverted the empty sledge and came on board, leaving the animals to themselves; and there they remained until their master had finished his visit.' This bravura performance was in fact stage-managed – Amundsen had sighted the ship from the shore, and, like Jehu, had descended on the scene (Gjertsen noted that 'never before had the speed been so great'). He could afford to be tongue-in-cheek about the disruption to their arrangements:

When the first man got to the top of the ridge, he began to wave his arms about and gesticulate like a madman. I understood, of course, that he saw something, but what? The next man gesticulated even worse, and tried to shout to me. But it was no use; I could not make anything of it. Then it was my turn to go over the ridge, and, as was natural, I began to feel rather curious. I had only a few yards more to go – and then it was explained . . . Now it was my turn to wave my arms, and I am sure I did it no worse than the two first. And the same thing was repeated with all of us, as soon as each one reached the top of the ridge. What the last man did I have never been able to find out for certain – but no doubt he waved his arms too. If a stranger had stood and watched us that morning on the ridge, he would·surely have taken us for a lot of incurable lunatics.

---

* Including Hjalmar Johansen, Nansen's companion on his famous Arctic journey. Nansen had persuaded Amundsen to include Johansen, who had fallen on hard times and into alcoholism.

† Levick described the photographs he took of *Fram*, Framheim, etc, as 'very indifferent indeed', due to his unfamiliarity with Priestley's camera. Those held at the Scott Polar Research Institute support his modesty.

The rival human teams behaved like Amundsen's dogs. After the first mutual shock of recognition had worn off, they circled carefully around one other, hackles raised, although courtesy and decorum were scrupulously maintained. Campbell, Levick and Pennell breakfasted at Framheim on 4 February, and this hospitality was repaid by lunch on board *Terra Nova*. Campbell's tight-lipped diary comment – 'The camp presented a very workmanlike appearance' – was an indication of his bitter chagrin, but compliments flew thick and fast from the other Britons. Gjertsen recorded laconically their enthusiastic reactions to the hut and their eulogies on the ship's spacious and comfortable quarters: 'When they saw that every man had his own stateroom and a saloon shared by all, their eyes grew very wide.' (The ratings slept two to a cabin and had their own large messroom.) The walls were adorned with photographs and embroideries, the library held 3,000 books, and the notepaper, crockery, cutlery and glass were all stamped with the ship's name. For their musical *soirées* they could choose between a piano, a violin, a flute, mandolins, a mouth-organ and an accordion – plus the essential gramophone.

The Norwegians' impressions of *Terra Nova* were somewhat muted. 'I must confess,' wrote Lieutenant Nilsen, Amundsen's second-in-command, 'it did not look very inviting, especially where comfort is concerned.' Lurid accounts of the British sailors' living conditions during the voyage out from New Zealand did nothing to change their view. Gjertsen commented incredulously: 'They all (the crew, that is) slept below the fo'csle with the ponies, which were packed tightly head to tail above the tables used at mealtimes. So they could not avoid "eau de Cologne" at any time during the day or night, nor did they avoid spices during meals.'

Niceties were preserved during these social calls, and in other circumstances mutual respect might well have developed into friendship. Levick was impressed: 'We found them all men of the very best type & got on very well. They are all very fair, with flaxen hair and blue eyes, very hard of appearance, and the officers most gentlemanly.' Men of their friend Tryggve Gran's kind, in fact – and of their own. As it was, the Norwegians' presence, if not a complete surprise, was a devastating blow. Both sides had much to ponder – Gjertsen called it 'a day rich in change to our programme'. Amundsen, who had not known exactly where Scott would make his base, yet had guessed correctly that he would plump for somewhere in the familiar territory of McMurdo Sound (the area colonised during the *Discovery* and *Nimrod* days), now knew for certain that his rival was starting from a point some sixty miles (one whole degree) further from the Pole than his own.

Naturally, both sides were cagey about the current state of their preparations and their future plans. Amundsen's main concern had been the edge he was sure Scott possessed with his motor sledges. Unfortunately, a member of the Eastern Party had let slip the fact that one of these machines was even then reposing on the floor of McMurdo Sound, a fact noted by Nilsen in his diary – 'at 200 fathoms on the ice they had lost their best automobile'. Amundsen must have been profoundly relieved to hear this snippet of news.

He would have drawn his own conclusions, too, from the amazement betrayed by the Englishmen at the strength, discipline and sheer number of his dogs. Ever since his visit to Quail Island in New Zealand, Abbott had seen them as the key: 'I feel sure that dogs are by far the swiftest & safest animals that can be used for transporting food supplies etc.' For Priestley this was the real facer: 'The principal trump-card of the Norwegians was undoubtedly their splendid dogs, and even then it was quite clear to us that if they won the race they would owe it to a great extent to these animals.' His assessment of Amundsen's chances was clear-headed: 'If they get through the winter safely, they have unlimited dogs, the energy of a nation as Northern in type as we are ourselves, and experience of snow-travelling that could be beaten by no collection of men in the world.' He concluded that the outcome would probably be a toss-up, decided eventually by luck and stamina; even so, he recognised the Norwegians as 'dangerous rivals' and that 'the news we have for [the Southern Party] will keep them on tenterhooks of excitement all Winter'.

Levick's reaction was in one respect typical: 'It is very unfortunate that Amundsen was not more aboveboard about his coming here.' But he also spoke of it as 'a wonderful day', and added: 'Anyhow it is going to be one of the finest races next summer that the world has ever seen, as the routes of both parties converge at the Beardmore Glacier and they may actually meet on the way.'* Browning gave the lower-deck perspective: 'There is plenty of talk on board now comparing our Expedition with the Norwegians and which is likely to succeed. We of course hope that Capt Scott will; anyhow he will have a good rival in Amundsen.' The awesome fitness of Amundsen's men and the efficiency and purposefulness of the preparations afoot at Framheim threw into sharp focus the crucial difference between reaching the Pole by hook or by crook under their own steam, and beating another team to it.

The confrontation in the Bay of Whales elicited gentlemanly offers from both sides. Browning fetched newspapers and magazines from *Terra Nova*, since the Norwegians had seen none since Madeira, and handed them over to Amundsen. Nilsen expressed his gratitude for chronometer readings more up to date than his own. Campbell promised that Pennell would

---

* This was a common misconception by the British – that Amundsen would use the tried and tested Beardmore route to the Pole. It does not seem to have occurred to them that he might instead follow the shortest and most direct line.

deliver mail in New Zealand for Amundsen and his team, while for his part Amundsen suggested that the Eastern Party should overwinter there as they had planned – reciprocal courtesies that were not taken up.

Given the importance attached by Scott to the exploration of King Edward VII Land, it seems curious that the opportunity to salvage this highly important part of the expedition's scientific work was not given more careful consideration. Certainly Campbell was sorely tempted to remain. But other members of the group, especially Wilfrid Bruce, felt that to trespass on their rivals' turf would be most inappropriate. Levick's view was similar: 'The "Fram" is in possession of our only possible landing place on the Barrier, & we have therefore to give up the idea of landing on it, which is a great disappointment to us, excepting Priestley.' Priestley himself played the moral card, asserting that 'we cannot according to etiquette trench on their country for winter quarters'. Campbell's bleak and inaccurate summary of their deliberations was that 'Amundsen suggested my wintering there, but I decided it would not do.'

In hindsight it was a classic case of Gentlemen v. Players – or in the rueful words of Dr Arnold of Rugby: 'My boys will always be out-louted.' Indeed, it is difficult to imagine anything more painful and embarrassing for Campbell and his men than to be present in the Bay of Whales when Amundsen returned in triumph from the Pole.

It is eerie to realise that if *Terra Nova* had succeeded in disembarking the Eastern Party at Cape Colbeck as planned, Pennell might conceivably have chosen to follow the same route back to Cape Evans, bypassing the Bay of Whales entirely. The British expedition as a whole would then have remained in complete ignorance of Amundsen's presence there until Scott reached the Pole thirty-three days after his rival. The surviving members of the expedition would have been enlightened only when they retrieved the letters and papers from the dead men's tent.

As it was (keeping Priestley on tenterhooks), they persisted at first in their search for a landing place on the Barrier close enough to King Edward VII Land to make exploration there viable. No safe haven offered itself, so on 5 February they gave up the fruitless task and headed out again into the Ross Sea to inform Scott, turning due west for Cape Crozier and reaching Cape Evans two days later. Their arrival was as dramatic as they could have hoped: 'We have exchanged news & astonished the natives with our startling budget & learnt their small adventures,' wrote Priestley complacently.

Reactions from the other expedition members when they broke the news were predictable. Cherry-Garrard wrote: 'For an hour or so we were furiously angry, and were possessed with an insane sense that we must go straight to the Bay of Whales and have it out with Amundsen and his men in some undefined fashion or other there and then . . . Our sense of co-operation and solidarity had been wrought up to an extraordinary pitch; and we had so completely forgotten the spirit of competition that its sudden intrusion jarred frightfully.'

Campbell's first and most pressing duty was to inform Scott of 'perfidious Amundsen's'* landing in the Bay of Whales, so he skied the fifteen miles over sea ice to Hut Point (inaccessible from Cape Evans by land because of its mass of glaciers) with Priestley and Abbott to deliver his bombshell and Levick's inadequate but telling photographs. Before this he ordered that the two ponies which were to have been landed with the Eastern Party on King Edward VII Land be pressed into Scott's service. Where they themselves now were bound – beneath the formidable Admiralty range – ponies had no place. So the unfortunate animals were lowered from the ship into the icy water and pulled ashore by the whaling boat, then warmed up with a brisk rub and half a bottle of whisky. (One, already weakened by the Great Storm, did not recover from his ducking, and had to be shot a few weeks later.) This thoughtful gesture was a final renunciation of the Eastern Party's grand design.†

Levick and Browning, meanwhile, were sent off on skis to Hut Point to leave extra provisions and tobacco for the Southern Depot Party. 'Our journey was rather a hard one,' wrote Browning, 'as we both were new to skiing, about 4 miles out a heavy wind came on blowing all the snow off the ice, at times we had to go down on our knees to prevent our being blown backwards, we abandoned our skis about 3 miles from Hut Point and proceeded on foot, the ice surface was like glass and on several occasions we came down a cropper; when we returned Mr Campbell was just thinking about sending out a party to look for us.'

One of the great fascinations in reading diaries is to correlate different perceptions of the same events. Levick's version of this excursion to Hut Point gave more details, and contradicted Browning's sparse recital in venomous detail. According to his reading, Browning proved so hopeless on skis that his superior made him remove them and proceed on foot, which was no improvement: 'I now had a fair example of the uselessness of the average bluejacket in using his feet.' It got worse. 'When the gusts came on, he simply stood rooted to the spot, and couldn't lift one leg off the ground without falling down.' Using a stick-and-carrot technique, Levick managed to haul, push, bully and cajole Browning up to the hut and back on the return journey to camp, in rapidly deteriorating weather. 'What made the situation worse', spat Levick, 'was that Browning, whom I now classed as a gutless swab, could not be got along at anything more than

---

* Wilfrid Bruce's phrase.

† Scott wrote generously to Campbell on learning the news, 'I heartily approve your decision not to winter in King Edward's Land, your courteous conduct towards Amundsen and your forethought in returning the two ponies to this station.'

8. Murray Levick, skier. A natural athlete, he was proud – even boastful – of his prowess at the sport, then in its infancy. The Norwegian expert Tryggve Gran, recruited as expedition coach, found most of his pupils ignorant even of its first principles.

2 knots.' It was all he could do to keep his temper. When they finally staggered into Cape Evans, they had been gone for twelve hours – 'I could have done the whole journey myself in five hours comfortably', was Levick's final bitter remark.

What would seem to lie behind this uncharacteristic outburst of bad temper on the part of the famously easy-going doctor was a combination of two things. First, he fancied himself as a skier ('I am becoming good at it', he had boasted earlier in his diary, 'and believe I shall be one of the best'). It was therefore more than irritating on a good long ski trip to be held back by a bumbling and frightened beginner. Second, it was his first opportunity to prove himself a competent leader, however minor the assignment. He must have felt a prize idiot as he and Browning returned to camp to find Campbell about to send out a search party. It was a long time before Browning was forgiven.

Bad luck seemed to be dogging the Eastern Party. On 9 January Browning reported in his matter-of-fact way: 'While engaged icing ship today a large piece weighing several tons fell away into the sea. Abbott was standing on top when it went, and got carried in with it he had a very narrow escape from being crushed to death.'

After the ship's return to Cape Evans, Cherry-Garrard suggested that Campbell was deeply regretting not being able to see Scott, since he felt sure the existing plans and parties would have been rearranged in response to the altered circumstances. In particular, 'Amundsen had asked Campbell to land his party at the Bay of Whales, giving him the area of the east to explore, and Campbell did not wish to accept before getting Scott's permission.' Campbell evidently did not feel able to accept Amundsen's offer on his own initiative, and Scott was not to learn about the Bay of Whales encounter until 22 February. The Eastern Party was thus forced to fall back on the final part of Scott's instructions: 'Should you be unable to land in the region of King Edward's Land you will be at liberty to go to the region of Robertson Bay after communicating with Cape Evans.'

# 3

# Confinement at Cape Adare

## 9 February 1911–4 January 1912

The Northern Party – as it was now permanently and properly known – set sail again on 9 February 1911. Ponting described their departure: 'We stood on the shore watching them until the boat was hoisted aboard. Then the good ship dipped her ensign, and, with three blasts of her whistle in salute, she stood away to the northward.' Those left at Cape Evans would not see the familiar outline of *Terra Nova* on the horizon for a long twelve months.

Campbell's instructions from Scott had been clear and unequivocal: 'The main object of your exploration in this region [Robertson Bay] would naturally be the coast westward of Cape North.' This was because no one had yet succeeded in landing on this outpost of South Victoria Land, where the great Admiralty range of mountains plunges down to the sea. Pennell, once he had dropped them off there, had been instructed to explore the shoreline still further west until forced to leave for his overwintering in New Zealand.*

In 1841 Ross had thrown down a tantalising gauntlet: 'We had a very good view of Cape North whilst close in with the icy cliffs, and observed that a high wall of ice . . . stretched away to the westward from the Cape, as far as we could see from the mast-head, and probably formed a coast line of considerable extent: a close, compact, impenetrable body of ice occupied the whole space to the northward and westward.' Behind, 'the lofty range of mountains appeared projected upon the clear sky beyond them beautifully defined.' Exploration here would be a reasonable compensation for the loss of King Edward VII Land.

The Northern Party had to reach their destination with all possible speed, as the ship's supplies of coal were running low. But their run of bad luck continued: from 12–15 February the ship was lashed by gales and

---

* In fact Pennell and his crew managed from the ship to survey a completely new stretch of coast west of Cape North (later named Oates Land), before being halted by heavy pack.

pushed nearly 100 miles north of Cape Adare, opposite Smith's Inlet. Dickason commented breezily: 'Hove-to in heavy sea, ship rolling very heavy, good old tub, heavy snow at times, we must be some way to the N.W. of Cape Adare by now, things are a bit more lively now.' The following day: 'Tonight it looks as though it would like to ease up a bit, if it don't and at this rate we shall soon be back in New Zealand again.'

They found nowhere to land on the precipitous and heavily glaciated coast from Smith Inlet to Cape North. Ross, scanning the coastline from the crow's nest, had thought the two deep adjoining bays of Smith's Inlet and Yule Bay promising. He had soon been disabused: 'The line of coast here presented perpendicular icy cliffs varying from two to five hundred feet high, and a chain of grounded bergs extended some miles from the cliffs.'

In the third major volte-face in the story of the Eastern-cum-Northern Party journey, *Terra Nova* was forced to retrace her steps and work her way anti-clockwise round Robertson Bay. There was no possible landing place on the ice tongue of the Dugdale Glacier;* Duke of York Island was inaccessible. Time was running out. Cape Adare was the only place where they were assured of finding a base, and then at a single spot – Ridley Beach, a flat basalt area strewn with pebbles, nestling against the sheer 1000-foot cliff face. They now faced an unpalatable choice: either they could settle for Cape Adare, or they could take a gamble and head back towards Cape Evans, aiming for the virtually unexplored and geologically interesting Coulman Island or Wood Bay. But if they were unable to land at either of those two places within the next three days, they would have to return with Pennell to New Zealand for the whole of the winter.

It was a dilemma, but there was no real contest. Their decision – or rather the decision taken by Campbell after consulting first Levick and then Priestley – was unanimous. They would go the farthest north they could beneath the great bulk of the Admirality mountains in Victoria Land and hope to build up a respectable body of research and exploration. It was a decision that Campbell was despondent about at the outset, and that he came bitterly to regret.

By 1911, Cape Evans and McMurdo Sound had become indelibly associated with the names of Scott and Shackleton, of *Discovery* and *Nimrod*. Cape Adare and Robertson Bay had their own ghosts – those of the *Southern Cross* expedition of 1898–1900, which had made polar history by being the first to overwinter voluntarily on the Antarctic continent. The Norwegian Carsten Borchgrevink had led the ten-man team, with Louis

---

* Luckily, as it turned out – some time later, as Abbott related, 'we found a huge part of the Dugdale Glacier majestically floating out to sea; so it was a lucky thing for us that we did not build our Hut on it, as we should have done, if there was a convenient place to land our stores, which I am pleased to say there was not.'

Bernacchi, a young Australian meteorologist and magnetist, as his second-in-command. Ghostliest of all was the party's zoologist, Nicolai Hanson, who had died during the expedition and been buried in the lee of a large boulder on the high plateau of Cape Adare.*

Borchgrevink was thus well known in polar circles, although rather more as a liar, mountebank and trouble-maker than as an explorer. He was an incorrigible fantasist – about his education, his qualifications and his achievements – and had made powerful enemies. Early in Borchgrevink's chequered career, Dr H. R. Mill, Librarian of the Royal Geographical Society, described him as 'of the most irrepressible persistency in gratifying his ambitions', while Dr Roy Lankester, Director of the Natural History Museum, called him 'a person with whom one would gladly have no dealings'. Most unfortunately for Borchgrevink, he also put up a black with Sir Clements Markham, President of the RGS, whose word in polar circles was law, and who evidently regarded him as a cross between a knave and a fool. Yet at the time his dogged determination and undoubted courage won him some admirers, and in 1930 the President of the RGS, Sir Charles Close, belatedly awarding him the Patron's Medal, was to acknowledge that Scott's Northern Party had made them realise that 'the magnitude of the difficulties overcome by Mr. Borchgrevink were underestimated . . . we were able to realise the improbability that any explorer could do more in the Cape Adare district than Mr. Borchgrevink had accomplished'.

Borchgrevink's account of the winter spent at Cape Adare was criticised, by Campbell among others, as lightweight and inaccurate, and for leaving out facts which might have been useful to future expeditions, whereas Bernacchi's fuller and more considered narrative was widely praised.† Scott and other members of the *Discovery* group, including Bernacchi,‡ had landed at Cape Adare in 1902 on their way to McMurdo Sound, visited Borchgrevink's hut and read his letter to the commander of any subsequent expedition. Already prejudiced against the Norwegian, they had ridiculed his claims, his sentiments and his grammar. Bernacchi, who was of the party, had remained loyally silent about his erstwhile leader.

Cape Adare lies at the end of a 20-mile-long peninsula sticking out like a bony thumb at the eastern end of the Admiralty Range, 2,500 miles from Australia and subject to every vicious weapon in the Antarctic armoury.

---

* Hanson was the first man to die in Antarctica. It took Bernacchi and the two Finnish members of the expedition two days to dig his grave to a depth of five feet, four of them through solid ice. Having broken all their tools, they eventually resorted to dynamite.

† Borchgrevink's *First on the Antarctic Continent, being an account of the British Antarctic Expedition 1898-99* and Bernacchi's *To the South Polar Regions* were both published in 1901.

‡ Unlike Borchgrevink, Bernacchi had established a good reputation in London's polar circles, and had later been enrolled by Scott as a physicist for the *Discovery* expedition.

Bernacchi had been struck by its dramatic topography, exposed to every freak of weather:

> As we approached the coast it changed continually in aspect. Sometimes dense clouds of mist would envelop it; at other times the clouds would roll up like a great curtain, disclosing to our eyes a long chain of snow-clad mountains, the peaks of which tapered up one above the other like the tiers of an amphitheatre or those of the Great Pyramid of Cheops . . . As we drew closer, the coast assumed a most formidable aspect. The most striking features were the stillness and deadness and impassibility of the new world. Nothing around but ice and rock and water. No token of vitality anywhere; nothing to be seen on the steep sides of the excoriated hills.

As the Northern Party's predecessors had warned, however, the dramatic beauty of their surroundings was a colossal drawback. The mountain range encircling the Cape Adare peninsula and Robertson Bay justified its formidable reputation: 'Rising to an average height of about 7,000 feet, and partly free of snow on its northern slopes,' Bernacchi had commented ruefully, 'it presents an impassable barrier to a sledge party.' The inland ice plateau visible beyond was tantalisingly inaccessible, as Campbell was fully aware: 'I was very much against wintering here, as until the ice forms in Robertson Bay one is quite cut off from any sledging operations in the mainland, for the cliffs of the peninsula descend sheer into the sea.' Viewing the scene from Ridley Beach, Levick corroborated this pessimistic assessment:

> Excepting when the sea ice is frozen over, which is only during the winter and spring, we cannot get off our little beach, because although we can climb up the cliff onto Cape Adare, this last mountain is separated from the mainland by what proved to Borchgrevink, inaccessible heights. The sea surrounding us, although . . . only frozen over in the winter & spring, is frequently covered with miles of pack ice during the summer, but this is kept constantly on the move and well broken up by the swirling tide which sweeps round Robertson Bay and so is quite impracticable for sledging or walking.

Although Borchgrevink and two companions had succeeded in penetrating some way into the interior, both on Cape Adare and at the southern end of Robertson Bay, where they had used the glaciers as escalators to gain the land mass behind, their sorties had been limited in duration and extent. Above all, they had failed to explore the area around Cape North, the conspicuous snow-covered bluff noted by Ross in 1841. He had (erroneously) thought it to be the northernmost point of the region, and it would make a satisfying area of study for that reason alone. This had been Borchgrevink's fault. Bernacchi, delivering a paper to the Royal Geographical Society on the topography of Victoria Land in March 1901, had replied to a question from the floor: 'I am very sorry to say that no expeditions were undertaken towards Cape North. I do not know for what reason. The commander was requested to allow permission to undertake expeditions to Cape North by various members of his staff, but for some reason he did not grant that permission. There is no doubt we could have undertaken these expeditions, because the surface of the ice was not hummocky in that direction, and was perfectly secure, and remained so until late in December.'

Borchgrevink's failure to explore Cape North provided the Northern Party's dream and great opportunity. Although they could not expect to fare any better in the territory around Cape Adare, locked as they were out of the interior of Victoria Land, they could set their sights on making a valuable survey of the coastline west of Robertson Bay, as Scott had intended. Levick was to write in his diary: 'There will be satisfaction in our journey across the sea ice, because, rightly or wrongly, Borchgrevink decided when he was here, that the risk made the attempt unjustifiable.' Priestley was decidedly less sanguine about their opportunities, either scientific or exploratory. He had written in his diary on 17 November, when the Northern Party were forced off King Edward VII Land: 'I have no doubt that I can find enough work at Robertson's Bay but Campbell's surveying work will be terribly reduced, if not cut off altogether by the difficulties of transport. I am much afraid my sledging here will be decidely local & confined to geology.'

Levick described the tantalising view from Ridley Beach:

> Facing us, about 15 miles across the Bay, is a magnificent range of snow covered mountains, with vast glaciers, moving their tongues into the sea. These are so badly crevassed as to be impracticable as a means of ascending to the heights, and possible plateau, of the unknown country beyond . . . Now far away to the westward, at the point where the range of mountains fades on the horizon, we noticed as we came along in the ship, that the ground became more undulating, lower, and less precipitous, and apparently offers a chance for a party to make their way through to the inland regions. This spot is about eighty miles from us as the crow flies, across the sea.

First they had to batten themselves down for the polar winter.

The Northern Party approached Ridley Beach at 3 a.m. on 18 February. The tide was running strongly in the bay, pockmarked with pack and fringed by pancake ice. Levick recorded their uncomfortable landing: 'Campbell & I pushed off in one of the whaleboats with a few seamen and pulled off for the shore. We found considerable surf breaking over a fringe of stranded floe ice along the beach, so we had to set our teeth, and at the word "jump" from him, he and I jumped from the bows, up to our waists in icy water, and after hauling the boat up a little way and leaving the men in her, we ran onto the little peninsula under the cliff.'

The ship carried with her the carcass of the hut that they had intended to erect on King Edward VII Land. They were also to make use of what remained of Borchgrevink's living and storage huts – the first of many tangible reminders of the *Southern Cross* expedition.* Ridley Beach was a triangular 400-acre gravel spit created by the strong tidal eddies swirling round Cape Adare. The flat, pebbly surface seemed a perfect place for a base camp; deceptively so, as it was plagued by winds from the cliffs behind and currents breaking up the ice in the bay in front. To the million penguins which colonised the area, however, it was an annual refuge. 'Campbell's men', wrote Teddy Evans, 'might for all the world have been erecting their hut on Hampstead Heath during a Bank Holiday, for the penguins gathered in their thousands around them in a cawing, squawking crowd.' Before they laid the floor of their new hut, Levick tried to bleach out the pungent smell of guano† with chlorine, nearly temporarily blinding himself in the process.

That first day, the six men and the ship's crew, especially Davies the ship's carpenter, worked like dogs for 22½ hours, during which time they unloaded the components of the hut, plus 30 tons of stores; the next day work started shortly after 7 a.m. and continued till dusk. Then, with little ceremony but heartfelt thanks, at 5 a.m. on 20 February the company stood on the beach to wave *Terra Nova* off. As a souvenir, Wilfrid Bruce took away with him a heavy brass dog chain left behind by Borchgrevink's expedition.

Scott's final instructions had laid down what would happen a year hence: 'You will not be expected to be relieved until March in the following year, but you should be in readiness to embark on February 25‡ ... Should the Ship have not returned by March 25 it will be necessary

---

* Ridley Beach had been named by Borchgrevink after his mother, a descendant of Bishop Ridley, the Marian martyr. This was a connection of which he was inordinately proud. According to Hugh Evans, the expedition's assistant zoologist, 'he never allowed us to forget that the "weins" of a Ridley flowed in his blood'.

† Guano (the Spanish word for the excrement of seabirds) is rich in digested salt-water fish. It was Victorian England's favourite garden fertiliser and made an enormous fortune for its importer, William Gibbs. His house, Tyntesfield near Bristol, was built at a cost of £74,000, half his annual income from Pacific guano. The senior branch of the banking family also benefited, giving rise to a popular ditty: 'Antony Gibbs / Made his dibbs / Selling the turds / Of foreign birds.'

‡ The Northern Party's departure date was evidently later revised, probably after Scott had received the news about Amundsen from Campbell. One of Pennell's sailing orders from Scott was to 'pick up Campbell and party about January 1 at Cape Adare'.

9. Hastily relocated to Cape Adare after finding Amundsen encamped on the Great Ice Barrier, the Northern Party waved goodbye to the ship and its crew on 18 February 1911 in the knowledge that they would not be picked up again for nearly a year. *Terra Nova*'s fragile lines shows clearly beneath her formidable hull and iron sheathing.

for you to prepare for a second winter . . . In conclusion I wish you all possible good luck, feeling assured that you will deserve it.'

Although twelve years separated Borchgrevink's and Campbell's expeditions, the two parties arrived at Cape Adare in the same month, February, within a day of each other, and only a month separated their departures.* The long year divided itself naturally into four seasons. From their arrival in mid-February until mid-May, the continent was moving from autumn to winter, with sinking temperatures and dwindling sunlight progressively curtailing outside work. From mid-May until the end of July, the sun

---

* The *Southern Cross* expedition landed at Cape Adare on 17 February 1899 and were picked up on 2 February 1900 (several weeks later than anticipated, due to adverse weather). The Northern Party were deposited at the same spot on 18 February 1911, and rejoined their ship on 4 January 1912.

disappeared and winter bit deep; the men's world shrank into the interior of their huts. Then, during the first week of August, the sun's globe showed itself entirely above the horizon for the first time for almost three months, ushering in a series of spring sledging journeys to the farthest corners of their circumscribed kingdom. Finally, in mid-November came the short and blessed Antarctic summer.

After disembarkation, the priorities for the Northern Party were to stow the stores and finish the hut. They hollowed out an ice house for their supplies of frozen meat, but although their first effort disappeared out to sea, Campbell recorded on 1 March: 'We managed to save the inmates and carried 40 stiff little corpses up to a new and still more beautiful icehouse Priestley built out of cases built in a hollow square, the inside all ice blocks.'*

Although the bones of their new home were assembled that first day, insulation and lashing-down were carried out after the departure of *Terra Nova*. Their carpentry efforts were workmanlike rather than professional, and made more difficult by the buffeting the components had received on board. 'Matchboarding', in Abbott's view, 'is excellent stuff if it has not been kicked about; but after being severely handled, as ours was, it makes the air turn a bit blue as it is put up, with cold hands.' But although it bulged oddly in several places, the hut stood up valiantly against the cyclonic winds sweeping down upon them almost continuously from the heights of Cape Adare, accompanied by tons of drift. They tied the building up like a parcel, with hawsers sunk into a barrel of oil and three anchors cemented into the gravel, which secured it to the ground on all four sides. These cables were their strongest lines of defence: Borchgrevink had noted nervously how the metal stays 'sang lustily during the fierce squalls . . . had they snapped we would probably have been shaken up like so many dice in a box'. Sure enough, on 20 March 1911, the Northern Party lost their magnetic observation tent, carried away by gusts of over 80 mph,† but this was junior league compared with some of the gales that struck just before the disappearance of the sun and the abrupt descent into winter.

The day following the loss of the tent was beautifully calm on land, but

---

* When it came to penguin-killing, they found that stunning them and then beating them over the head was the best method. Although Priestley admitted that it looked like 'a brutal attempt at mutilation', the alternative was worse: 'On a former occasion when we had been more gentle I returned after ten minutes and found a penguin croaking dismally with only half of its head left.' A sword, he felt, would have been preferable; a gun would not work, as the victim would have made off before they could get the second shot in. He did not discuss Ross's tried and tested method – poison.

† Levick did not bemoan its loss: 'It is lucky it did so, as we would probably have taken it sledging later on, and it might have happened with us in it, which would have been serious. It is evident that dome tents are useless and unsafe for Antarctic work.'

a tremendous surf was rolling up the beach – 'the biggest we have had since we came here', wrote Levick, 'and it has brought up enormous blocks of pack ice which are wedged along the beach and form a solid wall in some places over which the waves, laden with brash ice, break, hurling up blocks up to a hundredweight twenty or thirty feet high'. Whatever the disadvantages of Cape Adare as a location, the dramatic changes in weather gave it a never-ending fascination.

Campbell was determined to make the most of the time available before the encompassing darkness arrived. As soon as the hut was completed, the six men quickly assumed their various scientific roles. Campbell put himself in charge of surveying their territory* and undertaking magnetic observations. Levick was appointed photographer, zoologist and stores officer – and, of course, doctor, although at this stage, as Campbell pointed out, 'his medical duties have been nil, with the exception of stopping one of my teeth, a most successful operation; but as he had been flensing a seal a few days before, his fingers tasted strongly of blubber'. Priestley's main duties were geological, meteorological and microbiological. Abbott was carpenter and kayak-builder, Browning assistant meteorologist and assistant cook (and took over from Levick the responsibility for keeping the acetylene gas lights burning†), and Dickason was cook and baker.

Priestley was generous in his praise of his own three 'adaptable helpers', Abbott, Browning and Dickason, who threw themselves enthusiastically into the laborious work of data collection, acquiring new skills as amateur scientists. In the foreword to his report on the physiography of the Robertson Bay and Terra Nova Bay regions, published by Harrison & Sons in 1923, he was quite specific about their contribution: 'The very complete Meteorological and Auroral Record, the collection of thousands of geological specimens, the gathering of a botanical collection which has made possible a Memoir on the lichens and mosses, the compilation of a continuous ice record, have only been accomplished at the expense of a great portion of the little leisure time which they might well have claimed for themselves.'

Spirits began to rise after the depressing circumstances of their arrival had given way to a regular programme. After they had been established for a few weeks, Campbell noted with surprise: 'It is wonderful how quickly the time is passing. I suppose it is our regular routine, and the fact of all having plenty to do.' Although not as arduous and exhilarating as the

---

* The maps which resulted were, according to Priestley, still in use in 1969.

† These had been refined from the cumbersome equipment used on both Shackleton's and Scott's earlier expeditions. Each burner now had its own generator and was economical to run, although the lamps needed constant watching. Priestley likened the noise when the gas was running low to 'a constant succession of motor-bicycles at 4 a.m.'

existence they might have had on King Edward VII Land, it was pleasant and fulfilling enough. Campbell's report in *Scott's Last Expedition* gives a reasonable idea of the range of their activities one Sunday in early March: 'This afternoon Abbott, Priestley, Levick and I climbed to the top of Cape Adare, and certainly the view over the bay was lovely, the east side of the peninsula descending in a sheer cliff to the Ross Sea. We collected some fine bits of quartz and erratic boulders* about 1000 feet up, and Levick got some good photographs of the Admiralty Range. On the way down I found some green alga[e] on the rocks.' On that occasion they failed to locate Hanson's grave, but much later Browning cleaned and levelled it, and worked an inscription in quartz on basalt as a mark of respect to the first explorer to die on Antarctic soil.

Skiing, climbing and walking were other enjoyable ways of passing the time while the light held. Abbott wrote on 31 March: 'In the evenings I have been up the mountains for exercise, it is simply grand. There is one place I go to every evening, high up amongst the rocks – I sit down & just feast myself on the glorious scenery.' (Decidedly there was something of Wilson in the petty officer's make-up.) Another handy walk was to The Sisters, two rock stacks – one tall and slim, the other portly and short – lying about 250 yards offshore from the Cape; the return trip could be made in an hour. The name was derived from a music-hall song:

> We are the sisters wot won the Prize
> The sisters Hardbake with the Goo-goo eyes
> My name is Gertrude and mine is Rose,
> We shan't be single long I don't suppose.

The meteorological measurements taken by Priestley, Browning and occasionally Dickason were the most time-consuming part of their scientific programme, occupying many waking hours each day with thermometer and barometer. As in Borchgrevink's time, measurements were taken every two hours. In fine weather it was just another chore, but in blizzard conditions the observer was lucky if he escaped a lambasting from stray objects hurled at him by the wind. Sometimes it took the unfortunate on duty fifteen minutes to struggle the 800 yards back to the hut, and then only by hanging grimly onto a guide rope.

On occasion Levick helped Campbell with his magnetic observations. He did not enjoy the experience. 'We do this in a tent under which we

---

* Rocks and boulders swept down from the interior of the continent by glaciers in an earlier age.

10. Raymond Priestley holding a geology class at Cape Adare. His two 'adaptable helpers', Petty Officers Abbott and Browning, became both adept at and interested in the work. They were also called upon to take meteorological readings (chilly) and trawl for marine specimens (unsuccessful).

have dug a pit, to make room for the legs of the instruments. It is a cold business as you can't move for fear of moving the Barrow dip circle. If you stir this the whole thing has to be started again. Campbell stood in the middle & I had to squat, half sitting on the snow at the side of the tent. After an hour without moving my position, I could have sat on a spiked iron railing and never felt it.' Under the pseudonym 'Bluebell', Levick later contributed a poem to the in-house *Adélie Mail*. Entitled 'The Barrow Dip Circle', the ending expresses the poet's opinion of his task:

> Then on our frozen limbs we rise
> and fill the air with joyful cries.
> We'll go and make a huge repast
> the beastly thing is done at last.

The meteorologists of the Northern Party had been taught their trade by an exacting taskmaster, the expedition meteorologist 'Sunny Jim'

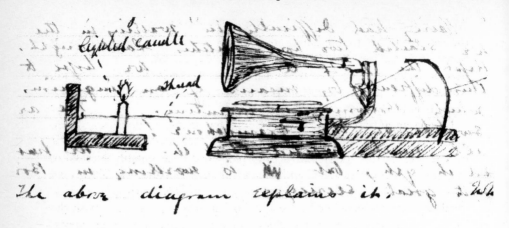

11. Browning's ingenious musical alarm clock, the 'Carusophone',
as drawn by Levick in his diary.

Simpson.* He had single-handedly raised the money for their state-of-the-art equipment, borrowed other instruments from major meteorological offices, set up the screens around Cape Evans on which the thermometers were mounted, and instituted a rigorous hourly programme of wind speed and temperature measurements which earned him the admiration of his colleagues, a future position as Director of the British Meteorological Office, and the abiding respect of his peers. Simpson's assistant at Cape Evans, Charles Wright, described him as having 'a supreme contempt for everything but Meteorology'.

The three amateur weather men were later to invent their own unorthodox meteorological aids. Wanting to duplicate Bernacchi's observations, Priestley decreed that the two-hourly shifts should continue throughout the winter months. Since Levick, who took the 2–4 a.m. shift, regularly overslept, Browning came up with an ingenious musical alarm clock of which Heath Robinson might have been proud. On 17 May Levick reported that they were all agog to find what Browning was working on 'in great secrecy' in Borchgrevink's hut. When the 'Carusophone' was unveiled by its inventor a week later, it was found to consist of a candle marked out in hours, a piece of thread and a bamboo cane, all linked to the gramophone. The device was activated by the person taking the midnight observations. Levick described its operation thus: 'When the candle burns

---

* Named for his distinctive quiff, which gave him a passing resemblance to a cartoon character of the period, rather than for his disposition. In fact deafness caused him to become increasingly morose and hermitic in later years.

down to the thread, it snaps it, releasing a piece of bent cane which pulls the catch off the gramophone, and starting Caruso off on the "Flower Song" from *Carmen* which I guarantee to wake the dead, or a man with his head in a sleeping bag, which is much the same thing . . . This invention works so well that I haven't worried about producing my own, though think it is really more scientific and exact.'

During an autumnal lull on 27 March they launched their Norwegian 'pram' (a light rowing boat) in order to try their hand at dredging for marine life. At this the *Southern Cross* party had been notably successful, catching all manner of weird and wonderful crustacea and fish. Their own efforts could have formed an extra chapter in *Three Men in a Boat*, involving a snow-shovel and a wooden bucket to sweep away or smash the ice, a net, a tangle of fishing lines, muscle cramps and swear words. Priestley also made a fish trap, which they lowered under the sea ice baited with penguin meat; this struck bottom at eight fathoms, but they caught nothing. Their total haul for the season being eight whelks, one sea urchin, one polychaete worm and a sea spider, they abandoned marine biology without regret.

Campbell was responsible for improvising the most successful effort in the nautical line – two kayaks, which were built to order by the nimble-fingered Abbott during April and May ready for their spring sledging journeys to the west side of Robertson Bay. Each consisted of a cover laced onto a standard sledge, the first made from canvas tenting material, the second from cotton curtain material. The canvas was dressed with blubber and remained reassuringly watertight. Levick took one out on a trial run, and she rose magnificently to his 12-stone challenge.

They also took soundings, and the beauty of their surroundings made up for the tedium and discomfort of the work. Abbott wrote after one morning's effort:

It was warm work – it made us perspire freely, & we got smothered in Ice from head to foot. I had the misfortune to lose a small crow-bar while I was making my fourth hole. I put my arm down the hole up to the armpit, to see if by chance it was lodged anywhere – but it had gone. My arm was soon as though it was cased in armour. We worked out as far as the Bay & it was one of the loveliest sights I have seen; it was like being in a beautiful garden . . . We went into the Bay through a large cavern & the sight when we were inside was indescribable.

Levick was also hard at work photographing the men, the hut, their environs and the magnificent icebergs making their erratic journeys across the bay. He discovered a blanket-lined cupboard in Borchgrevink's hut which he appropriated for his own use, although it was so cold in this primitive darkroom that he lost all feeling in his fingers; when he was loading slides he had to keep holding his breath or blow it away out of the corner of his mouth, to prevent it crystallising on the surface of the plates and ruining them. However uncomfortable, it was absorbing and rewarding. On 6 April he reported: 'For the last few days I have been working hard at photography, chiefly illustrating the different formations and curiosities of the ice foot, and at last I have taken a few dozen plates which are quite perfect. Fortunately they are also very beautiful, which is lucky as I have been taking them chiefly for Priestley who wants geological pictures. Altogether I have been at work from early niner till frosty eve, Sunday included.'

Levick was unable to resist continuing his rather bizarre experiments, the precise significance and usefulness of which were unclear. In mid-March he started making a weekly recording of the hand-grip of each man with a dynamometer, boasting with childlike pleasure: 'and I head the list by a good deal'. He even beat Abbott, the physical training instructor. More usefully, he instituted a weekly weigh-in, 'as it is very important for us not to get soft', and proposed to hold a regular Swedish exercise class. Later he and Campbell took to jogging before breakfast, although the combination of rough ground and worn-out boots made this a bit of a trial. Other martial arts were contrived. A punching ball was rigged up in Borchgrevink's hut, 'which is a good thing to warm oneself up before starting work in the morning'. Fresh from his triumph with the kayaks, Abbott devised two tin helmets made from biscuit boxes, worn over a woollen helmet, and made some sabres out of split bamboo. Leather mitts protected their hands. 'I think', concluded Levick modestly after one bout, 'I am a slightly better fencer than he is.'

It was a civilised time in the hut. Although the bother of heating water curtailed their washing activities, Levick reckoned that they kept themselves 'pretty clean on the whole', and they carried on the Edwardian tradition of dressing for dinner. 'My favourite costume for this', he wrote, 'is sea boots (to the top of my thighs) and my old blue naval blazer with brass buttons, which Priestley declares gives me the appearance of the "Admiral of the Dogger Bank Fishing Fleet".' After listening to a concert on the gramophone or dipping into a book plucked from the library shelves,* they retired to eiderdown sleeping bags reinforced by an inner lining of blankets.

The Sunday service was another fixed point. Campbell and Levick

---

* Abbott's reading matter included a clutch of novels unknown today: *The Virginian* by Owen Wister, *The Fighting Chance* and *Maids of Paradise* by R. W. Chambers, *Forest Lovers* by Morris Hewlett and *The Illustrious O'Hagan* by Justin McCarthy.

12. Levick at ease with book and pipe in his cubicle at Cape Adare. The naval tradition of segregating the ranks obtained even in these cramped conditions, and would do so when they moved to their final billet underground. The doctor is surrounded by the tools and medicine bottles of his trade, with the sledging flag given to officers at the start of the expedition as decoration.

chose two weekly hymns from their limited repertoire of known tunes. On one adventurous morning they tried a new one, 'Hark, Hark, My Soul', which Levick recognised from home – 'some cottagers used to play [it] on the harmonium all Sunday afternoon'. Alas, they had over-reached themselves. 'When the tune came, after the first few lines I found that my own beautiful bell like voice was singing all alone, the others having dropped out of the running.' He soldiered on, and the others chimed in intermittently in later verses; they struggled to the end 'with just the occasional disagreement in the harmony'.

As autumn began to yield to winter, the temperature dropped and frostbites increased (still a novelty, they were not treated with due deference – Dickason's rallying-cry was: 'Just the sort of weather to keep one on the move, "what ho" *the noses!*') and tensions began to surface. In early April, Levick reported Priestley in a sulk over Campbell's decision that all photography must be done in Borchgrevink's freezing cold hut, where the blubber stove made a mess and was apt to ruin plates. Levick persuaded Campbell to rescind this edict, but had to use his peace-keeping skills a few days later.

> At lunch the other day we were having quite a friendly argument as to whether girls ought to play hockey with men, and Campbell lost his temper and was exceedingly rude to Priestley in front of the men and P. replied in the same strain. Campbell told me afterwards that he thought of speaking to Priestley about it, but I got him to let me do it, as I felt sure, knowing Priestley's temper, that he would lose it still further if Campbell spoke to him, and probably create a most uncomfortable situation.

Levick dealt with this spat with no-nonsense common sense: 'I spoke pretty plainly to P. and told him he had put himself absolutely in the wrong, and got him to promise me that if ever he was going to have trouble with Campbell, over complaints or anything else, he would do it privately and not in the presence of men.' He continued: 'I have tried as far as possible to make my position rest between Campbell and the others, which seems right as I am no. 2 of the party and ought to act as a buffer to both sides in case of unpleasantness arising.' It was doubly fortunate that Levick was possessed of a placid, easy-going nature, and that, Campbell excepting, he was older than the rest of the group. Would-be combatants accepted his stepping in with good grace; neither Priestley nor Campbell seems to have felt inclined to shoot the peace-maker on that occasion.

Given Campbell's irritability, Priestley's tendency to sulkiness and Browning's observed shortcomings ('Browning though very clever and useful, I have already commented on in my account of our ski trip to Hut Point'), Levick was consciously evolving a way to maintain the group on a psychological even keel. He allotted Abbott a key part in this. He recognised the large, gentle and intelligent petty officer's worth, just as Wilson had done: 'He is quite one of the most splendid men I have had the luck to know, and I am quite fond of him.'* Ruminating on the implications of the Campbell–Priestley spat, he wrote: 'With Abbott to keep the two other men in their place we ought to get on all right, and there isn't much chance of their losing their heads through living and messing with officers.'

Levick's strategy was evidently geared to defusing unpleasantness firmly

---

\* The two men remained on excellent terms, and Abbott felt able to rib Levick as did his peers, recording one day in his diary: 'The Doctor is going to try to beat my record for fetching Ice, but am not startled as his motto is "Festino lente".'

and fairly before personal dislikes took hold and ruined the harmony of the group – he would mediate between Campbell and Priestley, while Abbott prevented unseemly behaviour from the junior seamen incurring the officers' displeasure. It seems to have worked. On 6 April, after Campbell had been rude to him several times, Levick recorded: 'as it occurred one morning at breakfast I followed him out of the hut, and as soon as we were alone fairly let him know he had overstepped the mark, and things have been different ever since. We are both excellent friends now.' He added kindly: 'He means to be a decent chap and is, on the whole, although rather small minded and lacking in guts.'

It is rare to find such frank comments on record in Antarctic diaries of the period (although Oates's letters to his mother, for example, are equally revealing about Scott); most are much more discreet, if not downright misleading. It comes as no surprise that neither Campbell nor Priestley mention these two quarrels, and Levick no doubt excised them from his own account in his fair-copy journal.

A fortnight later, he noted with relief: 'We are all getting along very peacefully now, and C. getting reconciled to P., I think. The latter had been moping a good deal for some time [probably at the thought of the winter soon upon them], but I started pulling his leg continuously at meals, which bucked him up quite a lot, & he has now started to pull mine in return and is altogether quite another person. He works like a nigger at his job I must say.'

He even enlisted Campbell in his therapeutic Priestley-baiting exercises. On 25 April, Campbell and Levick were enjoying an after-breakfast pipe when the doctor noticed Priestley, the only non-smoker of the party, looking disgusted at a habit he considered both revolting and a waste of time. Levick winked at Campbell, who twigged at once, and the following conversation, with a strong whiff of Lewis Carroll about it, took place:

| | |
|---|---|
| I | 'I think pipes have distinct characteristics like human beings.' |
| Campbell | 'Undoubtedly. I once had a pipe that was continuously getting lost. I never had any trouble that way with my other pipes, but this one in particular got itself mislaid nearly every time I smoked it. My keeper knew it by sight, and whenever I smoked it out shooting he kept a special eye on it and as I walked away from each drive, he would pick it up from the ground where I left it behind, & restore it to me.' |
| I | 'This pipe I am smoking now won't draw. I cursed it some time ago as it wasn't drawing properly, and it has never worked well since.' |
| Campbell | 'That would account for it. One should be very careful how |

71

|            | one speaks to one's pipes, they are so sensitive.' |
| I          | 'Do you think they have souls?' |
| Campbell   | 'Undoubtedly. I think they probably first came into this world as common or garden shilling pipes, and then if they behave themselves well, they re-exist as Benlays', Loewe's or B.B.B. own make.' |

At that juncture, Priestley got up and walked away.

It is interesting in this context to read, in a book written by Louis Bernacchi's granddaughter, his intimate and revealing diary kept during the *Southern Cross* expedition.* Any hint of animosity was expunged from Bernacchi's own book, but his personal notes laid bare a riveting story of high farce and high drama. Bernacchi took to referring to Borchgrevink as 'the individual' or 'the booby', and his disgust at his leader's truly staggering displays of incompetence, cowardice, greed, drunkenness, bluster, lies and egotism rose to a crescendo of fury. Eventually he came to the conclusion that Borchgrevink was, quite simply, mad. Bernacchi's writings reveal the contemporary lack of knowledge and understanding of the effects of cold, anxiety and boredom on the psychology of the individual and the group. This applied throughout the *Southern Cross* expedition because of the singular character of 'the booby', but the onset of winter was clearly beginning to threaten the harmony of the Northern Party too. Levick was wise to be both concerned and vigilant.

He stuck to his guns over less explosive matters too. He became convinced of the importance of keeping the hut well aired, and insisted from mid-April on opening the inner and outer doors for a few minutes each day, only letting the fug rest unmolested when a blizzard was blowing. Two months later he was still fighting his corner: 'I have been insisting on our keeping the hut at a decently low temperature . . . Campbell likes it at a fearful heat. However I got him to agree to 45°F though he wanted it at 50° . . . unfortunately he really feels the cold more than we do and says he cannot write or do anything in that way at the lower temperatures. What he will do during spring sledging the Lord only knows. Priestley is as hard as nails & doesn't care how cold the hut is.'

From mid-April, the freezing of the sea – the gradual transformation of evanescent ice crystals into more stalwart saucers of pancake ice and finally into an impenetrable block – marked another milestone in the approach of winter, although individual gales were still able to blast the solidifying ice out of the bay. On 15 April (Easter Sunday), for example, a gale tore in

---

* *That First Antarctic Winter: The story of the Southern Cross Expedition of 1898-1900 as told in the diaries of Louis Charles Bernacchi* by Janet Crawford, South Latitude Research Ltd, New Zealand, 1998.

without warning – beautifully fine at noon, fifteen minutes later it was gusting at 60 mph. 'This is most typical of the Antarctic climate,' wrote Levick. 'When the air is still, the sun shining, and everything looking fine and wonderful, nature is simply lulling you into a false sense of security, and crouching ready to spring on you when you can be taken unawares.'

In 1911, as in 1899, the disappearance of the sun in mid-May – the true harbinger of winter – was preceded by an almighty blizzard. On 5 May Borchgrevink had recorded a terrific natural upheaval: 'The ice-fields were screwing, and at the beach the pressure must have been tremendous. Already a broad wall some 30 feet high rose the whole length of the N.W. beach, and coming nearer we saw that the whole of this barrier was a moving mass of ice-blocks, each several tons in weight. The whole thing moved in undulations, and every minute this live barrier grew in height and precipitated large blocks on to the peninsula ... The roar of the screwing was appalling.' The prolonged blizzard which struck the Northern Party, coincidentally also on 5 May, was of equal ferocity. Levick described it as 'the most tremendous hurricane we have had yet, or any of us experienced before. The din outside kept us awake half the night, & very often small stones hit the side of the hut with a crack. Some of our outside wall of cases blew down. In the morning ... it was impossible to stand up straight in the wind, and one had to drop to all fours in the squalls.' The 14-stone Abbott was tossed against one of the hawsers securing the hut like a piece of sacking. 'Lately', wrote Levick, 'we have all been laughing a great deal at Borchgrevink's descriptions of the conditions he met with here, thinking that he was simply piling on the effect, but now we are beginning to feel a little more respect for what he says.'

For Borchgrevink the departure of the sun on 15 May had been an apocalyptic moment: 'The refraction of it appeared as a large red elliptical glowing body to the north-west, changing gradually into a cornered square, while the departing day seemed to revel in a triumph of colours, growing more in splendour as the sun sank, when the colours grew more dainty, and surpassed themselves in beauty. It imprinted itself upon the minds of us ten so strongly that it made life possible for us through those dark days and nights to come.'

The Northern Party lost the sun on 17 May, but the darkness was not absolute. At midday each day the reflection of the sun's rays reached them even though the sun itself was below the horizon, and they were granted a period of daylight; only Midwinter Day was absolutely pitch-black. Levick described the scene on 27 May: 'The skies lately have been perfectly beautiful. Towards noon, we get the appearance of a most wonderful sunset over the region of the horizon where the sun reaches its highest altitude. These "sunsets" have been, lately, various shades of amber, burnt sienna, and gamboge, fading at the edges into delicate apple green and blue.' Their nights were also lit up by the cold glow of the moon. 'Imagine', wrote one observer, 'a perfectly still evening with forty degrees of frost, the air perfectly dry, and a brilliant moon surrounded by a halo in which the colours of a rainbow are represented twice over, and which shows up perfectly clearly against an indigo sky, while the light of the moon is doubled by the reflection from every point of every ice and snow crystal.' Bernacchi's earlier description of these nights had revealed a powerful *chiaroscuro* element: 'There is something particularly mystical and uncanny in the effect of the grey atmosphere of an Antarctic night, through whose uncertain medium the cold white landscape looms as impalpable as the frontiers of a demon world.'

The clear skies prevailing during winter also gave the best opportunity to observe the spectacular fireworks of *Aurora australis*, to which they were treated on most nights. At Cape Adare – situated on the northern rim of the continent (at 71° 185' latitude) and fairly close to the South Magnetic Pole, where the magnetic activity which generates the displays is at its most intense – they had the best seats in the whole of the southern hemisphere. The show might last from 6 p.m. to 3 a.m., and the 8–9 p.m. slot provided most of the drama.

The officers of the Northern Party would almost certainly have gone through *The Antarctic Manual* of 1901 – required reading for all polar explorers of the period – and the chapter on auroras must have gripped their imagination. The phenomenon is catalogued in all its guises – an arch of tender light pricked through with stars, a band twisted into intricate convolutions, broad flaming streamers, narrow stripes of red and green enclosing a brilliant white centre, rays flashing and flaring around the magnetic Pole, slender threads of gold woven into a veil, a sea of red, white, green flames ... Accompanying the pyrotechnics of light and colour, the author noted the uncanny silence, and also the sense of desolation at the aurora's departure:

Nature displays before us such an exhibition of fireworks as transcends the powers of imagination to conceive. Involuntarily we listen: such a spectacle must, we think, be accompanied with sound. But unbroken stillness prevails; not the least sound strikes on the ear. Once more it becomes clear over the ice, and the whole phenomenon has disappeared with the same inconceivable rapidity with which it came, and gloomy night has again stretched her dark veil over everything. This was the aurora of the coming storm – the aurora in its fullest splendour. No pencil can draw it, no colours can paint it, and no words can describe it in all its magnificence.

Priestley, who had experienced 'colourless displays' at Cape Royds, was not holding out high hopes for Cape Adare. In the event, he could not contain his excitement when describing in his diary what was unanimously voted the finest display of the winter. Although not as extensive as others, it was

magnificently coloured, all the colours of the spectrum being represented except blue, while several compound colours were present, of which the most noticeable were lilac, purple, pink, and a bright golden green. These changed with inconceivable rapidity, melting into each other almost imperceptibly, and not only the lower portion of the filaments, but whole curtains, were often a brilliant deep crimson, rose pink, or violet, while frequently a large portion of an arch would appear as a chequered pattern of brilliant green and gold, and red or pink. It might truly be called an opalescent aurora.

These auroras left those who observed them a unique and priceless legacy of movement and colour, but they could not eradicate the boredom and discomfort that was winter life at Cape Adare. Borchgrevink had demonised it as 'the dark period', when 'the sameness of those cold, dark nights attacks the minds of men like a sneaking evil spirit'. At a moment requiring inspired leadership, he was, needless to say, found wanting. For the *Southern Cross* group, dirt and idleness, punctuated by quarrels and insults, were the order of the winter day. Even in his expurgated version, Bernacchi was unenthusiastic:

Very little work was possible during the dark cold months, so we waxed fat and apathetic out of pure inertion and sloth; it was a life of merely bovine repose. Whilst our godliness was indisputable, as much could scarcely be said for our cleanliness. Ablutions were rare on account of the difficulty of melting the snow to procure water, so we were soon disguised in dirt; a disguise made more effective by the growth of long patriarchal hair and beards, which really saved a peck of trouble in the way of shaving.

By contrast, Campbell's strategy for dealing with the cold and tedium smacked of his public-school past: firm discipline and immutable routine. Each man had a bath once a week and a brisk snow-wash every morning, although Priestley admitted: 'I fear it was only a spirit of emulation and a desire not to be outdone by Campbell which kept me up to scratch for the greater part of the winter.' The daily pattern was described by Levick as follows:

We turn out at 8.15, run out of the hut & clean our teeth etc. Then in. Breakfast 8.30. During the morning we generally do duties which take us outside such as (according to our several vocations) geology, magnetic observations, photography, zoology, soundings through the sea ice, etc. This applies mostly to Campbell, Priestley and me. Lunch is at one. After lunch we work in the hut till tea, or outside if there is anything going on. After tea, we read, write, draw, while Campbell and I generally have a game of chess as well. Dinner at 7. After dinner, same as tea, but the gramophone is always turned on about 8.30 to 10.30 or eleven.

Meals consisted of many of the same staples as those enjoyed by a middle-class Edwardian household, with porridge, potted meat and plum duff putting in regular appearances among the seal and penguin steaks and cold roasted skua. Alcohol was strictly rationed to a glass of sherry or port on Saturdays in which to drink the traditional naval toast of 'Sweethearts and Wives'. On birthdays the allowance was more liberal, and Campbell was certainly stretching things when he ordained that a bottle of sherry be opened to celebrate the Fourth of June. But on 22 June all the rules were waived for Midwinter Day. There were parcels from home, decorations, a formal and satisfyingly large champagne, brandy and crême de menthe dinner, with cigars and crystallised fruits on the side, and an extended sing-song.

On Saturday mornings the 'men' scrubbed out the hut, while the afternoons were devoted to running repairs. On Sundays work was suspended. Breakfast was put forward an hour to give the cook a lie-in, a church service followed at 10.30 a.m., and, moonlight permitting, a brisk walk took them along the coast or up to the icebergs stranded near the beach, all under the clear winter sky lit up by a succession of magnificent auroras. On 4 July Abbott and Dickason enjoyed an afternoon's skiing down the slopes near the hut in bright moonlight.

The occasional accident also added spice to life. On 15 June Levick was playing chess with Campbell in the hut, 'when suddenly, in burst Browning, staggering a few steps towards his bunk, and then fell senseless on the floor'. Levick got him in a squatting position, forced his head between his knees and, when he came round, put him on his bunk and dosed him with brandy and water. 'I then got the following history out of him. He had been sitting at work [in Borchgrevink's hut], with stove on and doors tight shut. The fire smoked a lot, and burned dully, and after a time his candle went out. He relit it, and it went out again. Then he felt sick, and came over to the hut, where he collapsed. Diagnosis – carbon monoxide poisoning. So simple, my dear Watson!'*

---

\* Bernacchi and two others had suffered the same fate in the same hut, which had later nearly burnt down altogether, when a candle was carelessly left burning on a bunk.

13. Exploring one of the magnificent 'cave-bergs' stranded in the sea ice after the freezing of the sea and watching the kaleidoscopic aurora displays were unforgettable aspects of the winter at Cape Adare. Experimenting with magnesium flashlight, while photographing inside a berg, Priestley succeeded in singeing off his eyelids and eyelashes and burning his face.

Campbell's insistence on creating a framework of order and structure undoubtedly helped to combat the lurking demons of depression and lethargy. Debenham had already categorised him as 'an instance of that rarity, an officer who could be a martinet on deck and a good companion on his watch below'. The ability to instil respect bordering on fear was a useful tool for an officer, but Tryggve Gran disclosed to Huntford that Campbell had 'a very nasty temper, and the nickname "the wicked mate" was a right one'. He was certainly a good man in a crisis and good company when things were going well, but long spells of boredom and discomfort were likely to tell on him more than on a man of slower pace and more even temper, such as Levick. By nature extremely shy and reserved, Campbell was a natural target for the sort of dark introspections suffered by Scott. In his obituary, Priestley commented on the considerable mental strain Campbell was under at this time, given the shock of the Bay of Whales and the frustrating limitations presently imposed on the party at Cape Adare. A remark made by Cherry-Garrard about Scott might be applied also to Campbell: 'Temperamentally he was a weak man, and might very easily have been an irritable autocrat. As it was he had moods and depressions which might last for weeks.' Like Scott, he kept his feelings bottled up, divulging them neither to his diary nor in his public writings. Priestley was equally uninformative about personal matters. Levick and Dickason alone, in diaries not intended for publication, suggested that there were undercurrents. It would have been strange if there had been none.

There is a hint at this time that Campbell had taken against Levick for some reason – perhaps a legacy of Levick's reprimand back in April. There is not much to go on, and what little there is takes the form of snide remarks in his diary, such as 'Levick spends most of his day at photography the results, I am afraid, doubtful as he usually forgets to wipe the lens or puts the plates in the wrong way.' This might have been meant as a joke, but comments like these are significant because they are not applied by Campbell to any other member of the team. Perhaps Levick's slow and thorough approach to life and decision-making irritated his mercurial superior; perhaps, as second-in-command, he seemed a legitimate target for Campbell's pent-up frustration. But the imperturbable good humour which had endeared 'The Old Sport' to his shipmates stood him in good stead now, and during the hard times to come.

Priestley was entirely different in character from the two naval officers. Charles Wright, another member of Scott's expedition and later to be Priestley's brother-in-law, wrote of him after his death: 'He had the common touch and he had learned how to obey and to command, a legacy of his days in World War I. But his character was not altogether a simple one. He was unassuming and not without ambition. He was very prompt to inform me whenever he had received any special advancement . . .' He was also a good raconteur and a natural diplomat; on many occasions he helped Levick to supply the glue which held the disparate band of men together during the long winter months. He was also enlightening about the character of the Abbotts, Brownings and Dickasons of the period, calling them 'naval seamen of the long service type, caught young and meticulously trained for many years in a specialized environment . . . Naval men of that particular vintage were the salt of the earth but they needed knowing and sympathetic and firm handling under the unusual Antarctic conditions.' He added: 'I sometimes used to think that he [Campbell] was occasionally too hard on the men for what seemed to be very minor peccadilloes' – although he went on to retract this remark. Priestley was thinking especially of Abbott, 'who was always getting into what I thought was too hot water for mislaying gear of all sorts'. Campbell's handling of his subordinates during that long winter was certainly firm – but knowing? sympathetic? That was Levick's forte.

The 'men' became adept at deception to avoid incurring 'Mr C's' displeasure. Dickason recorded gleefully on 14 June: 'I very near caused a sensation in camp this morning, instead of turning out when called I lay on and dropped off to sleep again, when next I woke it was a quarter past eight and I had to have breakfast ready by half past, so by flying around and putting the clock back twenty minutes I had things ready when the others turned out. Of course I readjusted the clock at the first opportunity, or at least "Rings" [Browning] did the trick whilst I screened him, very narrow shave. "You blighter".'

By the end of July all six men, in the prime of life and peak of fitness, deprived of light and cooped up like battery chickens, were sick and tired of their sedentary existence. It was with profound relief and palpable eagerness that they prepared for the spring sledging journeys that would follow hard on the heels of the returning sun. Levick, still concerned about his relationship with his superior, was relieved that winter had passed off with no major confrontations. He confided to his diary on 2 July: 'On the whole we are getting on quite well together. Priestley and I are really good friends. I am, I think establishing an ascendancy over Campbell, which has been a good thing in many ways, as I am gradually getting him out of many of his fads. He is not a bad chap but hopelessly out of place as a leader, being much too self-conscious and lacking most sadly in guts.' He added: 'I feel rather a beast sometimes when Priestley and I get away together and crab him to each other, whilst all the time he and I remain outwardly friendly. Campbell and I have more in common to talk about on general subjects than Campbell and Priestley, and as the latter can't stand having Campbell with him on his peregrinations, C. and I generally take our walks together, though *I* would rather go with Priestley. That pretty well sums up our general relations I think.'

Levick was also concerned about Dickason ('a fine chap'), whose duties as cook confined him indoors far more than the others, and who might therefore be out of condition for the start of spring sledging. Once again Levick had his way, writing on 12 July: 'I have after a good deal of difficulty got Campbell to arrange for Browning and Dickason to take turns over the cooking, so that now Dickason gets outside work on at least three days a week.' Abbott was not enthusiastic about the arrangement: 'Had a day's cooking, relieving Dick so that he could work in the open – have just finished the business – I wouldn't be a cook for any money.'

The following day came a bad bout of polar *ennui* (a medical complaint diagnosed early on in Arctic and Antarctic exploration), the first for many months thanks to Levick's vigilant defusing of potentially inflammable situations. It started, trivially enough, with an absurd argument about the number of times Levick had trimmed coal aboard *Terra Nova*. Campbell evidently feeling that his status as the ship's first mate was being impugned, got into a tremendous sulk and refused to speak to Levick. The doctor bore this for two days, but when he realised Campbell was starting to get into 'a sort of neurasthenic condition', he decided something must be done. When Campbell left the hut to get some exercise, he followed him out, caught him up, and tackled him.

I said, 'Look here Campbell, you've got the hump'. He stopped and faced me, and out it all came, that weight on his mind which had been loading him down for two days! He said – 'well I must say I was vexed at your saying at breakfast the other day, that you had been down coal trimming as often as twice a week on the way out, when I knew quite well you hadn't. I was in charge of the routine of work and surely I ought to know,' etc etc.

I said, 'Now look here, I am not going to open up that argument again, but I am going to speak to you very plainly, and I want you to understand that no offence is meant, and I hope you won't take any. We are a small party, cooped up together for a long time in a very small space, and it is only natural that we should get tired of one another, and apt to exaggerate in our minds, the small faults which we see in one another, repeated so often. You yourself have had perhaps a duller time than Priestley & I, as we have both had attractive jobs to keep us going, whilst you are still waiting for yours, and this dullness is beginning to get on your mind, and to put it plainly, you have got the hump. Now we shall soon be sledging and have plenty to do, and when you look back at the little things that worry you now, you will simply laugh to think that they annoyed you. Many a fine chap has been taken the same way before, and it's nothing out of the common. You've been looking rotten lately, and I am going to give you a tonic, which will make you feel another man.' I then repeated that I meant no offence & hoped he had taken none, and he said he hadn't, and we came back to the hut the best of friends again.

Ironically to present-day readers, Levick went on: 'I have given him a tonic with strychnine in it [nux vomica] and he has been better and much more cheerful ever since.'

Levick's sensible treatment of a disagreement that had threatened to fester into a serious breach was in character. But it took some courage to lecture his superior officer, and some nerve to suggest that Campbell was marking time while he and Priestley were achieving useful and fulfilling work. On the other hand, mentioning spring sledging journeys to their leader, and promising a tonic to a man with hypochondriacal tendencies, were both masterly touches.

Levick's return to favour suffered a set-back when they nearly fell out again over the vexed question of ventilation.* Although Campbell vetoed Levick's proposal to extinguish one of their two stoves, he permitted the door to be left open for longer periods, and even promised to have a small kind of cat flap made in the inner door. Perhaps the fact that he was putting lap bindings onto his skis in preparation for their forthcoming trips had put him in a good mood.

While the Northern Party were still in the grip of winter, Levick had pondered on the sledging plans master-minded by Campbell. These focused on two major journeys to the westernmost end of Robertson Bay – Cape North and Cape Wood – which Scott had been so anxious for them to explore. Levick wrote: 'Our only chance of success in this direction, lies in making the whole journey in the spring, and in getting back before the sea ice breaks up. We must thus start in the very early spring, which is the most trying time for sledging, owing to the very low temperatures, frequent hurricanes, and short periods of daylight.' Campbell may have been raring to go, but Levick was looking forward to this period 'with much the same sensations that I used to feel when looking forward to exams'.

There were to be two separate sledging parties, the first consisting of Campbell, Priestley and Abbott, the second of Levick, Browning and Dickason. Levick summarised the plan of campaign thus:

> Some time about the middle of August, both parties are to start off together, each hauling two sledges laden with their provisions, and make for the western end of Robertson Bay, i.e. the coast between Duke of York Island and Cape Wood.
>
> Arrived somewhere about there, I part with the other party, and bringing back just enough provisions to get us home, return here, rest for a day or so, load up with more provisions and then make the journey again to our place of parting. Campbell will have taken his party on for extended exploration, and I will leave a depot of provisions for him to

---

* Levick continued to worry at the problem, ascribing rheumatic pains suffered by him and Abbott to 'our ridiculous means of ventilation, by which the hut is frequently cooled down from 60° . . . to below freezing point, in a few minutes, instead of being kept at least approaching an even temperature.'

get home on, and then return with my team along the coast, making a photographic survey of the mountains as we come along.

This programme will take my party the whole of the spring, pretty well. Campbell should pick up the depot I leave for him, on his way back, about the end of October, and then come straight back here, provided always that the ice is still safe. If it has gone out, he will have to stop at the depot until the ship comes for us at the end of the summer [i.e. at the beginning of January 1912].

Levick's party, in other words, was to be to a large extent nothing more than a support party, ferrying supplies for the major exploration effort. He was, however, also intending to pursue his zoological researches. 'During the summer, and the end of spring, if I get back in time, I am hoping to put in great work among the breeding penguins here, and the other birds and seals etc.' So, 'this is our programme, and it will be interesting to see how it develops.' Not as planned, inevitably.

Sledging fever was upon them. On 24 July Dickason tramped out to The Sisters to get himself fit. Whiskers were shaved off, since they would become uncomfortable as their owner's breath froze on them during hauling. Levick lectured the party on breaks and fractures, and Dickason listed a hundred and one other things to do: 'sledges and harness, canvas "kayaks" to go with them, weighing up food, each man's allowance per day, what clothes to wear on the march and in the sleeping bag, which is lightest and best . . .'

An immense amount of preparation and meticulous attention to packing went into each sledging trip – unsurprisingly, since on one of the two major journeys made by the Northern Party during the spring of 1911 the total weight hauled (including their two sledges) was 1,163lbs. All the gear had to be stowed so that it could be unloaded or reloaded in order of need and at top speed – essential on foul-weather days. The rapid provision of shelter, light and hot food, in that order, took precedence. So the tent was carried on top of the load, and the primus lamp and the stove were also ready to hand. Then the delicate scientific instruments had to be boxed up out of harm's way, and the weight distributed evenly over the centre of the sledge. As the rations disappeared down ravenous gullets, the space released would be filled up by the same volume of geological and other specimens. Other bulky items were gallon tins of oil and the shovel and ice axes needed to erect the tent on frozen ground. Each man was also allowed to squeeze in 10lbs of spare clothing. These mighty loads were pulled by harnesses of canvas and leather – shoulder straps buckled onto a waistband, one for each man – stitched together by the deft fingers of Abbott and Browning.

Given Campbell's orderly mind and organisational skills, the Northern

Party and their laden sledges probably looked reasonably tidy as they set out each day, compared, say, with the Western Party under the leadership of Griffith Taylor. 'Old Griff on a sledge journey', wrote Cherry-Garrard in a delightful passage, 'might have notebooks protruding from every pocket, and hung about his person a sundial, a prismatic compass, a sheath knife, a pair of binoculars, a geological hammer, chronometer, pedometer, camera, aneroid and other items of surveying gear, as well as his goggles and mitts.' And, just like Lewis Carroll's White Knight, he also carried his own lethal weapon: 'in his hand might be an ice-axe which he used as he went along to the possible advancement of science, but the certain disorganization of his companions'.

'The question of clothing for these spring journeys', wrote Levick as their preparations were in full swing, 'has been occupying us a great deal, and everyone is using his own judgement entirely in clothing himself.' As they were to discover, the major and insoluble problem was the cumulative build-up of sweat during the march, which then froze and thawed alternately, so that after a few days the men were lying in pools of water. 'The misery of turning out in the morning with wet clothes, into a temperature . . . on an average between −20° and −30°F, and sometimes colder, is no joke, and it is this that makes spring sledging what it is.'

The Northern Party's rations owed much to those previously worked out by Shackleton for Professor David's Magnetic Pole Party – a judicious combination of protein and carbohydrate. Pemmican – a mixture of 40% dried meat and 60% fat – decanted from dozens of frozen tins (a frightful job) and mixed with biscuits put through the mincer was the staple of their diet, supplemented by whole biscuits, cheese, raisins, sticks of chocolate, sugar, cocoa and tea. The pemmican mixture was served hot for breakfast and dinner, washed down with hot cocoa or tea. 'Cheese at −20°F', Levick was to note later, 'is peculiar stuff, & cracks in your mouth like toffee, and the emergency biscuit is so hard as to require very careful worrying, and I realized then, with months of sledging before me, how lucky I am to have a magnificent set of teeth. I shall always be most particular in future, if ever I have to examine candidates for these expeditions, to see that their teeth are strong.'

Cooking was itself fraught with dangers. Writing as 'Primus' in the *Adélie Mail*, Dickason's light-hearted account of the tribulations of a sledging cook lists the hazards: incinerating the tent, knocking over the lamp, causing the pemmican to boil over into the stove, dropping a pot of hoosh* onto the filthy floor. He concluded: 'I could write several paragraphs on the subject of the inconvenience due solely and simply to

---

* An onomatopoeic term coined a few years earlier to denote a thick soup or thin stew.

83

the low temperatures . . . I have not forgotten the blisters on my fingers, the result of grabbing the cooker with my bare hands.'*

Before the two major journeys outlined by Levick were undertaken, Campbell had decided on making a couple of trial runs to break in the sledgers. Campbell, Priestley and Abbott set off first, to the southern end of Robertson Bay. The *Southern Cross* party had made several journeys there and had warned of the perilous nature of sledging on the sea ice, due to the early and uncertain break-up of the pack. This outing, which lasted from 29 July to 4 August (several days longer than anticipated, owing to bad weather and worse surfaces), took them as far as Duke of York Island, and brought a taste of the blizzards which they could expect to descend upon them without notice. Pulling for home near Warning Glacier on the eastern side of the bay, Campbell was 'awakened by a terrific din and found the lee skirting of the tent had lifted the heavy ice blocks we had piled on it and in another minute would have gone. I had just time to roll out of my bag, grab the skirting of the tent and shout to the others to do the same'. While he and Priestley sat on the skirting, the unfortunate Abbott had to crawl outside to pile on more ice blocks. He had much the worst of the night, climbing back into the tent sopping wet and being disturbed at regular intervals in an absurd sequence of events:

I managed at last to doze off although my head was getting shook about by the bellying of the Tent. Got wakened again & was asked to change places with Mr P as he could not get any sleep in his billet, so after a struggle shifted round gradually in our bags & managed to exchange positions. Mr P said he was no better off in his new position. I was soon dozing again when I was awakened by Lt C asking me to look out for the skirting his side as well as mine (a bit of a job). I said alright & continued to battle with my side which kept bellying in & flapping violently. Once more I heard a voice & Lt C said I had been asleep – it is a puzzle to me if I was, under the circumstances; however, I continued to keep watch & at last the wind eased & we all got to sleep.

Meanwhile, Levick and his two companions remained at Cape Adare. At 11.15 a.m. on 31 July they saw the sun for the first time since the autumn. 'There was at that time a great mirage effect all round, and bergs, sea ice,

---

* Similar trials had beset the mealtimes of the *Southern Cross* party. On one occasion, as Bernacchi took a nip of port wine from an aluminium flask, the bare nozzle stuck to his flesh, tearing away part of his lips and tongue. Earlier, as they breakfasted in the splendid natural surroundings of a vast cave, one of the party had been 'avidiously eating some frame food jelly which, being partly frozen and very viscous, clung tenaciously to his teeth. On pulling it away, behold, much to his horror and our amusement, a large front tooth came away with it.'

and mountains appeared jumbled about in a very queer manner . . . It was infinitely cheering to see it again. I took its photograph.'

They kept themselves busy. Levick set Browning and Dickason to scrubbing the hut, and himself to 'a great feat of engineering, consisting of hewing a road through the ice boulders on the South beach, for sledges to pass on & off the sea ice. With the debris from the boulders I have made an embankment leading down in a gradual slope to the sea ice, and both cutting & embankment look most imposing.' With their own sledging journey in sight, Browning overhauled his skis and sleeping bag, and Levick made himself a nose guard from a piece of red flannel he discovered in a case of wax matches – 'tonight in consequence my nose is dyed a brilliant vermilion'.

On 2 August they were struck by the same blizzard that was pinning Campbell's party into their tent. As the weather worsened, Levick went out to retrieve a lantern he had placed at the top of his new slipway to guide the others in. He soon lost his bearings in the thick drift.

> I . . . began to feel very uncomfortable, and was congratulating myself on having just had tea, in case I had to wander about for several hours. The wind was blowing then something like 60 miles per hour, and I reflected that my best course was to walk about in a circle to keep warm, until the snow had got blown off the peninsula as the drift would then ease up and I could probably see the light from the hut. However, just as I was figuring this out, something dark loomed ahead, and it proved to be the meteorological screen, which is about 70 yards from the hut! A guide rope leads from this to the hut, and so I was safe. But it just shows how careful one should be about wandering out in a blizzard, as you can get hopelessly lost, 20 yards from the hut door.

As with so many others, the White Death had come close to tapping him on the shoulder.

With winds up to 100 mph and the barometer at 28.126 and still falling, it was the worst hurricane they had yet encountered. Levick was not yet anxious about the sledge party, thinking (correctly) that they had probably holed up to wait out the gale; instead he read up on Scott, Shackleton and Borchgrevink, 'picking up as many tips as possible'. On 4 August he was sufficiently concerned to go out looking for Campbell's group, and met them walking back, having depoted their sledge, tent and most of their gear. That night he weighed the three travellers. Campbell had lost 3lbs, Priestley 5lbs and Abbott 9¼lbs.

The first major western journey had originally been scheduled to leave on 20 August, but as with all the Northern Party's plans – to date, and to come – this now had to be changed. They had discovered just how difficult the surface was in Robertson Bay, alternating between high pressure ridges and salt-flecked ice (the most difficult sledging surface imaginable, since the granules stuck to the sledge runners). The conclusion they had been forced to draw was that any notion of an extended journey over the sea ice was impossible: travelling was so slow that they could not carry enough provisions to last them out. 'There is nothing like the Antarctic for sending the schemes of mice and men all to blazes,' wrote Levick.

Campbell decided to add Dickason to his team to help with the hauling. Dickason wrote on 5 August: 'I was informed by Mr. Campbell that I should be attached to his party for the long trip to the W., as three men was not enough to pull a loaded sledge over the bad surface, which greatly alters his plans . . . now us four will have to take as much as possible and get as far as we can.'

It had proved a tough introduction to sledging for Campbell and Abbott, and even for the seasoned Priestley, an experienced spring sledger from *Discovery* days. It cannot have done much for Levick's pre-exam nerves, since he was to be in charge of the second trial expedition. He was relieved that Priestley had been loaned to them by Campbell 'to show us how to look after ourselves, as none of us have had any previous experience'.

They set off on foot on 8 August, making for the depot left by the earlier party, which they would adopt for their own four-day journey. Levick found himself lumbered with some 37lbs of gear, which he carried on his shoulders, slung between two ski sticks; Browning ended up carrying his on his head; Dickason was sure his load was getting heavier with every mile. Reaching the abandoned tent and sledge at about 4 p.m., they pitched camp under Priestley's tutorial gaze.

In essence the procedure was very like that on any field trip, with a few minor differences. The steam from the cooker froze solid to the walls of the tent, as did the sweat on their clothes and the medicinal brandy in its bottle, although their brisk post-prandial walk was made in a (relatively balmy) temperature of −15°F. Then it was time for bed. Levick removed his day clothes, all frozen stiff as boards, donned his night gear: woollen pyjamas, rabbit's wool helmet, dry socks and finnesko,* and snuggled down into his reindeer sleeping bag, into which he had sewn a blanket bag. No boy scout could have been more comfortable.

His enquiring mind had led him to decide that the pools of water accumulating in sleeping bags on sledging journeys was due to breath rather than sweat, and proved this to his satisfaction by sleeping with his head outside his bag, contrary to established custom. 'I was a little nervous about it, as Priestley assured me I should lose my nose while I slept!' In

---

* Soft shoes made from reindeer skins.

fact he did wake up in the middle of the night wondering if his nose was frostbitten; however, a quick rub reassured him that it was still there, and 'in the morning my bag was dry inside, & so it was the next night, whilst all round my face on the outside of the bag, was a thick layer of ice from my frozen breath'.

The following day Levick was introduced to the discomforts of photography on the march – 'whenever you touch any metal part of the camera with bare hands . . . you get a "burn", the tips of my fingers being now well blistered owing to this'. Still, Warning Glacier, with its hanging wall of ice, was dazzlingly beautiful: 'it would be profanity to attempt any description of it'. Although hauling the sledge on the return journey was as troublesome as it had been for Campbell's party ('the beastly thing felt as if it had about six ice anchors out'), they returned to Cape Adare in great spirits on 11 August. For them at least it had been a most satisfactory introduction to spring sledging.

The following day the party gathered around the fire by Abbott's bunk (he was suffering painfully from rheumatism of the knee), 'and had a very lively conversation on the chances of Capt. Scott & Amundsen getting to the Pole'. Their conclusions were somewhat bizarre: that Amundsen would have to use manual power for getting his sledges onto the Barrier 'as the dogs will not be able to do it' and would have to man-haul all the way to the Pole, while their four British rivals 'will not be required to pull sledges, the extra hands doing this for them' and should therefore win the race. 'The final result of our consultation was that it would be a near thing. I say jolly good luck to those who get there whoever they are.'

Their revised plan suffered a further set-back on 15 August with another almighty gale; at one point during the night they feared for the safety of the hut. The next morning, 'lo & behold! All the sea ice has gone out of the Bay, leaving just a narrow strip, from half a mile to a mile or so in width, at the very end, under Cape Adare; and in place of our usual white expanse, wavelets of black ice were beating on the ice foot.' Dickason could hardly believe that the wind could shift ice like that – 'it was between three and four foot thick and much thicker at the ridges, and stretching across a distance at the narrowest part of twenty miles or more'. As Levick realised, the implications were serious: 'This was the most awful blow to our hopes of sledging along the coast, but if it had happened ten days later, Campbell, Priestley, Abbott & Dickason would certainly have been dead men, as they would have gone out on it.'

Inspecting the damage, they found that their outer wall had suffered but that their gear and provisions remained intact, while Borchgrevink's store house had lost its roof and a 20-ton beam had been hurled 20 yards away.

The effect of a hurricane of this sort on, say, London, would be awful. Half the houses would be wrecked, buses would be overturned, vehicles like hansom cabs would be picked up from the road and carried along in the air. This sounds an exaggeration, but it is not one, as anyone who has crawled along on hands & knees in one of these blizzards knows. Priestley, who is a reliable authority, says that the hurricanes experienced by Shackleton's party at Cape Royds, and by sledge parties on the Barrier, have fallen far short of these Victoria Land winds, and we who used to laugh at what we thought were Borchgrevink's fairy tales, no longer do so.

Levick continued his enjoyable routine of photography and zoology: 'Have been reading up all I can find about penguins . . . My great ambition now is to work them up thoroughly and write a book on them when I get back.' Campbell meanwhile was assessing the chances of succeeding in the sledging ambitions for which he had been waiting all winter. They would now have to add on hundreds of extra miles to reach their destination, skirting right round Robertson Bay on the strip of safe ice which fringed the steep coasts. On 21 August, harking back to their original decision, he wrote gloomily: 'Altogether the outlook made me wish more than ever that the ship had had sufficient coal to take us back to Wood Bay' – conveniently forgetting that they themselves had decided on their present location.

Levick recorded yet another set-back on 25 August: 'This morning on going out of the hut we found that the ice had gone out right up to the end of Cape Adare, and the open Ross Sea was beating on the edge of the narrow strip of sea ice which remains with us, extending only a few hundred yards from the edge of the beach. The noise of the breakers was distinctly audible, and a dense bank of dark "sea-smoke" was rolling away off the open water.'

It was not until 8 September that Campbell, Priestley, Abbott and Dickason finally set off. They were to be away for ten days. Dickason was clearly apprehensive: he added a note to his diary: 'In case I should not return from this sledging trip . . . I entrust this log to the care of F. V. Browning who will cause it to be delivered to my mother, failing her my Brother. Address 42 Hazelhurst Rd., Lower Footing, London S.W. No letters. H Dickason.'

Levick and Browning travelled with them as far as Warning Glacier, due south of Cape Adare, to photograph and geologise for a few days, before returning to the hut on the 13th. That first night the two men camped some seven miles from Cape Adare, and were joined by Abbott, who had been sent back to the hut to retrieve his ski boots (no doubt with a flea in the ear from Campbell). Although it was −30°F, Levick recorded that they

14. Given scale by the tiny figure semaphoring at its foot, the spectacular 'marbled' face of Warning Glacier – so named by their predecessors at Cape Adare because the clouds of drift blowing off its top was the reliable herald of a blizzard to come. Levick and Browning made many excursions there to photograph and collect geological specimens.

spent a convivial evening in their sleeping bags, smoking and singing shanties. 'The atmosphere in the tiny little tent, with three pipes going and every means of ventilation lashed up tight, can be easily imagined, and we all coughed a good deal. Abbott remarked "my word, it is so thick you can hardly breathe – it's lovely".' The following morning, Levick and Browning returned Abbott to his group, and set off to photograph the glacier and mountains which surrounded them. Then started three days of terrifying weather, 'which', admitted Levick later, 'I remember more as a bad dream than anything else'. It started with a warning cloud over the top of the glacier. This they treated as an interesting photographic subject, but, accompanied by puffs of wind, soon started to make their way back to their tent. At first 'it was a dignified retreat, as we stopped several times to take photographs of interesting parts of the glacier as we passed

89

them, even up to the last moment, when our retreat had broken into a run'.

They decided to stay with their tent, which was impossible to shift in the gale-force winds, rather than to take their sleeping bags to the shelter of the cliff, although they kept ready to 'make a hop for it', as Browning euphemistically put it. Levick described the ordeal which followed:

And now began the most trying night I have ever spent, I think. We could feel the ice rising and falling under us, whilst that abominable crack on our lee side tried to cheer us up by playing all the tunes it knew, the wind on top of the cape made a noise like a huge waterfall, the canvas of the tent roared & banged an accompaniment in such bad taste as to frequently drown the noise of the principal performers outside, to whom we were most anxiously listening; whilst the slowly piling pressure ice on the ice foot joined in occasionally, as second fiddle to the orchestra, though its notes were only to be expected, and not as alarming as some of the other instruments.

The tone of Levick's account might have been light-hearted, but the two men were in serious trouble. Effectively, they were quite alone, since the other four were out of reach and hearing, and most probably in equally dire straits. The cup of tea provided by Browning, that 'most indefatigable cook and general "bucker up"', although encrusted with reindeer hair, was as welcome as a glass of vintage champagne.

They decided to head for Cape Adare with all speed – although not before Levick had taken two more photographs for Priestley's benefit. Exhausted and hampered by salt-flecked ice, they struggled homewards, to find the topography entirely altered:

The ice had completely changed its formation during the blizzard . . . The whole surface had the appearance of having been churned up, whilst cracks had formed, and been sealed up again by the freezing of the water which had oozed through them. At Seal Point itself, enormous slabs of ice had been thrown up on end; in fact a general break up had taken place . . . and it seemed a miracle that the whole lot had not gone out. For hundreds of yards out from the cliff of Cape Adare, basalt stones had been showered down upon the ice by the wind, and were in places so thick as to resemble a pebble beach . . . I firmly believe that this was the record blizzard of the year.

During their dash for safety Levick had strained his leg, and Browning was suffering from some undiagnosed complaint, so they did not move far from the hut. 'I think we both feel a little lonely,' wrote Levick on

17 September, 'but Browning is a cheerful companion and is working like a nigger. He is an excellent cook and lays himself out to please me with all sorts of surprises in the way of dishes. He is a Devonshire man, having spent his boyhood on a farm before he entered the Navy. He is a qualified torpedo instructor, and first class petty officer, and is certainly gifted with brains, and runs the meteorological observations exceedingly well and intelligently during Priestley's absence.'

Meanwhile, the senior sledge party had travelled anti-clockwise round the bay past Dugdale Glacier, before curving north-west across the three bays which looped into the coast on the way to Cape North: Relay Bay, the Bay of Bergs and Providence Bay. The scenery of glaciers backed by mountains was magnificent; Priestley described it as their chief solace during the frustrating time that followed. They then pushed on past Cape Wood at the northern end of Providence Bay, only to be halted at Cape Barrow by a dangerously thin surface, to which they were alerted by the alarming noise of a seal gnawing the ice beneath their feet.

They had no choice but to retrace their steps to Relay Bay, camping in the spectacular cave at Penelope Point. Since it was a Sunday, they loosed off a volley of hymns. 'I turned in my bag without swearing tonight,' revealed Dickason, 'the first time this trip, I suppose the hymns had something to do with it as I was turning in whilst singing.' The next day they struck out for home across Robertson Bay – the ice able now to bear their weight. The two watchers at the hut spotted them approaching on 18 September, and learned over a glass of champagne that they had had no wind at all while Levick and Browning were being pounded by the blizzard 30 miles away.

A few days later Levick returned to Warning Glacier with Priestley, Browning and Dickason, to be subjected to the same wearing winds and snowstorms as before. A gale on the 25th kept them in their tent – 'this laying up business shakes the tobacco pouch up a bit', complained Dickason, 'as I cannot go to sleep every time I turn in so I get the pipe under weigh [sic] and read a little'. Even so, Levick felt that the thirty photographs he had taken of the glacier made the journey well worth while. The geologist concurred, and Levick reported with modest pleasure on 2 October: 'Priestley says that his notes and my photographs of Warning Glacier make up the most valuable piece of work we have done since we came.' He was kept so busy that he had no time to wash any clothes, and set out as part of the support group for Campbell's second big sledging journey on 4 October in the same things he had been wearing for the past three weeks. 'It can't be helped.'

Levick and Browning travelled together, for the following ten days, and as before encountered severe weather and bad surfaces while making their way across the bay to Penelope Point. They then split from the other party, and having made a trip on skis westwards to Cape Wood and photographed from afar the major landmarks that the others would encounter, they turned eastwards towards the Dugdale, Murray and Newnes Glaciers at the southern end of the bay. Levick was still suffering leg pains and his diary entries are notably less cheery than before. The pair were relieved to reach Cape Adare and the hut just before another blizzard struck on 13 October. 'We are both as hard as nails', crowed Levick, 'though our noses have suffered by sun & frost!'

Campbell's second western journey followed the same route as his first. Although they made far quicker time to Cape Barrow, the four men were again halted there by rotten ice too dangerous to trust. Campbell wrote: 'It was a bitter disappointment, for I had expected at least to be able to get beyond Cape North this way.' There was a faint hope that, by scrambling up a glacier, they might get up onto the plateau and continue by land. Day after day they scrutinised the coastline, but the verdict was always the same: the glaciers were all too 'wall-faced' to climb. The Admiralty Range had beaten them on all fronts, and Scott's expectations would remain unfulfilled.

With the reunion of all six men at the hut on 20 October,* exploration in any meaningful sense was at an end. Robertson Bay had become honeycombed with mushy holes, while to the north-east and north-west winds and currents were creating widening stretches of open water. Thereafter, until *Terra Nova* arrived at the beginning of January 1912, their theatre of operations shrank to familiar territory. 'Our work', wrote Campbell unenthusiastically in *Last Expedition*, 'was now restricted to the immediate confines of the beach and the peninsula of Cape Adare, and this time was principally occupied in taking routine observations and adding to our biological collections.' He was still harping on about it weeks later, commenting enviously on 10 December that, compared with Borchgrevink's group, 'it seemed as if we must be having a very open season'.

They managed a final few short sledge journeys. The first, composed of Levick, Priestley, Browning and Dickason, lasted from 28 October to 4 November and was, according to Priestley, agreeable from beginning to end. Their main purpose was to explore Sir George Newnes Glacier near Duke of York Island, a beautiful and fascinating place; the panorama from their camp encompassed spectacular ice falls, towering cliffs and a steep gorge. Levick and Priestley photographed the glacier from every angle, and bore back with them 400lbs of rocks, including a piece of quartzite

---

* Dickason: 'Arrived at the hut about 6 pm and took Dr. Levick and Rings by surprise as they had not seen us approaching, had a good dinner, wee doddle and gramophone concert, all feeling up to-date.'

which Browning and Dickason asserted vociferously to be seamed with gold.

Priestley was by now well content with the notes he had made and the collections of rocks and lichens he had amassed at Cape Adare, and Levick was equally pleased with his data and photographs, especially relating to penguins. During this last trip he had discovered a supposedly extinct rookery on Duke of York Island, and his observations there, added to those made at Cape Adare, made him confident of producing a worthwhile book on the subject. Priestley had also asked him to supply the photographs for a book he intended to write on the glaciology of the region. All in all, Levick was able to dismiss light-heartedly the trials they had endured: 'We as a party have undoubtedly hopelessly failed in our object (exploration) but Priestley and I are settling down to get as much scientific work as possible done, to try as much as we can at any rate to justify our existence.' One's sympathies must lie with Campbell.

During the final ten-day sledging trip, starting on 7 November, Levick was left in sole occupation of the hut as the five others set off once again for Duke of York Island and the less familiar Dugdale and Murray Glaciers. Having surveyed and photographed there, they paid a final visit to Penelope Point and Relay Bay before making tracks for home. Campbell, tired of waiting for Priestley to finish his geologising, walked back alone a couple of days before the rest. On their return Dickason was struck by the fact that the thaw had begun in earnest, and above all by the smell rising from the rookery – 'it brings back to my mind the day we landed here. I thought at the time that we would not be able to stick it but of course one soon gets used to it.' The year had come almost full circle.

The six weeks which preceded their departure from Cape Adare were days of glorious summer. The winds abated and the sun shone continuously. To work outside was now a positive pleasure, and for Priestley and Levick each day brought fresh opportunities to observe, photograph and note down the changes taking place in the unique – and suddenly well-disposed – land surrounding them. Campbell's kayaks added considerably to their mobility and enjoyment as the patches of open water multiplied around the bay.

Levick was becoming increasingly absorbed in the zoological aspects of his duties. In early spring he had produced a notebook for communal use. The amateur zoologist had stressed the need for accuracy and the importance of animal welfare, adding a characteristic footnote: 'N.B.– Please remember that we have every reason to believe that birds feel pain as much as we do, and that it is well worth half an hour's laborious chase to kill a wounded skua rather than to let it die a slow death.'

By the time the penguins had begun flooding back to Cape Adare in

October, Levick had carried out a post-mortem on a crab-eater seal and a white seal, chloroformed and skinned an emperor penguin ('on my bedstead', noted Priestley indignantly), and skinned and mounted a rare Isabelline penguin. But inevitably, since they were living cheek by jowl with the Adélie penguins for much of the year, these charming birds became his special interest.

'Imagine a little man', a member of an earlier expedition had written, 'standing erect, provided with two broad paddles instead of arms, with head small in comparison with the plump stout body; imagine this creature with his back covered with a black coat ... tapering behind to a pointed tail that drags on the ground, and adorned in front with a glossy white breast-plate. Have this creature walk on his two feet, and give him at the same time a droll little waddle, and a pert movement of the head; you have before you something irresistibly attractive and comical.'

Levick turned his notes – the most comprehensive yet made on the Adélies' habits – into a delightful little book, a model of simplicity, clarity and humour. In it he described the pattern of their year, from their arrival at Cape Adare in the middle of October, through the building of nests and rearing of chicks, to the mass departure four months later for the relative safety of the pack ice off shore. He illustrated it with graphic photographs which brought every detail of the Adélies' behaviour vividly alive. (His photographic skills had evidently improved since Campbell's tart comment; indeed he was regarded by some – after the master, Ponting – as the most accomplished practitioner of the whole expedition.)

The charm of *Antarctic Penguins* lies in Levick's study of their social habits. A few of his comments based on hours of acute observation distilled into a few well-chosen sentences suffice to bring the birds vividly to life.

When the penguins arrived at the rookery in October, 'the whole air of the line at this time was that of a school-treat arrived in sight of its playing fields, and breaking into a run in its eagerness to get there'.

As a doctor, he understood how the birds' anatomy dictated their actions: 'Suddenly those that walked would flop on to their breasts and start tobogganing, and conversely strings of tobogganers would as suddenly pop up on their feet and start walking. In this way they relieved the monotony of their march, and gave periodical rest to different groups of muscles and nerve-centres.'

The charmingly frivolous side of the Adélies reveals hours of ornithological enjoyment: 'Small ice-floes are continually drifting past in the water, and as one of these arrived at the top of the ice-foot, it would be boarded by a crowd of penguins, sometimes until it could hold no more.

15. Penguins started to arrive at the Cape Adare rookery in October. Levick took hundreds of photographs of the birds and copious notes, capturing every aspect of their delightful personalities.

This "excursion boat" . . . would float its many occupants down the whole length of the ice-foot, and as it passed close to the edge, those that rode on the floes would shout at them in reply, so that a gay bantering seemed to accompany their passage past the rookery.'

He noticed how, caught out in the act of stealing pebbles to furnish his own nest: 'The consciousness of guilt . . . always makes a penguin smooth his feathers and look small, whilst indignation has the opposite effect.'

Once the birds were on their nests, they evoked a picture of a more adult educational kind: 'If I walked by the side of a long, nest-covered ridge, a low growl arose from every bird as I passed it, and the massed sound, gathering in front and dying away behind as I advanced, reminded me forcibly of the sound of the crowds on the towing-path at the 'Varsity boat race as the crews pass up the river.'

The photographer in Levick noticed the strange beauty of one bodily function: 'The nests themselves are never fouled, the excreta being squirted clear of them for a distance of a foot or more, so that each nest has

95

the appearance of a flower with bright green petals radiating from its centre.'

The anthropomorphic tendency which penguins always seem to arouse in man was taken to considerable lengths by the Northern Party as a whole. On their arrival at Cape Adare, Campbell and Levick initially slept in Borchgrevink's old hut, sharing this with a lone penguin, 'Percy', which had retreated there for its moult. Unlike other Adélies, he was a rebarbative creature who spurned their offers of food and friendship and, according to Campbell, waxed 'very indignant at being turned out and stood all day at the door scolding us. He also did showman to the crowds of sightseers who came to watch us.'

Although the penguins were the most entertaining, vociferous and numerous inhabitants of Cape Adare, summer brought other wildlife. Seals instructed their young in the arcane art of swimming; on 30 November Levick spotted the first killer whale of the season; Abbott, catching a snowy petrel, was treated to its unpleasant defensive trick of spitting a noxious liquid at its enemies. For Priestley a red-letter day was 2 December, when he discovered a colony of small red insects sheltering beneath moss and stones on the slope of Cape Adare.

But the penguins were their constant and much appreciated companions, and it was fitting that the Northern Party should have called their newspaper the *Adélie Mail*. Although nothing like as ambitious, lavish and beautifully illustrated as *The South Polar Times* slaved over by Shackleton and Wilson during the *Discovery* days and continued at Cape Evans by Cherry-Garrard, they succeeded under Priestley's editorship in turning out a respectable body of poetry, prose and jokes. Levick ('Bluebell') penned a valedictory ode, and Campbell contributed an 'advertisement':

I regret very much that pressure of business calls me away from this fascinating neighbourhood which I have found it exceedingly hard to leave. You will find the house, which was erected by my family under my supervision, very strongly put together, and never, during the hardest blow, have I known more than six boards removed from the weather side on the same day.

Mysterious noises have been heard from time to time, and these were at first put down to the fact that a pipe had been walled between two of the layers of matchboarding,* but I am able to prove that these are not supernatural in origin, but owe their occurrence to the return of some of our neighbours after the closing of the public houses.

---

* Levick's favourite pipe, which he was distraught at losing.

I have much enjoyed the fishing in the neighbourhood and may say that while wielding rod and line I have never been free from frostbites.

Apply to Messrs Lettem and Allcomb

HOUSE AGENTS

CAPE ADARE

But if Levick and Priestley were absorbed in their scientific chores, and the three 'men' appreciated the diminution of theirs, Campbell was undoubtedly fretting during this extended summer holiday. He was first and foremost a man of action and of command, and unlike Scott his diary entries do not reveal him to have been especially interested in the minutiae of natural history. He featured in Priestley's book and Levick's diary at this time only when action was called for: when he shot two sea leopards, 'turned all hands out' to help put scores of badly injured penguins out of their misery after a catastrophic cliff fall, and instituted a round-the-clock watch for the ship high up on Cape Adare immediately after Christmas Day. In his own report for *Last Expedition*, Campbell devoted just four paragraphs to these six weeks.

Priestley may have entitled the relevant chapter in *Antarctic Adventure* 'An Ideal Antarctic Summer', but he recognised that undercurrents of dissaffection and dissatisfaction were building up. Cape Adare was getting on their nerves and they perceived their results as inadequate, themselves as failures. This perception may or may not have emanated from Campbell, but he as leader should have concealed it in himself and nipped it in the bud in others. Neither Shackleton, nor for that matter Scott, would have allowed the miasma of failure to infect the men under their command. The demoralisation of the party was particularly unfortunate in view of Scott's warning that they might have to spend yet another winter at Cape Adare. To what depths would morale by then have sunk?

But for the first time, their luck was in. On 3 January 1912 Levick, on look-out duty, noted at 8.30 a.m.: 'I sighted her and hoisted a flag to alert the five men in the hut,' and soon afterwards *Terra Nova* was anchored off the beach. 'Robertson Bay is not a nice place from a seaman's point of view,' Pennell revealed in *Last Expedition*. 'The tidal streams are strong, the pack ice heavy, there are very many grounded bergs about, and gales are frequent and fierce, while the uneven bottom suggests the likelihood of unknown pinnacled rocks.' The last night in the hut was crowded and uncomfortable, since the crew members detailed to help with the loading were marooned on shore when heavy pack ice forced *Terra Nova* to put further out to sea, but the newcomers were royally entertained by the usual penguin cabaret.

Alas, loading time was so short that there was no opportunity to get all their precious specimens on board. Levick was particularly sad to leave behind his taxidermist's gear, the penguin skins he had so carefully collected, and a sample taken from the lake near the hut, which he had hoped would make his name as something of an authority on single-cell algae called protococci – 'it seemed a sinful shame'. As Ridley Beach and the high bluff of Cape Adare dwindled behind them, Levick and Priestley felt relief tinged with regret. Campbell's emotion was probably closer to Bernacchi's: 'We were not sorry to leave that gelid desolate spot, our place of abode for so many dreary months.'

# 4

# Working the Glaciers from Evans Coves

## 4 January–15 February 1912

For the Northern Party, 4–8 January – the four days it took *Terra Nova* to ply her way southwards from Cape Adare – was in the nature of a pleasure cruise, giving them the chance to read and reread letters from home, appreciate a different diet and new faces, and catch up on local gossip and national and international news. Less welcome was the new intake of dogs and mules which had been embarked at Lyttelton to replenish the stock.

They were travelling back along a coastline seamed with landmarks familiar to them from their previous journey north to Cape Adare. They passed Possession Island, whose rugged cliffs and standing stones reminded them of their old abode and of The Sisters, Gertrude and Rose; the imposing 1,000-foot bulk of Coulman Island, guarding the entrance to Lady Newnes Bay; and Wood Bay, where the hospitable harbour provided a fine setting for Mount Melbourne, a snow-covered version of Etna. Ross had seen all these in 1841, and in 1900 the *Southern Cross* explorers had visited them briefly, but had not lingered.

Campbell by this time was desperate to produce something of significance for Scott. To date his two attempts to out-trump Shackleton – on King Edward VII Land and at Cape North – had failed. Now he was treading in his rival's footsteps once again: the *Nimrod* expedition had explored the McMurdo Sound area with considerable thoroughness in 1908, and the 1,300-mile return journey to the South Magnetic Pole that October had been a notable 'first' for Professor David and his leader. But David had only needed to travel as far north along the coast of Victoria Land as the Drygalski Ice Tongue, lying two-thirds of the way between Cape Adare and Cape Evans, before turning 250 miles inland across the polar plateau to seek his goal. The territory north of the Drygalski was both fascinating and unexplored. Success here would go a long way towards tilting the balance – but it was positively Campbell's last chance.

As the ship neared Evans Coves, she hit heavy pack ice in Terra Nova Bay. Campbell conferred anxiously with Pennell. The captain's orders from Scott had been to deposit the Northern Party there, then pick up the Second Western Party, who had been expanding on their previous work at the western end of McMurdo Sound, and deposit them at Evans Coves in their turn. They would then supplement the studies they had already made of the Ferrar and Koettlitz Glaciers with a study of the Ross Glacier and its flanking mountains, Nansen and Larsen.

As he had been after the debacle in the Bay of Whales, Campbell was faced with an unenviable alternative: if they could not land on 8 January, they would have to hitch an unwilling lift back to McMurdo Sound and, their numbers swelled by the Second Western Party, try again one final time. Such a delay would eat into their precious six weeks. (In fact, *Terra Nova* did not succeed in picking up the Western Party until 15 February, too late for them to go to Evans Coves; they returned instead to Cape Evans.) The Northern Party were thus a whisker away from missing out on their six-week sledging trip. But they would have avoided the nightmare to come.

Another incentive to get to grips with the territory north of Evans Coves was the intrinsic interest of the place. Some past upheaval had bunched the land up into a tangle of peaks and glaciers – for Priestley the geologist the whole area promised to be a fascinating study. If only they could effect a landing they could expect a strenuous and exhilarating six weeks. Having already come through the trials of autumn, spring and early-summer sledging, a further bout of summer sledging held out nothing but the prospect of pleasure. From the ship Campbell had taken particular note of Melbourne Glacier, sweeping diagonally away from the southern slope of Mount Melbourne. Since the terminus of this broad highway was within easy reach of Evans Coves, he felt confident that it would lead them over to Wood Bay.

The Northern Party was indeed to put their stamp on the place, for several distinctive features were subsequently named after the six men, their order of importance seemingly governed by hierarchy. Thus the most impressive, Melbourne Glacier, was renamed Campbell Glacier in 1913 in a graceful act of recognition by Professor David, while Priestley was awarded the smaller, but most interesting, glacier swinging away to the west. To Abbott, Browning and Dickason fell three minor peaks, while Levick merited a more substantial summit (9,133 feet) further to the north.

And, as Pennell seized the fleeting moment, land they did on 8 January – not at Evans Coves, but slightly further to the north-east, at a spot they called Depot Moraine Camp and later, more appositely, Hell's Gate.

16. Campbell's party encamped during one of their excursions from Evans Coves, in the sort of fine, clear conditions that made spring sledging pleasurable. In a blizzard the routine of pitching and striking the tent, cooking and sleeping disintegrated into a nightmarish scrabble. The sledging flag hangs at the entrance to the tent.

Pennell and some of the crew helped the six men to drag the heavy loads across half a mile of sea ice and up the steep slope of a snow drift onto the piedmont. Priestley revealed later: 'We had prepared a large depôt at Cape Adare which was to have been landed with us here, but it was necessary to sledge all our gear about half a mile over sea ice before it would have been possible to depôt it, and as Campbell did not wish to delay the ship, he decided to land only such spare food as could be taken in one journey by ourselves and a sledge party from the ship's crew. In the light of after events this proved to be a grave mistake.'

Their stores had already been divided into two. First came six weeks' worth of equipment and provisions, bagged up in advance and stowed onto the two sledges ready for an early departure the following day. The second mound contained a month's skeleton rations and a miscellany of emergency kit, including two weeks' worth of pemmican, 56lbs of sugar, 24lbs of cocoa, 36lbs of chocolate, 210lbs of biscuit, some Oxo cubes, a few spare clothes, reindeer and dog skins for patching mitts and sleeping bags, and bamboos for marking depots. These extra supplies were a precaution against the remote possibility that *Terra Nova* would not be able to pick them up around 18 February as planned. Campbell was so sure that this would not happen that he did not feel justified in broaching cases which were earmarked for the main party at Cape Evans.

Pennell was anxious to leave, so the unloading was a brisk affair. It was 2 a.m. on the morning of the 10th before the six men turned in, turning out again a bare four hours later. The emergency depot was secured and marked, a letter left for Debenham confirming their own plans. At all costs Campbell wanted to avoid the two teams tripping over each other in this small corner of Victoria Land.

Campbell decided to divide the party as before. He, Priestley and Dickason were to be the lead team in charge of the main exploratory and scientific efforts around Mount Melbourne, while Levick joined forces with Abbott and Browning. As Scott had done before him when he had teamed up with Lashly and Taff Evans in *Discovery* days, he was discovering that sledging journeys brought individuals closer together – or drove them further apart. Scott had written then: 'I learn a great deal about lower-deck life – more than I could hope to have done under ordinary conditions.' Levick at least was content with his lot: 'Thank God my party is a cheery one, & Abbott & Browning just about as good companions as any man could wish for.' He was not so happy at being palmed off with the 10-foot, iron-runner sledge, which had proved on average a worse performer over the wide range of surfaces they encountered, and complained in his diary that it was carrying more than their fair share of the load, partly because of the weight of his photographic equipment. He qualified these comments at the time: 'Of course the others are the last people to wittingly put more than a person should on my sledge – I know that' – and later deleted them altogether.

The two groups set off together in the best of spirits. As they tackled the approach to Melbourne Glacier, Levick wrote: 'We started at once on unexplored land, and hope that this piedmont will lead us far inland. The going was very good at first – clear hard blue ice, with small & not dangerous crevasses & little chasms formed by the thaw streams.' When they stopped for lunch, Levick's team opted for a cold picnic in the lee of their sledge. 'I think I shall make a practice in future of lunching in this way in fine weather, when the pitching of a tent seems to be an unnecessary luxury but I may change my mind later! (Note: I did!!!)'

That first day, however, turned out to be a false dawn. Their 'very good at first' progress slowed to a crawl as they were caught in a snowstorm and lost their bearings, while the 'small & not dangerous crevasses' increased in size and tiresomeness, and the 'thaw streams' appeared to follow them inside their tents as they settled down to a soggy night, with their sleeping bags soaking up water on the tent floor. One tedious result of the snowfall was that they had to relay the whole of the following day and the next, but at last they found themselves at North Fork, the crossroads between Melbourne Glacier stretching across to the west and the aptly named Boomerang Glacier curving round to the east.

They tackled the Melbourne Glacier on 13 January, but two days later were confined to their tents for four days by a snowstorm. 'Here we are at the gate', wrote Campbell despairingly, 'and can't get on, and with our five precious weeks slipping by.' A minor consolation for Levick was that his beard seemed to be coming along nicely. 'I think it is of that shape known as "The Clarence".'

On 20 January, climbing a peak in order to try to map out the route ahead, Campbell, Levick and Dickason discovered to their dismay that the crevasses they had already encountered were replicated further up. Levick recorded: 'we got a fine view to the North'ard and saw that the ice between us and Mount Melbourne was impassable – right across more ice falls and ridges, a perfect tangle of crevasses'.

Meanwhile Priestley, Abbott and Browning had been dispatched to investigate the Boomerang. This too was pitted with deep and treacherous crevasses. In the first of these, Priestley recorded ruefully in his diary, 'I was landed more like a half-drowned perch than anything else, and felt as if the snow which had been driven down my neck must have been coming out of my boots.' Another twist of the glacier revealed a series of magnificent views in every direction save towards Mount Melbourne, but Priestley estimated it would take at least a week to reach the base of the mountain, with no certainty of success. Campbell's decision was inevitable: 'considering our limited time we decided to work along more to the westward in the hopes of finding a larger and easier glacier. Even if unsuccessful we should be breaking new ground and Priestley could put in some good collecting from the different moraines, while I surveyed.'

Then came a parting of the ways for Campbell and Levick, psychologically as well as physically. Since the object now was to quarter the ground to the south and west of their present position as thoroughly as possible in the time remaining, Campbell decided that he, Priestley and Dickason would work their way back down the western side of the Melbourne Glacier, collecting geological specimens and surveying as they went, while Levick, Abbott and Browning would steer south-east, making for the eastern foothills. The two groups would join forces again, according to Campbell's diary, 'at the south west entrance' of the glacier. Levick's understanding was that his party would wait on the south-eastern side for

Campbell to join them. The ensuing wire-crossing was to sour relations between the two men.

As they set out on the afternoon of 21 January, Campbell's party were felled by a severe attack of snow blindness.* 'Only one eye between us,' Campbell scrawled in his diary, 'and that belongs to Dickason.' For Priestley it was the worst bout in his sledging career. The pain was so intense that it continued to head his list of the trials they were to endure over the next two years – no mean achievement. When they got going again they encountered heavy sastrugi,† which slowed them down considerably. It was with relief that they rounded the tail of the glacier on 24 January and camped, waiting for Levick's party to catch them up from the east.

They waited for three interminable days, with Campbell becoming increasingly exasperated. On 26 January, he spied through his binoculars 'the truant party calmly camped on the east side of Melbourne Glacier'. The sighting sparked off a tantrum and swift retribution: 'returning to camp we packed food for 18 days and depoted . . . a note for Levick telling him my proposed plans . . . and directing him not to attempt them unless he caught me up but to photograph and collect at the base of the mountains.' Meanwhile, the object of Campbell's displeasure was himself becoming more and more confused and flurried. He observed the behaviour of the distant Lilliputians with perplexity through his own binoculars, repeating 'my orders are plain' to himself like a mantra. On the 29th, his nerve finally cracked: 'I mean to go in chase of the others now. I have stood long enough on the burning deck.'

Campbell's anger and Levick's anxiety were the result of a genuine misunderstanding about their meeting place, complicated by undulating terrain in between. The episode highlights the primitive nature of their communications. They had no loud-hailers, no flares, no signalling devices – nothing but a couple of flags and bamboos. They could only watch one another impotently through field glasses. Levick was incapable of despondency, however. He was satisfied with a stream of rock and lichen specimens, which he hoped would please Priestley, and delighted to have discovered 'the most marvellous drink that ever descended the throat of man: an Olympian beverage. It is made by dissolving half the luncheon allowance of chocolate in a pannikin of hot tea, and adding three lumps of sugar. I found it out three days ago, and now think of hardly anything else during the morning's march, knowing that I shall get it at lunch.'

---

* Levick was forever nagging them, but his audience was unreceptive: 'I repeatedly warn them all but they are very perverse about wearing goggles.'

† Solid waves of snow whipped up on the sea ice by the action of the wind and revealing the direction of the prevailing wind. Experienced Siberian travellers used them as a guide, but to the Northern Party they were merely a hurdle.

Decisions concerning Campbell had to compete with this culinary breakthrough, and also with a bout of philosophical musing. Trudging along hour after hour had put Levick into an introspective frame of mind:

Sledge journeys in themselves are terribly monotonous when there is little change of scene – in fact when there is no collecting or other scientific work to occupy one's mind, and one is pulling hour after hour with nothing but glaring white ahead, darkened by snow goggles, it is simply a form of mental starvation. The only way to relieve this starvation is to let your mind run over scenes of your past life . . . [I] am in fact becoming an artist in chewing the mental cud of past scenes and actions . . . This habit which I have acquired, owing to the many hours which I have devoted to it during the last six months, has I firmly believe done me an immense amount of good.

He continued:

I have come to regard my life rather in the light of a very serious play in two acts. The first act was over, and the curtain rung down on it when I left civilisation to enter this blank antarctic. Now comes the interval during which I am given ample time to reflect upon the scenes of the first act – to perceive its weak spots, and the way in which I as the chief character must avoid making such mistakes in the second; for the second act, unlike the play we go to see at the theatre, is not yet written, and I, in the principal part, have come into the audience, seen myself act, made my criticism, and decided as far as lies in my power, on my comportment when the curtain rises again. If only for this reason alone, it would have been well worth while to have come here, as I don't believe that anything but a real break in the ordinary routine of life would produce the state of mind necessary for this sort of reflection . . .

This may be no great shakes either as a piece of self-analysis or as a piece of prose, but it reveals how Antarctica was affecting the self-awareness of one decent, prosaic, capable individual, for whom the 'ordinary routine of life' was about to change dramatically.

The misunderstanding between Campbell and Levick spawned a chain of misadventures for Levick's team. Having decided to hare after the others on 29 January, they became hopelessly ensnared in a 'perfect network' of crevasses. 'I really believe that for miles together there was as much crevasse as solid ice. We would cross six to twelve feet of crevasse, then about six feet of solid ice, then another crevasse and so on. Had we not been on ski, I dont believe we could possibly have got along, & must have gone down one after another of the "D'd Hell Holes" as Prof. David christened them.'

Pitching their tent that night was no respite:

We had to spend over half an hour sounding with an ice axe before we could find a solid patch big enough to pitch the tent on . . . So here we are, perched on a little island, the tent surrounded about 1 yard away in every direction (except in front for 3 yards) by crevasses whose lids we have smashed in, in places, with the ice axe, and apparently they are of good depth, as we cannot see the bottom of any of them, and a piece of ice chucked down any of them, produces no sound till it hits something a very long way down. I have marked out a little circle round the tent, and absolutely forbidden either of the men to cross it until we are roped up again.

Not the night for a quick pee outside – or for sleep-walking.

Campbell and crevasses notwithstanding, Levick's irrepressible cheerfulness reasserted itself as he scribbled the day's events in his diary: 'I want to get a little way further west, as there is the most magnificent mountain scenery, with glaciers and ice falls which should make very fine photographs, and I am going to get them at any cost.'

The following day, reading Campbell's terse instructions, they were determined to rejoin the other party, who were making for the glacier which would later bear Priestley's name, hoping to find a way through to Wood Bay. Trying to cut corners, they became embroiled once again in a minefield of crevasses. There was one particularly dicey moment when the sledge became wedged in a bridge or 'lid' of snow concealing a chasm at least forty feet deep with tapering sides. 'Owing to the great weight of the sledge, and the fact that we were pulling up the further slope of the lid at the time, I am sure that if the sledge had gone through, it would have pulled us all back after it, as of course we were harnessed to it.' Priestley's comment on hearing this tale was that 'The feeling of the party when they found they were safely over must have been very similar to that of an elephant whose foot has just dislodged the covering of one of the African natives' big-game traps.' Levick's own reaction was somewhat unexpected: 'I am sincerely glad this little accident did not happen early yesterday, as we should have taken greater care then, and spent goodness knows how long over getting this far.'

Meanwhile, the other group was heading north. Having set up camp on one of two parallel moraines stretching from the Priestley Glacier, Campbell related how, after supper, 'I went out with Priestley to collect and the sun being hot I took off my vest and turning it inside out put it on over my sweater where it dried beautifully. I remarked to Priestley at the time that this ought to bring me luck, and sure enough immediately

17. The segment of pine trunk fossilised in sandstone, found by Priestley in the glacier subsequently named after him, was instrumental in helping to establish Antarctic climate patterns in past ages.

afterward I found a sandstone rock containing fossil wood which Priestley was very pleased with!' Priestley explained why it was such an important find: 'There can be no doubt . . . that several times at least during past ages the Antarctic has possessed a climate much more genial than that of England at the present day . . . while as an antithesis we have equally definite proof that at other times the extension of ice has been infinitely greater than it is to-day.' The pieces of fossil tree trunks which they were to unearth, photograph and bring back to England were important clues in deciphering the past of a continent in a permanent state of flux.

In a lecture delivered to the Royal Geographical Society on the fiftieth anniversary of Scott's death, Priestley put Campbell's find in context: 'One sliver of wood formed the subject of a whole memoir and controversy about its exact age still goes on.'

At the time Edith Sitwell was the *enfant terrible*, not yet the *grande dame*, of the English eccentrics. She and Raymond Priestley were exact contemporaries. It is not known whether they ever met, but it is tempting to imagine that she crafted a few of the lines in her poem *The Shadow of Cain* after a conversation with him:

107

And now in memory of great oscillations
Of temperature in that epoch of the Cold,
We found a continent of turquoise, vast as Asia
In the yellowing airs of the Cold: the tooth of a mammoth;
And there, in a gulf, a dark pine-sword

To show there had once been warmth and the gulf stream in our veins
Where only the Chaos of the Antarctic Pole
Or the peace of its atonic coldness reigns.

The discovery of this pine-tree fossil was not only important in unravelling some of Antarctica's mysteries, but also turned out to be an unknown genus related to the monkey-puzzle tree, and as such was given the species name *Araucaria priestleyi* by the author of the report on Antarctic plant fossils discovered during the *Terra Nova* expedition. Priestley had earned his ticket.

Before pursuing this exciting lead, Campbell's party decided to make a detour to explore the steep, deeply crevassed glacier, which they named Corner Glacier for its shape, descending from the western slopes of Mount Dickason. They succeeded in getting to the top of its first ice fall, where a fine panorama of a valley and steep glaciers, two of which seemed to emanate from the hills above the Boomerang, unfolded before them. But it was impassable by sledge: they would have had to carry everything on their backs. They returned to camp footsore and disappointed.

At last, on 31 January, after more rough going and bad language,* the miscreants succeeded in catching up with the others, who were marching again for the Priestley Glacier to resume their searches, '& there were great rejoicings at the reunion'. Either Levick was glossing over a chilly reception, or Campbell had got over his pique (perhaps the fossil find had mended his temper). The newcomers were regaled with lurid details of their snow blindness, learnt about their collecting efforts, their investigation of the Corner Glacier, and above all, the exciting discovery of the fossil wood immured in sandstone. ('It is perhaps one of the greatest discoveries made in the Antarctic up to date', was the impression gained by Levick, and 'Priestley is in great fettle about it.')

Campbell had by then abandoned his master plan: 'I had now given up all hope of getting through to Wood Bay this year, our time being too short to get over by the Boomerang, which I consider the only passable route for a sledge.' The discovery of the fossil wood was therefore all the more

---

* Levick was later to confess: 'I have got into the habit of using very bad language at the sledge I am afraid, and the men have taken this as permission to open the flood gates of their own inexaustible [sic] repertoire, so that when things are going badly, we fill the air with melody worthy of a pack of hounds.'

momentous, and the following day the party united to seek out more fossil specimens in Pine Tree Glacier, as they had christened the future Priestley Glacier. Campbell, Abbott and Dickason transported a large piece back to camp, and Levick took photographs of the actual tree trunk and imprints of the fossil in its sandstone bed.

It was hard but satisfying labour. Levick wrote on 1 February: 'We came back laden with specimens and got back to our respective tents about 9.30 p.m . . . We get through plenty of work nowadays . . . We shall have very heavy loads, going back to the main depôt with all these geological specimens, and will probably have to relay most of the way.' They had also amassed a quantity of lichens at a site they named Vegetation Island, and Levick found time to record progress of a hirsute nature: 'This morning, looking in a thaw pool, I found that my beard was coming on finely. It has a copper tinge.'*

By now they were getting the first intimations that summer was drawing to a close. Levick noted with regret: 'The sun is getting lower at night & the temperature a little lower than a few weeks ago.' They had only fourteen collecting days before the ship was due. Once again, they had a decision to make – whether to go northwards and climb as far up the Boomerang as time permitted, or to make their way southwards to explore the area near their landing site. They chose the latter, making a wide detour to avoid the crevasses Levick's unit had encountered in their dash to rejoin the others, which he pointed out to Campbell through binoculars.

Reaching their base at Evans Coves on 6 February, it was pleasant to pitch camp for lunch, washed down by hot tea, on the side of the little lake of clear green ice which had formed in the hollow of the piedmont near their depot. Their contentment was compounded by the kill of a young Weddell seal, whose liver and undercut transformed their usual pemmican hoosh. As well as the group of Weddells, they also spotted skuas and a snowy petrel – the first wildlife they had seen for three weeks. To round off this productive period, Abbott found some sea-worm casts on the piedmont, which reinforced another of Priestley's theories, that the sea had at one time reached the level of their camp.

Their stores were unmolested, but why was Campbell's note to Debenham untouched? The Second Western Party had clearly for some reason been prevented from carrying out their plans. Had something happened to them – or, worse, to *Terra Nova*?†

---

* He was not alone. Priestley reported that all the party save for Campbell, who remained resolutely clean-shaven, sported respectable sledging beards, 'though Abbott's was only represented by a few hairs which he said reminded him in numbers of a football match, the two teams being only "eleven a side" '.

† In fact Pennell and the tough little ship were making the first of several desperate attempts to rescue the Northern Party. On 15 February she picked up the Second Western

On 7 February Campbell, Priestley and Levick climbed over 1,300 feet to the summit of the Southern Foothills;* from there they could dimly make out what they thought was the Nansen moraine, which Priestley was keen to visit. As the Second Western Party did not appear to be in the locality, there was nothing to prevent them sledging over, and so Priestley set off with Abbott and Dickason the following day. Two days later they were back: what they had seen was in fact the moraine to the Priestley Glacier, with which they were already familiar.

Levick was bent on pursuing discoveries of his own. Setting off southwards to investigate reports of a skuary on 11 February with just Abbott for company, he found himself in 'a beautiful little cove with a pebble beach running down to the sea, and a small Adélie penguin rookery, with skuary attached, all complete. The small and seemingly recent rookery was still inhabited this late in the season, by moulting or moulted adults and de-downed and nearly de-downed chicks, which were splashing about the shallow water and gaining their first experience of the sea.' He continued excitedly:

> Now for the important discovery. At the Northern end of the beach are quite a large number of skeleton or mummified seals. They are mostly very old: so old that the bones and teeth are crumbling away, and I saw some of a more recent date. They all lay well up on the beach, at a considerable distance from the sea. Some were of great length: one twelve feet in length, but there were two very small ones, evidently sucking youngsters, by their size. The teeth of most of them were too disintegrated to distinguish their species, but I made out both crab eaters & Weddells, and the sucking youngsters were both crab-eaters. There were many Weddells sleeping about the ice foot and on floes near it. I have to up anchor and join the others at the foothills tomorrow†, but shall request to return at once and spend the rest of my time till the ship comes, over investigating this most interesting find.

Party at Granite Harbour, turning north for Terra Nova Bay four days later. They met heavy pack 15 miles south of the Drygalski Barrier; 'the alternative of leaving the ship in the ice and letting her drift with it past the Barrier was too dangerous to be more than thought of and cast aside,' wrote Pennell. Gran described the scene of 23 February: 'When we awoke this morning we had a bit of a fright. The ship lay dead still in newly frozen ice . . . The prospect of a winter on board, imprisoned in ice, sent shudders through us.' The implications for the Northern Party were obvious: 'The relief of Campbell is not going to be easy. He will have to tighten his belt for a time, perhaps even for months.' *Terra Nova* returned to Cape Evans, mission unaccomplished.

* An island which formed the western shore of Evans Coves, and later renamed by them Inexpressible Island – a place which was to have a profound impact on their future existence.

† No question of disobeying Campbell's order.

Indeed, the two men returned on the 15th. Although a snowstorm had obliterated their finds, they managed to dig up nine of the skeletons, two of them being of enormous size.

By now the weather was definitely on the turn. On 6 February all the ice had gone from the bay, gales started to blow with monotonous regularity down from Reeves Glacier opposite their camp, and on the 13th the snow started, pouring out of the sky for days without respite. This was both good news and bad. If the bay was clear, Pennell stood a fair chance of forcing his way in, but the heavy snowfalls would be a deterrent.

On one of the many days when a blizzard kept the men in their tents, Levick instigated a series of debates with Abbott and Browning to help pass the time. There was one proposer, one opposer, and an arbitrator, who swapped roles from topic to topic. These included: 'That every man in England should be allowed to shoot rabbits on anybody's land.'* (Motion defeated.) 'That aeroplanes will be commonly in use for commercial purposes, five years from now.' (Motion defeated.) 'That white men should not box black men for the world's championship.' (Motion carried.) 'That batchelors [sic] over 28 years old should be taxed.' (Motion carried.)

While Levick was playing parlour games in his tent, Campbell was talking over the position with Priestley, and asking him to take charge of doling out all rations for however long it took before they were rescued. Priestley was flattered on both counts. At this turning point in their fortunes, Levick – Campbell's fellow naval officer and second-in-command of the Northern Party – was clearly not yet restored to favour.

---

* The opposer in this case was Levick: 'My argument that there wouldn't be a rabbit left in England at the end of twelve months, was met by the proposer [Abbott], who said that shiploads of live rabbits could be imported from Australia by the Government, and turned [out] on the lands.'

# 5

# The Igloo on Inexpressible Island

## 15 February–29 September 1912

From mid-February to mid-March 1912, the Northern Party lived in limbo. Their hopes of being picked up by *Terra Nova* began to evaporate; certainty shaded into doubt, then anxiety and finally a cold, consuming dread.

At first the six men made light of their predicament. On 18 February they shifted their waterlogged tents higher up onto snow, to a position where they could catch sight of the ship, due that day. Campbell wrote on the 23rd, 'Personally I hardly expect to see the ship until the weather ends. Pennell would hardly make this place in such thick weather.' Two days later Levick was still managing a fair assumption of insouciance: 'We are now a little anxious . . . However, the ship has probably only been driven northwards by the gale, and ought now to be on her way here.' Twice *Terra Nova* was definitely sighted on the horizon – twice it proved to be the shadow cast by an iceberg.

On 29 February* Levick recorded with heartfelt relief: 'The blizzard is over for the present, we having been practically confined to our bags for 13 days – a record I believe for any Antarctic party, and it has been absolutely miserable. Every day our bags and all things in the tent have been covered with fine granules of ice . . . and the wind has been well below zero, judging by the way all the metal articles have "burnt" our hands.' For some of that time there was such a gale blowing that the men in Levick's tent dared not stray far outside for fear of getting lost, and (since Priestley was now doling out the rations from Campbell's tent) they ran miserably short of food.

---

*Pennell left Antarctica on 29 February with the convalescent Teddy Evans and assorted scientists on board. (Evans, who had been in the last contingent laying depots for the Polar Party, had nearly died of scurvy on the way back to base, and had been saved only by the heroism of Lashly and Crean.) The ship made for Evans Coves, to be brought up short

As he surveyed the options, Levick's tone became more desolate, his conclusions more desperate: 'Should the ship not appear by the 6th March, there will be small chance of her reaching us owing to the pack freezing in, and we shall conclude that she has gone down or been injured somehow, as of course she would never dream of leaving us here for the winter with only four weeks' provisions.' The normally phlegmatic doctor dreamed that he was on board the ship as she was crushed and sunk by pack ice. As she went down, 'I nerved myself for a header into the icy water, thinking to myself that I would take a deep breath under water and end it quickly.' He dismissed this as 'a very natural sort of dream ... considering that we are all thinking about the ship all day.'*

The frustrations of waiting for the ship that never came, which Levick described as 'the period of disappointment, and of anxiety', were as nothing compared with the awful prospect of facing a winter in that desolate region with no permanent shelter, no winter clothing and virtually no provisions. If the ship didn't come, the alternatives became starkly simple. Either the spirit of survival kicked in and they secured for themselves a place of safety and a sufficient store of food – or they died. In his report in *Last Expedition*, Campbell outlined the position as March wore on: 'The conditions are gradually but surely becoming more unbearable, and we cannot hope for improvement until we are settled in some permanent home for the winter. The tents we are living in at present are more threadbare than ever, and are pierced with innumerable holes both large and small, so that during the whole time we are inside them we are living in a young gale.'

The men discussed the form and location of their shelter. The choice was between an overground hut and an underground igloo, and there were precedents for both. Some twenty years earlier, the great Fridtjof Nansen and his sole companion Hjalmar Johansen† had overwintered on the

---

35 miles from their destination. On 4 March they tried again; the ice was thicker than ever. Bruce wrote: 'We knew it was hopeless. Campbell's position was such a serious matter, though, that we could not afford to miss the very faintest chance.' Three days later they gave up and headed for New Zealand, arriving on 1 April to learn of Amundsen's success.

* Levick's dreams were usually straightforward. On board *Terra Nova*, when she had been 'bumping and ricocheting from floe to floe', he had had three vivid dreams in the course of one night: '1. That I was being shunted about in a goods train, 2. That I was on the bridge of the "Terra Nova" crossing the bar of a harbour in the most mountainous seas, 3. That I was travelling from Kings X to Newcastle in an express train, which kept coming off the rails and bumping along over the sleepers.'

† Johansen was at that moment on his way back to Norway, having been sent packing in disgrace from New Zealand by Amundsen on a variety of charges ranging from insubordination to drunkenness.

Arctic ice cap, building for themselves a hut from boulders, moss and snow, which they had roofed with walrus skins.* The excavation of underground rooms had already featured in the lives of the Northern Party: once after the arrival of the whole party at Cape Evans in 1911, when the two rooms had been dug out to house the animal carcasses brought from New Zealand and to conduct magnetic experiments, and again when they had tried unsuccessfully to build themselves a deep-freeze at Cape Adare. There was also a contemporary example unknown to them. Amundsen and his men had excavated a positive warren of ice caves at Framheim, which they called 'the great underground works', including a petroleum cellar, a pendulum observatory and that essential Scandinavian adjunct – a sauna.

Levick was one of the overground brigade, voting for a stone hut with a wooden roof fashioned from skis and sledges and insulated on the outside by a covering of snow. 'Fortunately for us, however,' he admitted generously, 'Campbell had a better idea, and to his plan of a burrow in a snowdrift we were later to owe our lives.'† It is certain that during the terrible winter of 1912 the notorious plateau wind blasting down from the Reeves Glacier, which was to whip over the ground for 180 days without remission, would have made short work of any rough-and-ready building that the men of the Northern Party had been able to erect.

Campbell, acting with his usual foresight and attention to detail, went out with Priestley and Dickason on 29 February to choose the site. They fixed on an island about 7 miles long and half a mile wide forming the western shore of Evans Coves; it lay $1\frac{1}{2}$ miles south of their present camp at Hell's Gate across the clear blue ice of the piedmont. Priestley later revealed how the name Inexpressible Island was coined: 'When discussing what name to give the island on which we spent such an uncomfortable winter, we had great difficulty in deciding on one which would at once express our feeling . . . and also be permissible in modern literature. We passed in review through our minds all the names we could think of that had already been given in the Antarctic, and the name "Inaccessible Island", given by Captain Scott to one of the Dellbridge islands in McMurdo Sound, suggested the one that we finally adopted.'

On 3 March Campbell, Priestley and Dickason moved their tent there

---

* Nansen's epic adventure was in fact to prove a source of comfort to the party safely ensconced at Cape Evans. Cherry-Garrard recorded that 'often and often during the long winter of 1912 our thoughts turned with hope to Nansen's winter, for we said if it had been done once why should it not be done again, and Campbell and his men survive.'

† Priestley likened their home-making to rabbits going to ground. Curiously, Campbell in his diaries persistently referred to his brainchild as 'the hut'.

18. Browning at the entrance to the igloo on Inexpressible Island, almost invisible from above. During blizzards, one of the bamboos projecting from the snow on the left would be thrust up the 'chimney' inside the cave and rotated frequently to prevent the men suffocating as they slept. A sealskin fixed to the hatchway protected the shaft from drifting up.

and started to dig into a drift of *névé,** using Priestley's geological ice axes. They combined this with fetching stores over from the Hell's Gate depot – a painful ordeal in the gale-strength winds. Frostbite, lack of sleep and semi–starvation (they were down to one biscuit a day and had not yet started eating blubber) made the name Inexpressible Island a distinct understatement.

From 7 to 17 March, Levick made no entries in his diary, 'a very exceptional thing for me, but it was a bad time that, for us all'. As he pointed out, 'If at this time we could have known that the ship was not coming, and turned our whole minds to the problem we were to face, I am sure we should have been the happier for it, but as it was, our minds were only half made up for what was to come, and uncertainty thus added its

---

* Granular snow not yet compacted into ice, and therefore easier to work.

tote to the sum of our misfortunes.' Priestley described moments of black despair, and when Levick took up his pencil again on 17 March, it was to write forlornly: 'This is the day we have talked about all along as the last on which we may expect the ship, and she hasn't come.'*

With the change of tack from rescue to self-help, morale at once improved. Levick's tone became more optimistic: 'As we . . . learnt to get over many little difficulties and hardships, we became undoubtedly stronger. Our plight was bad enough, but the almost insupportable anxiety and discomfort of the late autumn had given place to a settled routine and definite plans, so that I think our former weakness had resulted in a large measure from mental causes.'

It was the start of a primeval round of killing, eating, sheltering, and preserving life and limb. Levick, Abbott and Browning remained at Hell's Gate to watch for the ship and lay in food stocks to last them through the winter. It had been settled that these three would do all the butchering, the others, 'Dickason excepting, being duffers at it and non-starters into the bargain'. (This was a bit unfair on Priestley, who was an old hand at seal-killing.) Because Campbell, who resembled Scott in his aversion to animal cruelty, had resisted giving the order before they had abandoned all hope of rescue, they only succeeded in despatching eight seals and about a hundred penguins† before the animals left for their winter quarters. This was by no means enough: Levick estimated that they needed at least twenty seals to see them out.

The unceasing, unyielding force affecting all their activities was the Antarctic weather – the seventh member of the party. The shrieking wind, biting cold and frequent deluges of drifting snow recurred day by day. Levick chronicled the four weeks of unrelieved misery before they finally moved into the relative comfort of their cave:

*February*
18th–23rd: non-stop southerly, bitterly cold blizzard. Eight days, 'during half of which time the drift was beating against the tent with a noise like a crew holystoning‡ decks'.
23rd: a lull.
24th–26th: easterly wind with heavy drift – 'we dare not go more than a few yards from the tent for fear of getting lost'.
The wind then dropped and the sun came out, 'we having been

---

* Two days earlier, 15 March, was the date Campbell recorded in his diary as 'the last day I give the ship'.
† Campbell's figure was 11 seals and 120 penguins.
‡ The naval tradition of scouring decks with a soft sandstone (the holy stone).

practically confined in our bags for 13 days – a record I believe for any Antarctic party.'

*March*

2nd and 3rd: violent gale of 'bitter Plateau wind'.

5th: 'the gale continues without intermission'.

17th: Levick's summary – 'the wind has blown now from the S.E. for a whole month excepting one day'.

Because they could see open water in the bay, they failed to make, or at least to think through, the obvious connection between this spell of severe weather and the non-arrival of the ship. They conjured up for themselves a series of hypotheses: perhaps she had been blown too far northwards; perhaps she was still waiting to pick up the delayed Polar Party; perhaps – worst of all to contemplate – she had sunk with all hands. The reality – that she had tried desperately to reach them in three separate attempts, only to be frustrated each time by pack ice massed for miles offshore – occurred only, as one of several possibilities, to Campbell.

On 18 March an alarming incident in the killing fields brought home forcibly the peril of their situation. Levick recorded it breathlessly in his diary:

Yesterday we had a terrible time. About 9 a.m. the wind increased to hurricane force, and suddenly one of the tent poles (on the lee side) broke with a snap, and then two others followed, and in a moment the tent was down on top of us, and we pinned down into our bags, with a fearful weight of wind on it. It looked like a bad disaster, with all our belongings loose in the tent, and we not in windproof clothing, besides which, the effect of being under a fallen tent in that hurricane, produced a helpless suffocating sensation which was very hard to suppress. However, we did suppress it, and one at a time struggled out of our bags and somehow groped round and got our windproof clothing on. After this Abbott & I managed to crawl out, leaving Browning lying on our sleeping bags in case the tent blew away.

Abbott & I, progressing mostly on 'all fours' as we couldn't stand up in the wind, tried to find a spot sheltered enough to let us put up the spare tent, but we couldn't find any place where there was a ghost of a chance of doing so. We got our faces & noses frostbitten continually, and eventually got back to our wrecked tent, under which we spent most of the day waiting in hope of a lull, and thawing out frostbites as they appeared. All we had to eat was some raw seal meat, and two sticks of chocolate amongst the three of us.

At 4 p.m., things being no better, we settled that we couldn't stand a night of this, so we crawled out again, piling stones on the tent to keep the sleeping bags safe, and then struggled across the piedmont towards the foothills. This was a difficult business as the ice was clear and polished by the wind, and we had often to lie down flat to keep our ground, and in the intervals did the whole half mile on 'all fours', and it took us $1\frac{1}{2}$ hours to do it. We got our faces badly frostbitten & it was impossible to keep them thawed, because as fast as we got one right, several more would appear, and I shall always remember the appearance of Browning's face, which was dusky blue, streaked with white patches of frostbite, & I suppose the rest of us were the same, and I got a nasty one where the wind had got through my windproof trousers.

When we reached the shelter of the foothills we thawed ourselves out, and soon got over to the igloo, where we found the others barricaded up and in their bags. [They] gave us a hoosh which warmed us up, and after that we spent a rotten night, two of us being just able to get half into each 'one-man' sleeping bag, and we all got very cold & slept very little.* Today, Abbott, Browning & I returned for our sleeping bags, the wind having moderated just enough to allow us to get across the ice with them, and we got our faces well bitten again. We are now established in the half finished ice cave, and are all of us feeling pretty miserable.

This frightening experience brought home to them the precarious nature of their present existence. What if Browning had been unable to hang on to the tent? What if one of them had been badly hurt? What if they had been unable to find their way back to the cave? What if their belongings, especially their sleeping bags, had disappeared by the time they returned to pick them up? It did not bear thinking about – yet that is precisely what they had to do. Thereafter, save for a few essential and painful sorties above ground, the six men became subterranean troglodytes.

Meanwhile, far away to the south-west and high above them, the same accursed weather was dogging Scott and his four companions in the doomed Polar Party as they struggled homewards after their heartbreaking discovery of Amundsen's success in the race. On the polar plateau, 9,500 feet above sea level, the minimum temperature from 27 February to 10 March dropped below -30°F every day bar one. Although this was on

---

* Campbell drew the short straw: 'Levick was my sleeping partner, though my bag was luckily a good one and nothing split, but I was squashed flat.' Three weeks earlier, on 23 February, the other group had had a similar scare: 'Campbell came over to say that they were afraid their tent wouldn't stand, and that they might all have to take refuge in ours. However, this didn't happen.'

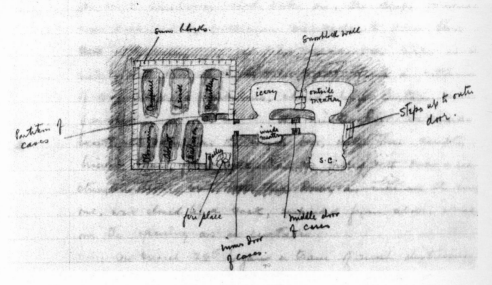

19. Levick's plan of the igloo. Officers and men slept on opposite sides and were further segregated by an invisible line drawn by Campbell down the centre of the cave.

average 20 degrees colder than those being experienced by the Northern Party, the winds which galloped down towards Evans Coves were equally savage and unrelenting.*

Levick wrote: 'Former experience of Antarctic regions had been that during the dark winter months, the temperatures are very low, [but] there was very little wind. Here, however, a different state of things obtained. For the whole seven months, during which we remained in the igloo, I believe we had hardly one calm day. Usually it blew a gale, seldom less than a stiff breeze.' The unholy trinity of bitter cold, fierce wind and driving snow had prevented their initial rescue. Its prolongation now threatened their very survival. Only anticipation, applied intelligence and a hefty dose of good luck stood between them and their maker.

By the end of March, although the igloo was by no means finished, they were beginning to settle into their underground home – 'and a dismal hole

---

* The outrageously bad weather which sealed the fate of the Polar Party is described in detail in Susan Solomon's book, *The Coldest March*. Denigrators of Scott may read it as a piece of special pleading, but the evidence is compelling, especially in her comparison of the day-by-day data orchestrated and meticulously collated by George Simpson with that amassed mechanically by Antarctic recording devices over decades since.

it is too', in Levick's opinion. He and Campbell made neat drawings, on plan and in section, but no drawing can convey the true nature of the extreme discomfort endured by its inhabitants during the long and cruel months of the Antarctic winter. The amenities consisted of a freezing latrine where diarrhoea held sway; a galley where the blubber used for cooking and lighting permeated hair, skin and clothing and gave the messmen acute conjunctivitis ('stove blindness'); and a sleeping/living area airless enough on two occasions to extinguish lamps and potentially life itself. This innermost room measured just 9 feet by 12 feet with an average ceiling height of $5\frac{1}{2}$ feet, and was entered through a doorway so low that Levick, Priestley and Abbott had to crawl in; those more vertically challenged could 'go through on an even keel'. 'Igloo back' also entered the vocabulary.

Reaching the inner room from the outside world was a cold and tricky business. First to be negotiated were the four steps leading down the shaft. This was eventually protected by a hatchway covered by a sealskin, which could be raised or lowered to allow access and was closed off in the evenings by a sack suspended from an ice axe. Beside the shaft, at the foot of the steps, was the euphemistically named 'round house'.* (On 10 March the previous year, at Cape Adare, Abbott had spent his thirty-first birthday digging out another round house, for use in emergencies, which 'turned out quite a comfortable place'.) Although the fittings of this latest unpleasant version were never described in detail, Levick mentioned them obliquely once in a medical context: 'I have been carefully noting as far as possible, the condition of our urine when it is poured onto the snow from the can, and also the stains left by us on the snow in the "round house".' On one occasion Levick and Priestley had to compete for the facilities. 'At 5.30 a.m. I had to run for the "round house", and was scarcely settled down when I heard a shuffling down the shaft, and Priestley appeared, in the last extremity. So I had to keep getting out and letting him in for a space whenever I could. Then he returned to his bag and I was out there altogether 40 minutes and got back very cold and in a bit of pain. The temperature was probably about −15°F in there.' Typically, he added: 'I am sorry for the others, who are worse than I am.'

The pressing need for a separate chamber became abundantly clear as soon as the six men moved into the cave. The acidity which resulted from the lack of carbohydrate in their diet had an unpleasant side-effect for the first couple of months. During the day they found it hard to control their bladders, and at night they would wake to discover that they had wet their bags in their sleep. This was initially a source of embarrassment as well as discomfort. One day in April, 'Campbell, in an endeavour to get things

---

* Literally, a lock-up, or a cabin on the after-part of the quarter-deck. To the men of the Northern Party it was indubitably more a place of punishment than a place of rest.

120

performed out in the wind in the middle of the night, had a bad accident in his clothing, and tried to change it outside; a very rash thing to do, and came in in a bad way, poor chap, being frostbitten in several places and half collapsed.' Levick followed suit: 'I turned out of my bag intending to go outside, but as I sat in my bag to get on my finnesco I lost all control, and wet my clothes right through. When I got outside they froze stiff and I was pretty miserable by the time I got back.' They resorted to keeping an oil can within reach of their sleeping bags, but that was not infallible. Levick wrote on 24 April: 'Last night I had more trouble over micturation, very suddenly having to rush from my bag for the empty oil can we now keep ready, but could not reach it in time.' Although things improved, Dickason noted incredulously one day in July: 'Seven fills in can.'

Once in the passageway leading inwards from the shaft, the men had to make their way through two doors, each one ingeniously constructed from three cases of sledging biscuits, two acting as jambs and one as a lintel, packed with blocks of snow. Both were also fitted with draught-excluding sacking. The passage had started life as an open trench, but a short stretch beyond the inner door was then roofed over with unflensed seal skins* laid over bamboos and ski sticks and covered with blocks of snow. Later a snowstorm filled the whole of the trench with drift. Instead of digging this out they burrowed through it, creating a tubular alleyway with a domed roof which they strengthened with more bamboos. Nature also lent a hand, deepening the drift overhead with successive snowfalls.

The innermost room served all their needs: cooking, eating, living, sleeping. 'Ice is a good conductor of heat, snow is not,' Levick wrote instructively, 'so in order to insulate the walls of the cave somewhat, we cut a lot of snow blocks almost a foot thick, and built them up against the ice wall, half way up to the roof, all round, excepting the galley corner where we brought some heavy flat rocks, and laid them on the ice to make a fireplace for burning blubber.' The ground was insulated by an equally imaginative use of scarce resources. First, as drainage, they spread pebbles and gravel, then covered this with dried seaweed and finally put down the tents' floorcloths. This layered flooring provided them with more-than-adequate insulation; it was one of the success stories of the winter. The seaweed, the only vegetable with which they were to come into contact, was to acquire an additional function as flavouring, although its degradation by the sun and mauling by generations of penguins cannot have improved its taste or appearance. Eco-friendly indeed the home which is not only 99 per cent biodegradable, but where even the underlay is consumed before being replaced.

---

* Skinned seals with the blubber left on.

20. The shaft leading into the innermost cave in which the men spent every winter hour, waking and sleeping. Unlike the shapely ice houses carved at Cape Evans, it was roughly gouged out in the Northern Party's frantic efforts to create a home when all hopes of *Terra Nova* were abandoned in March 1912.

It is impossible to read the various accounts of the setting up of this extraordinary abode without a mixture of admiration and amusement. It is a marvellous, macabre parody of suburban life, including the house-move from hell. Certainly, no first-time buyers could have been prouder or more relieved than the six men as their labours drew to a close and they found themselves settled into their brand-new, well-insulated and weatherproof home. From April the familiar rota of repairs and maintenance began, with refinements and refurbishments continuing throughout their tenancy.*

---

* It was on 17 April that Atkinson, Wright, Keohane and Williamson set out from Hut Point to try and relieve the Northern Party. The break-up of the ice at Butter Point forced their retreat, in blizzard conditions. Leaving a depot of a week's provisions, they returned to

'Nothing happens, nobody comes, nobody goes, it's awful!' The tragi-comic void at the heart of Samuel Beckett's *Waiting for Godot* was the keynote of the Northern Party's igloo existence also. Levick's diary entries for April set the tone for the winter to come. His preoccupations during that month were: incontinence, cooking with blubber, books, boots, the departure of the sun, tobacco yearnings, food rations, seals/penguins/saltwater ice, food dreams, frostbite, blubber fumes, cheery evenings, diarrhoea. It was a litany that would be repeated month after interminable month. The nightmarish nature of their existence is made, curiously, all the more vivid by the matter-of-fact tone of the diary entries. Igloo life had its own logic – until you remind yourself that it was not life at all, merely the grimmest kind of survival.

The six men had succeeded in building themselves a refuge, but immediately problems began to surface. On 1 April, Levick wrote: 'We are having great trouble over cooking.' They had a primus stove, but only enough paraffin to light it once a day. For the evening meal they had to devise a blubber stove. Levick's first attempt involved suspending a lamp wick made of tarred rope onto a float in a tin of melted blubber, but this model left much to be desired – 'We cannot get blubber to burn well, and it makes so much smoke as to nearly choke us and inflame our eyes.' They opted instead for an oil tin sawn through a few inches from the base, the bottom section serving as a stove, the inverted upper part holding the cooking oil. By trial and error they gradually learnt how to control and maintain the heat and cook the seal or penguin and blubber into a fairly respectable semblance of a stew. What they never managed to get rid of were the painful and debilitating fumes that caused so much distress to the two 'Peggies' on duty each day. First they isolated the cooking area, then dug out a small area in the shaft outside the main cave, extending this towards the end of April into 'quite a decent kitchen'. Levick came up with a palliative solution: 'I . . . have succeeded in carrying out a plan by which I can burn blubber on seal bones without the awful fumes . . . This simply consists in holding a piece of blubber on the end of a spike and letting the oil melt down onto the bones in hot drops which are thus at a lower flash point than the old lumps of blubber.' This worked moderately well, depending on the weather.

At the end of April, however, the smitch* was so bad that they took the risk of building a chimney to let in air and draw out fumes. With an ice axe, Priestley punched a hole a few inches wide through the roof which

Hut Point six days later. Atkinson's verdict was: 'I have never known any other journey have such an effect upon a party in such a short time.'

* A piece of West Country vernacular introduced by Browning which was enthusiastically appropriated by the party to describe the dense and oily pall caused by the fumes.

they plugged at night with rolled-up penguin skin.* The crack opened up and widened day by day, but they were at least able to breathe. This physical threat to the roof was accompanied by ominous noises, 'like distant 12 bore guns', according to Levick. He added that Priestley put them down to the still further cooling of the earth during winter. Priestley himself wrote that 'we are quite at a loss to account for the present fusillade' – perhaps he was trying to reassure the others by advancing a plausible-sounding geological theory.

The problem of smitch persisted. Levick advocated lighting only one blubber stove, instead of two, both to cut down on the smitch and to save on blubber, which they were consuming at an alarming rate. His greatest moment as inventor came in early June, when he boasted of having built a capital new stove with a carburettor. Sadly this contraption, named the 'Complex' to distinguish it from the original 'Simplex' model, had a short and inglorious career. On 5 June he reported sadly: 'I am sorry to say that the new patent stove went abominably and made a smitch all day.' The *coup de grâce* came just three days later: 'FOR SALE, or would exchange for a small piece of biscuit or half a lump of sugar, a BLUBBER STOVE. Quite a new invention, known as the "Complex". Has been thoroughly tried by the inventor.'

Unfortunately, the disgusting blubber was essential to their survival, not only for cooking and heating but also as a source of light. Without the glow from the stoves and the flickering light from the blubber lamps† dotted around the cave, they would have been in total darkness twenty-four hours a day; before the lamps were lit first thing in the morning, they were able to distinguish each other only by their voices. 'Within the igloo, it was quite dark, the little blubber lamps showing little small points of light, and it was only possible to read or write when we held the paper close against them. The walls and roof became blackened with soot from the blubber cooking stove, and enhanced the darkness of the cave.' It makes the faithful keeping of diaries all the more amazing. On April Fool's Day Priestley set a blubber lamp too close to the edge of the snow wall, and as the heat thawed the surface, the lamp tilted and poured most of its contents over his rucksack and the floorcloth under his sleeping bag; for the rest of the winter his bag and floor space were always greasier than the others'.

---

* Later, as the hole widened, a penguin skin was not sufficient to fill it and, recorded Priestley: 'one of the messman's most unpleasant duties was the endeavour to plug it up with a wad of refuse, which was as much as he could lift and full of grease, and "Placing the Plug" has been immortalized in song and diary as one of the most strenuous of Antarctic exercises.'

† The lamps consisted of Oxo tins filled with oil, over which lamp-wicks made of tarred rope were suspended. According to Levick they survived the winter without improvement.

Browning's lamp displayed even greater acrobatic powers, precipitating itself and its contents right inside his bag.

Since it was used for every daily activity, blubber was handled constantly, becoming smeared about the surface of the cave and trodden round with the men's finneskos.* 'It is dreadful stuff', Levick concluded, 'having a tendency to creep all over the place and pervade everything like a bad smell.' The men tried their best to keep it away from their clothes, since it made them 'a misery to wear' and caused them to lose much of their warmth. Their fur mitts became soaked with the stuff and when they went outside froze as hard as wood ('it is just like putting your hands into wooden boxes, to wear them'), so that the cuffs too stood out stiffly and the wind bit into their wrists. Its effect on sleeping bags was equally disastrous, ruining the fur and rotting the skin.

Another worry was that the constant burning of stoves and lamps would eventually cause the igloo to melt; when a duvet of drift piled up on the outside, the inside temperature rose still further. Drips started to fall from the roof in May, and by August this had become quite severe in the stove area. Being on the galley side, the three 'men' were worst affected, and one day Browning found that a sizeable icicle had deposited itself inside his sleeping bag. But since the drips froze where they fell, they could usually be plucked off the sleeping bags as little pancakes of ice before they had time to melt, and over time the under-surface of the roof glazed itself and became hermetically sealed.

On 25 May a new, and potentially lethal, danger surfaced – asphyxiation. The previous night and the whole of that day, a blizzard had raged from the south-west, with the result that the cave was gradually cocooned in a solid, wind-hardened drift. When they woke at 7 a.m. the blubber lamps were difficult to light and burned badly for the next five hours; this, however, was attributed to moisture in the wicks. Then, when the messmen lit the blubber stove at midday, it too failed to get started, and one by one the lamps went out. Alarm bells were starting to ring for Levick and Priestley, who suggested that the air might be getting thin and that it would be wise to burrow through the drift. Campbell, however, pooh-poohed this, so they decided to use the primus instead. It too went out, followed by all the lamps, and when Dickason struck three of their precious matches in succession, none of them would burn, and they were left in complete darkness. Levick, taking Campbell aside, said quietly but firmly that in his view they were fast running out of oxygen. In the nick of time Campbell was persuaded to go out and make a small hole through the drift. A few minutes later a match was struck and burnt, and the lamps

---

* Levick was in the fortunate position of having two good pairs, which he hoarded for the return journey, and one further pair liberated from Shackleton's hut, which he wore around the igloo like a favourite pair of ancient slippers.

were lit and burnt well. Apart from slight headaches the men were none
the worse, but Levick at least took the lesson to heart. 'I am convinced that
we all had a very narrow escape.' He was still brooding on it the following
day: 'I am certain we must not again have a fire going without free air entry
at the entrance, as evidently asphyxia from depleted air gives one no
premonitory symptoms. It was only by good luck we didn't all snuff out
yesterday like the lamps and matches.'*

Although keeping drifts at bay was added to their list of priorities, they
allowed the same thing to happen again one day in July. When Browning
went to the outer trap door leading out of the shaft he found the cave
drifted up, and as the blizzard persisted, they were obliged to clear it away
from the trap door every couple of hours during the whole of that day and
night, standing watches of two hours each. Levick reiterated the danger,
and the message seems to have sunk in; thereafter they made sure that the
bamboo projecting through the chimney was waggled about at regular
intervals to keep an airway to the surface permanently clear. (The wind
frequently did the job for them.)

Within the igloo, life revolved very largely around meals – the whole
process, from slaughter through butchery to cooking and eating. From first
to last the men were on the cusp of malnutrition, as the exceptional and
persistently severe weather meant that the seals stayed offshore. As soon as
any were spotted on the ice foot, the chase was on. The kill made, Levick
would heave a sigh of relief, optimistically asserting that they had enough
to see them through. But the blubber never lasted as long as expected,
some of the meat would be condemned, and the whole miserable business
started all over again. On 31 March, a never-to-be-forgotten day,
Browning had cut open a seal to find thirty-six edible fish inside, so every
kill thereafter was attended by hopes of a fish supper; it never happened
again. It added an item to the growing igloo mythology, however.
Whenever a seal was sighted thereafter, someone would shout 'Fish!' and
all would scramble to reach the beast first.

Fetching the slaughtered animals off the ice was in itself a nightmarish
business. Levick recorded one such sortie, when he and Campbell tried to
fetch the carcasses of two seals off the ice foot half a mile from the igloo.
Campbell, on culinary duty that day, returned with his load of meat, and
Levick was left to grapple with the corpses until help arrived.

I got two large bits of the skin into safety, getting blown down
repeatedly on the slippery surface, and sometimes about ten yards along
before I fetched up . . . I was just going to give it up, when Priestley
arrived on the scene, and we did it together, mostly by crawling on our

---

* Much of this account is quoted from Levick's rough diary; in the fair-copy version he
moderated his description to omit any criticism of his superior officer.

hands and knees, and pushing the skin along in front of us against the wind ... Then Abbott and Browning arrived, so I took them to the remaining skin which was whole, and we made a line fast to its tail, and tried to get it clear of the sea ice, but it was frozen down too hard, and we couldn't move it, chiefly because we had to hang on ourselves to prevent our being blown over the ice edge into the sea, ten yards off. So I took up the seal's head and returned to the cave. I was glad to get back ... having been out in the wind for two hours, and got my face and nose well bitten.

The culinary day started for Dickason, the acknowledged genie of lamp and primus stove, at 7 a.m. At 8.15 he doled out the morning hoosh, which had been prepared the night before, after which the party sat in their bags and talked among themselves for a couple of hours until it was time for the two cooks of the day to set to. One kept the blubber fire going, melted the day's blubber for the lamps, and cooked the hoosh; the other had to prepare the meat and blubber for that evening's and the next morning's hoosh. This was a fearsome business. A mass of frozen seal meat was brought into the shaft, where, exposed to the outside temperature and only partly sheltered from the bitter wind, the unfortunate operator got to work with a chisel and a geological hammer. The process was described by Levick with feeling and in detail:

The meat was as hard as the wood of the toughest yew tree, without its splintering properties, and sometimes it took several minutes to chip off one small piece, which would at last come away, all ragged and frayed out from the hammering it had received. To chip up enough seal for the two hooshes would take nearly all day, during which the wretched messman's fingers would be frostbitten time after time, and blistered from contact with the cold iron chisel, as he often had to remove his mit whilst the belaboured piece of meat danced and flew all over the place under his attack.

This butchery method involved a lamentable amount of waste, but Levick later devised a way of thawing the meat out in advance. An old biscuit tin was rigged up on some bamboos over the blubber fire, and each day the cooks placed in it the following day's ration. After the blubber stove had been going for some hours, the meat in this tin 'oven' would have warmed up enough for the assistant cook to start work on it with a knife, and even to handle it with his bare hands. To make the hoosh itself, the meat and blubber were chopped into small cubes and placed in the container over the blubber fire, together with lumps of ice, and boiled for several hours. Levick's aim was to keep the proportions of the hoosh to half blubber and half meat, but he had an uphill struggle to prevent the cooks from overboiling the brew – Browning and Abbott were the worst offenders. 'When overboiled, the hoosh is darker in colour, when gently simmered for a short time, light chocolate in colour, so I know the difference at once, besides which the flavour is distinctive to the two cases.'

For cooking purposes the men were divided into three pairs, on duty every third day. 'Great rivalry', wrote Levick with gusto,

> exists between the three 'firms' as they are called, over the performance of their duties, and each firm has its own reputation.
>
> The 'C & A' (Campbell & Abbott) firm are a sound, old established and respectable concern: very conservative, and never departing from the methods pursued by the firm during many generations.
>
> The 'B & D' (Browning & Dickason) firm have something of the American dash and enterprise about them, and taken all round, I think the general opinion is they are the best of the lot, though none of the other firms would actually go so far as to say so.
>
> The 'P & L' (Priestley & Levick) firm are, generally speaking, the experimental firm. It was for us to bring out the 'Complex' stove, and incidentally it still remains for us to prove its value! The enterprising 'B & D' firm took it up at once, but hove it out through the door after less than an hour's trial, during which they say they nearly went blind. The respectable C & A firm could not be persuaded to move in the matter at all, feeling, no doubt, that the stove which was good enough for their firm when the concern was first founded (we think about the beginning of the 15th century), is good enough for them now.
>
> There is one point I think, on which we are all agreed, and that is whatever their methods all three firms run each other very close in the grand consummation of their labours – the evening hoosh.

By 3.30 p.m. the hoosh was generally pronounced to be ready. The rest of the party, who, weather permitting, had been out hunting seals and doing odd jobs, would by then have returned home, stuffed the sack up the chimney to exclude the draught and got out their sleeping bags. Then, by the light of the little blubber lamps, the cooks served out to each man his pot of hoosh. Lumps of blubber floated in a couple of inches of oil at the top, and however well the pot was stirred, those helped first got most of it, as it continued to float to the top like cork. Seal and penguin (usually Adélie, occasionally emperor) were invariably on the menu. If a seal had been killed, the blood-soaked ice was scooped up to thicken the hoosh. Less nutritious constituents were hanks of reindeer hair from the sleeping bags,* sennegras† from boots and finneskos, fragments of rock picked up in the meat during its punishment on the floor – in fact any extraneous matter that could get itself into the pot. Fortunately the light from the blubber lamps was dim and fitful, so that much was swallowed in blissful ignorance. On one unfortunate occasion they discovered an ancient penguin flipper which had been used to clean the pot – although Campbell, who with Abbott was 'Peggy' of the day, was able to assure the diners that it was 'a fairly clean flipper'. Dickason renamed the guilty A & C firm 'the Armour Canning Co'.

They may have turned the procurement and cooking of their food into a joke, but their hunger was so acute as to be painful. The pangs returned as soon as they had finished eating, and a minor spillage became a major disaster. The hoosh was gobbled up no matter what accidental debris it contained. Rotten meat was described as 'gamey' and consumed unless it was actually oozing out of the door. Walking any distance made them feel faint with fatigue. They were hungry all the time.

Had it not been for the minimal extra stores depoted in Hell's Gate in January, the Northern Party would not have survived the winter. Without their 210lbs of biscuit (each one, weighing 2oz, had been specially baked by Huntley and Palmer for the expedition) they would have had virtually no carbohydrate in their diet. Messrs Huntley and Palmer were thus directly responsible for saving at least one life – that of Browning, who had a history of intestinal problems. He started to suffer bouts of dysentry early on in their igloo life, his system being unable to cope with seal meat and salt water, and these attacks increased in frequency and severity as the months progressed. Without the luxury items – the cocoa, tea, chocolate, raisins, Oxo cubes and tobacco – their mental health would have been much more fragile. As it was, the smallest treats gave pleasure on a gigantic scale.

Although Priestley, as stores commissar, kept the supplies beside his sleeping bag, and was responsible for doling them out, it was Levick who drew up their diet sheet and dictated the actual quantities. These he wrote out as follows:

Feb. 24th to March 17.‡
　　　Morning.　　1 pint of hoosh (sealmeat & blubber)
　　　　　　　　　1 spoonful of cocoa in a pint of hot water.

---

* Scott has been accused of buying inferior reindeer skins, possibly the thinner summer coats which tended to shed, instead of the thick winter coats. One member of the expedition complained: 'Our bags, like the fur boots, have been badly selected and moult continually.'

† Sennegras or senne-graas: dry Norwegian hay used as packing in boots to keep feet warm and absorb moisture.

‡ i.e., until they decided they would have to overwinter on the ice cap.

Evening.    Ditto.
At first 3 biscuits a day, afterwards reduced to 1 biscuit per day.

March 18th to July 31st.
    Morning      $1\frac{1}{2}$ pints of hoosh. $1\frac{1}{2}$ biscuits.
    Evening       $1\frac{1}{2}$ pints of hoosh.
                1 spoonful cocoa in $\frac{1}{2}$ pint of water
       Excepting.    Sunday.    1 spoonful tea instead of cocoa
                Monday.    The same tea reboiled.

In addition to this ration we had –
    Every Sunday 10 lumps of sugar.
    Every Saturday 1 stick chocolate ($\frac{1}{2}$ ounce)
    Every other Wednesday $\frac{1}{2}$ ounce chocolate.

*During August*   Two pints of hoosh morning & evening, but no biscuit.

*September*   Two pints of hoosh morning & evening. 1 biscuit per day.

On the last day of each month, we had ten raisins apiece. On birthdays, 25 raisins apiece.

On June 22nd, being midwinter day, we had extra rations, all round. One of the memorable days of our lives.

Maintaining the delicate balance between fats, proteins and carbohydrates assumed for Levick a major importance. Initially, as their supply of carbohydrate was limited to a meagre biscuit ration and they found blubber deeply unpalatable,* they had to consume huge quantities of lean meat to satisfy their hunger. In time, however, they became used to the 'nauseating flavour' of the blubber, and even to crave it. 'This desire for blubber fluctuated in each individual. One morning he would request a large quantity, and drink and gobble up half a fistful of it. The result would be what we termed a "set back", which meant that the thought of any blubber at all nearly made him sick. Gradually the desire would return, the quantity increasing day by day until another "set back" took place, and so on.'

Flavouring the hoosh was difficult, but important if it were to be even remotely palatable. Their one precious tin of Cerebos salt they kept for emergencies, using instead seawater ice dug out from the shore. The percentage of salt varied considerably, according to the time it had been

---

*Although when Campbell tasted it for the first time in February, he 'rather liked it, while Abbott and Browning declared that it had a very strong flavour of melon'.

frozen and the depth at which it was obtained, so they had to balance it out with chunks of freshwater ice, hacked off an internal wall. The immediate effect of too much salt was an epidemic of diarrhoea, Browning – starting a melancholy trend – being affected worse than the rest (the others gradually became immune). As for the 'precious biscuit', this was served out at the morning meal, and treated by each man according to individual taste.

As a rule, the men ate theirs at once, chewing it up in a few large mouthfuls. The officers acted differently. We used to fondle ours, & smell it, perhaps nibbling a tiny corner. Then as a rule we ate our hoosh, then the biscuit, but generally we kept half for the evening meal. There was a great art in biting off very small pieces of biscuit and taking as long a time as possible to chew them up. The sensation of eating this biscuit can only be described as an ecstasy, and became a pleasure of the intellect rather than the enjoyment of a sense.

Levick even had the strength of mind (or perhaps it was scientific curiosity) to forego his biscuit ration for a full week to observe the effects on his health. This started on 25 May; the following day he noted proudly: 'Today I resisted both my allowance of biscuit and chocolate, and also asked Priestley not to serve me out my weekly allowance of 12 lumps of sugar. I had a vivid carbohydrate dream last night, but on the whole don't hanker too much after it. It is useful to have trained a lot in former days [as an athlete], and got used to resisting little temptations!' At the end of his experiment, seven days later, he decided that they could easily stop the ration of biscuit if necessary, and keep fit on meat and blubber alone, 'but that probably we could not do much work on it, and that it certainly would not be enough for a full ration out sledging'. When the biscuit ration was abolished during August, to conserve the remaining supply for the sledging journey ahead, all except Browning suffered painful bouts of constipation.

For the smokers in the group, the loss of regular supplies of tobacco was grievously felt. Already by the end of March Levick was lamenting: 'We have a very little tobacco which we eke out with every possible substitute. The tea leaves we have used have all been boiled 3 times and are now being smoked. We all smoke wood shavings, a piece of teak proving the best flavoured, but I have at the present moment some raisin stalks mixed with an old pipe heal [sic] burning merrily in my pipe, and it is very passable.' He even wrote a short piece about the joys of smoking, which he contemplated turning into a book.

I lie here in my sleeping bag and gaze into the darkness which is relieved somewhat by a little blubber lamp whose smoky flame casts fitful shadows and little dancing points of light upon the roughly hewn walls of our ice cave. My pipe is in my mouth and as I puff slowly at it I am sensible of a feeling of calm comfort and enjoyment, and a tendency to look on the bright side of things. This last is most like the tendency produced by alcohol (I have often felt that too!) which while it cheers, dulls the mind for caution and induces us to ignore the more serious or unpleasant aspects of a position . . .

No doubt as I write, some wretched member of my club in London is miserable because one of the casters is off the only available armchair in the smoking room. Perhaps that gentleman would be surprised to hear the figure I would give for that chair as it stands. The leather would make me a pair of windproof trousers, of which I stand badly in need, with enough spare perhaps for a pair of moccasins. Whilst the uses to which I can put the previous woodwork are too numerous to mention. I could smoke the stuffing!

Dickason was the other addict, and his diary is peppered with withdrawal symptoms. On 31 May: 'there is no mistake in saying that I long for tobacco as much as anything', and on 21 July: 'N.B. Feel the want of tobacco very much!' Campbell redeemed himself in Dickason's eyes on several occasions by slipping him an extra pipeful, and on 23 September Levick made the ultimate sacrifice: 'Rings and I had the last of the tobacco this evening the doctor and Tiny [Abbott] standing out from sharing as it was so small.' Priestley, the only non-smoker, presumably knew better than to rejoice openly when supplies eventually ran out.

The evolving relationships between the members of the party is one of the fascinating aspects of their story. Thrown together as they were, night after rotten day, conventions and niceties became, if not obsolete, at least compromised. You cannot watch one of your naval superiors vomiting, shitting himself and wetting his sleeping bag, and hold him in quite the same awe and esteem. Anarchy, or a *King Rat* scenario, might have ensued. As it was, the extraordinary nature of their confinement upheld the traditional naval hierarchy while bringing the group closer together. As in any vulnerable institution – hospital or nursing home – the terrors and traumas of others evoked sympathy rather than derision. There, but for the grace of God, went they all.

Depression could not always be kept at bay. There was also the fact, as Levick pointed out, that 'excepting our three days on the ship [the journey from Cape Adare to Inexpressible Island], we had seen no other faces for a year, and already had spent one polar winter together.' Who knows how they might cope with being cooped up together for another six months in infinitely worse circumstances?

As it turned out, they coped remarkably well, partly by maintaining the traditional divisions between officers and men. Priestley, in a 1969 article for *Nutrition Today*, described how this came about:

> Campbell, using the sole of his boot, drew a line down the centre of the cave. Pointing to the area occupied by the enlisted men, he said, 'That becomes the messdeck.' Pointing to our side, he said, 'This will be the quarterdeck . . .' Once each week, I shall inspect all quarters. As on board ship, everything that is said and done on the messdeck will be the responsibility of the men and it shall not be heard or paid attention to or interfered with by any of the officers who reside on the quarterdeck. And the opposite is true.'

Good walls, even invisible ones, made good neighbours here too.

Priestley, the only civilian, was in sympathy with the apartheid policy, on grounds relayed later to Charles Wright that the men 'would be much happier that way, because of the great difference in their upbringing'. In a later lecture, he went further, arguing that Taff Evans, 'the only representative of the rank and file [on the polar journey], was virtually in a thought-tight compartment by himself. His mental life inevitably ran on different lines from that of his companions.' Among Priestley's fellow civilians, Wright disagreed strongly with his views while Debenham upheld them.

Campbell was a fine leader of men – intelligent, decisive and courageous. He was not so good at coping with individuals. This was especially noticeable in his inflexible treatment of the three ratings. They were accustomed to obeying orders without question, but they were very far from being lumpen navvies; Scott had after all taken infinite pains to select the best men available, lower ranks as well as officers. As their diaries show, Abbott, Browning and Dickason were well-read, intelligent and articulate. Browning was a sensitive observer of men and wildlife, and a natural writer. He not only gave them the immortal 'smitch' but also possessed a fund of earthy and irreverent stories, jokes and repartee. Priestley considered that: 'I think we all justified our existence during the long months of this winter, but Browning perhaps did so more than any of us.' The stoicism and good humour he maintained throughout his appalling and continuous bouts of diarrhoea is very moving.

Abbott, who had made many friends of all ranks and classes on the outward journey, had clearly won the respect of the two junior seamen, as Levick had anticipated he would at Cape Adare. Largely thanks to him, the three 'men' would hold the line against fear and depression. Abbott himself displayed courage and fortitude of a high order in the face of a badly injured right hand – a disastrous thing to befall a serving seaman. Although he managed to hang onto his sanity when it mattered most, it was he, not Browning, who suffered a breakdown on the way back to England.

Dickason, a more pugnacious character than his two friends, seems to have got on well with Priestley ('Mr P', but also the more familiar 'P') and Levick ('the doctor' or 'doctor'); he uttered not a word of criticism against 'Tiny' Abbott, while he and 'Rings' Browning became extremely close. But although Campbell provoked nothing near the farcically dangerous level of antagonism stoked up by Borchgrevink during the *Southern Cross* expedition, dislike of the man himself began to simmer in Dickason early on. On 30 May he wrote: 'Mr C is continually waking up in the early hours of the morning and starts again to the doctor, it is either about the time, hoosh or he has something the matter with him. It gets on my nerves to have him morning after morning, I don't know what sleep he gets.' On 12 June: 'Mr C had a bad attack he dropped hints about sea water ice and penguins this morning so we all turned out to get them. He did not worry about it yesterday, his lay in.' Later he wrote darkly: 'Have nicknamed one of this party Ananias.'*

Levick wrote in his rough diary early on in their confinement, '[Campbell] is, I am sorry to say, getting into a broody and irritable state of mind, and I rather fear trouble in the future. He has not a good constitution.' It seems to have been Dickason who, in the unnaturally close confines of the cave, objected most to being bawled out by Campbell. His mutinous mutterings increased as winter wore on. He wrote in his diary during August and September: 'Had bit of argument with Mr C about my sleeping billett . . . Mr Campbell used the word "piracy" to me when he told me in front of the others that I did not answer him in a proper manner. I am only putting this down in case of any thing turning up later . . . Mr C had a bump at Rings yesterday because hoosh was not ready at 4.10 p.m., and logged him, making doctor sign it. Rings did not answer in an outburst or out of hand manner.'

Dickason's irritability was both minor and understandable, and most of the time the six men got on famously, but Campbell seems to have been temperamentally incapable of bending naval rules to fit the realities of their uniquely awful existence. His disciplinarianism jarred on Priestley too: 'I sometimes used to think that he was occasionally too hard on the men for

---

* The husband of Sapphira; the pair were struck dead for trying to cheat St Peter. *The Oxford Dictionary of Phrase and Fable* states that 'his name is used allusively to denote a liar'. Dickason, well versed in the Scriptures, may have been thinking of a particular passage: 'And Paul, especially beholding the council, said, Men and brethren, I have lived in all good conscience before God until this day. / And the high priest Ananias commanded them that stood by him to smite him on the mouth. / Then said Paul unto him, God shall smite thee, thou whited wall: for sittest thou to judge me after the law, and commandest me to be smitten contrary to the law? (Acts 23: 1–3). Had Campbell been caught out in a lie, or had he thumped a member of the party?

what seemed to me to be very minor peccadilloes.' The decision to 'log' Browning evokes a truly Hogarthian picture. The villainous-looking criminal is ceremonially hauled in front of the two equally filthy villains sitting in judgement over him, before being formally reprimanded (and fined?). One of the magistrates produces a grimy sheet of paper on which the prisoner, straining in the smoke-filled gloom to read the awful details of his crime, affixes his name in a pencilled scrawl. Sentence pronounced, all return to their sleeping bags.

Levick's relationship with Priestley is tantalisingly unclear. He evidently developed a great regard and affection for the genial geologist, describing him as 'a fine chap with a sound head on him', and this seems to have been reciprocated, if Priestley's entry on Levick in the *Dictionary of National Biography* reflects his true feelings: 'During that long-drawn-out trial, when all were extended to the utmost, physically and psychologically, Levick was a tower of strength ... he was a chief contributor to the cultural life, confidant of the rank and file seamen; loyal and wise adviser to Lieutenant Victor Campbell his leader and friend.' These last few words do not quite ring true, nor does his assertion that Levick as a doctor was adequate but underemployed. But, true to form, in *Antarctic Adventure* Priestley hardly mentions Levick and gives very few instances of any interaction between them.

Responsible for maintaining the party's health, Levick was also instrumental in maintaining their morale. The dire nature of their predicament seems to have aroused in him qualities which had so far lain dormant. In retrospect it was a stroke of luck that Levick rather than Atkinson had been chosen for the Northern Party. Levick was not only a surgeon – useful for butchering seals as well as treating humans – but had also made a study of diet and exercise. Atkinson was equally qualified as a surgeon, but his specialities were bacteriology and parasitology, and his natural reticence might have been less useful in dispelling the inevitable bouts of gloom and uncertainty than Levick's unquenchable optimism.

Although Campbell had belittled the doctor's medical function initially, this became increasingly important to the welfare of the group. There were many possible sources of infection, many accidents waiting to happen. Scurvy was perceived at the time to be a serious threat, yet despite James Lind's pioneering work in the mid-eighteenth century, there was still no firm agreement on how to tackle it in polar regions. Lind described it as 'a foul and fatal mischief', and wrote that 'a very intense degree of cold, as in Greenland, &tc. is experienced to have a most pernicious influence in heightening its malignity'. Scott had itemised the symptoms during the *Discovery* expedition as follows: 'the first sign is an inflamed, swollen condition of the gums ... Spots appear on the legs and pain is felt in old wounds and bruises; later, from a slight oedema, the legs and then the arms, swell to a great size and become blackened behind the joints.'

There were two main schools of thought. Wilson and Atkinson were ranged on the side of those who believed that infected tins and poor ventilation were the likely suspects. Levick joined Lind and Shackleton in fingering the lack of vitamin C as the probable – and as we now know, the actual – villain, curable by a sizeable intake of fresh meat and fresh fruit. The latter was not an option for the Northern Party, the nearest equivalent being their seaweed flooring, the infrequent celebratory handful of raisins and Levick's meagre supply of citric acid and lime-juice tablets, which he started serving out in June as 'good for us in the absence of vegetable acids'. Fresh meat, on the other hand, they had a sufficiency of. Seal liver and brain are reckoned to be particularly rich in vitamin C, and this formed a regular part of their diet. On 29 May, reported Levick, 'we had an excellent hoosh with seal's brain in it, which was very good indeed, and tasted rather like soaked bread'.

In the event, during their igloo period none of the men suffered the symptoms described by Scott, although Levick may have suspected the onset of scurvy when towards the end of June Campbell disclosed a sore place on one of his gums. On investigation Levick found a darkish patch like a small scab, which brushed off but left the gum bleeding slightly. Earlier in the month he had confided with relief in his diary: 'We are nearly half way through the winter now, and our health, considering everything, A.1. I am sure that with an ordinary diet, we should be rotten by now . . . and that the carnivorous diet must be accountable for our well being.'

Levick recorded and worried over a series of complaints suffered by the party during their incarceration. The number of ailments and accidents with which he had to deal is miraculously small considering their hazardous predicament and the pitifully restricted supplies on which he could call. His medicine chest contained several treatments for diarrhoea: chalk powder, bismuth and lead compound (all with opium), a tonic containing strychnine, sodium lactate and chlorodyne. Then there was quinine for fever and chills, cascara for constipation and calomel for purging, mercuric chloride as an antiseptic and liquid cocaine for stove blindness. 'Newskin' was used by the doctor to mend a chronometer, and his supply of mustard plasters was pressed into service to pep up an evening hoosh. The experiment was not a success.

Levick had no resources (other than his own) to deal with life-threatening disasters. He was occasionally assailed by the potentially nightmarish outcome of their stumbling about in near-blackness among the boulders on their way to fetch meat from the depots: 'I sincerely hope I don't have any fractured legs to deal with under these conditions.'

Frostbite – a daily occupational hazard as the men fetched in sea ice, tracked, killed and butchered seals and penguins, or relayed corpses from depot to larder as supplies ran low – could also have had serious consequences. By the beginning of April, when the bitter wind had been blowing ceaselessly for forty-six days, they had all acquired 'horny and desquamating nobs [sic]' on the ends of their noses. A graphic picture was painted by another member of the expedition: 'If a frostbite gets below the surface tissue of the hand or foot the result is a water blister, exactly as in the case of a bad burn* . . . If the frostbite is deep-seated then the blood-vessels do not recover and the last stage is gangrene and the only hope amputation.' This must have been Levick's underlying fear when at the end of April Browning's hand was frostbitten right up to the wrist – 'quite dead and white'. Luckily the doctor was not called upon to wield his knife on that occasion, and the hand recovered.

Dickason contributed a heartfelt song on the subject to the Northern Party's literary output:

> Here's to the blizzard at plus seventeen
> Here's to the calm minus fifty
> The lower degrees that are still and serene
> The Blizzard so furious and drifty.
>> Hear the wind yell
>> Hang on for a spell
>> If you let go the rope it may blow you to Hell.
>
> Wrapped up in your windproof your body's all right
> With your hand lying snug in its mitten
> But your beautiful nose is exposed to frostbite
> And as often as not is frostbitten.
>> Hear the wind yell
>> Hang on for a spell
>> If you let go the rope it may blow you – away.
>
> Whatever you wear in the wind there remains
> The ever-insoluble puzzle
> Of how to be happy though blue in the face
> With the icicles stuck to your muzzle.
>> Hear the wind yell
>> Hang on for a spell
>> If you let go the rope it may blow you to Hell.

---

* A frequently reproduced photograph of Atkinson's hand, taken after he had lost his bearings and one of his mitts at Cape Evans in July 1911 and had wandered around outside for several hours, is a horrifying sight, described by Scott as 'immense blisters on every finger giving them the appearances of sausages'.

The men's 'bites' increased in size and severity as their blubber-soaked clothing degenerated into rags. 'My own clothes in which I am lying now', wrote Levick in May, 'I put on on Jan 8th on board the ship, and have not removed since, which makes 4 months, and I don't expect to change them till we leave here in the spring. This does not apply to my socks, which I changed three months ago, and which I remove occasionally to cut my toe nails (and lately at night).' Footwear was a more serious, if less aesthetic problem. 'Our leather boots became worn, and burst out at the sides, and it was torture to wear them, especially as often they were so iced up inside as actually to pinch our toes, [which] at length become quite senseless from being continuously very cold and frequently frostbitten.'*

Snow blindness, another threat, was avoidable, but Levick could not persuade the others to wear their balaclava helmets and goggles as a matter of course. The effect of the glare on their retinas could be prolonged and extremely sore – Wilfrid Bruce had compared it with having needles driven into his eyeballs, and had noted a curious side-effect: at first he could not stand the light, then for months afterwards he could hardly see at all in the dark. This was bad news for any sufferer trying to pick his way through the winter darkness.

With half an eye to scurvy and the other half to dysentery, Levick was meticulous about cooking and hygiene. Early on in the winter he wrote out a list of dos and don'ts, decreeing:

(1) That the meat brought in is to be thawed over the fire, should not be put on the floor as hitherto. (This is a mix of filthy blubber, round the fire.)
(2) That the meat should be used up as it is thawed, and small bits not allowed to accumulate.
(3) That the blubber board should be well scraped each day.
(4) That the warm water from the outer cooker which is poured over the next morning's hoosh each night, and allowed to stand all night, should be iced so that the board should not run the risk of bacterial incubation.

Dysentery was the main enemy; all suffered bouts from time to time, and Levick's diary records instance after instance, treatment after treatment. Browning's suffering was particularly severe, and the conditions in which he endured it make grim reading. Levick recorded the details with concern and compassion – in all, he refers to Browning's condition nearly fifty times.

---

* When Oates's body was found, it was discovered that he had cut his boots open across the front, the easier to force his feet in; the pain only started as the feet began to thaw.

Month after month this diarrhoea continued and I can give you little idea of what Browning must have endured during this time, as often he had to turn out of his bag and grope his way out in the darkness seven or eight times during the night, each time having to grope for his windproof clothing & frozen boots, and crawl down the shaft, undoing and replacing the frozen doors as he passed through them. One night of this would be bad enough, but for the whole seven months I do not think he had more than half a dozen undisturbed nights. Most men must have succumbed, but nothing seemed ever to shatter his determination to be cheerful and take his share of the duties of the party. All the remedies at our disposal were tried, and though at times these alleviated, they never cured him. He became very thin, and somewhat weak at times, though never so weak that he could not walk. Occasionally a little blood was passed in his stools, and tender patches were discovered in palpating the abdomen . . . As far as possible, it was thought best to encourage him in his desire not to become an invalid, and I have no doubt that it was this determination of his, more than anything else, which saved his life.

Priestley paid tribute to the doctor's assiduous care of Browning, saying: 'there is little doubt that but for Levick's unremitting care he would not have survived the winter'.

Levick's job as expedition doctor was at times a lonely one. He kept his own bouts of ill health to himself, writing on 17 May after a further bout of bag-wetting, 'I haven't told anybody of my accident, as they are all thinking too much about ailments, and are becoming imaginative.'* For the same reason he did not voice his theory, on hearing that Campbell, Abbott and Dickason had been passing blood in their stools and seeing it in his own, that they might have caught intestinal parasites from the seal meat. Noting the bad effect his early policy of explaining various symptoms was having on the others, he became more reticent and circumspect. 'One of our number is apt to get anxious about himself,† and I have been regretting the way in which I talked physiology to the party at the beginning of the winter, as it has in this way done harm . . . I have stopped this, and two days ago I had to refuse point blank to answer any more questions on the subject,' adding rather pompously, perhaps from feelings of guilt: 'A doctor under these conditions should be most

---

* In his rough diary, he was more explicit: 'I haven't told anyone as C. gets into panics about himself very easily and will be imagining he is going to do the same if he hears about it.'

† Omitted from the later version: '. . . and imagine that he has impossible complaints.' Another clear reference to Campbell.

tactful, and whilst freely giving his opinion when asked, avoid stating his reasons as far as possible.'

The greatest test to Levick's skill as a surgeon came on 10 July, when he and Priestley, as cooks of the day, were in the throes of preparing the hoosh. The rest of the party were outside, enjoying one of the rare periods of lull, and had the great good fortune to come upon a bull and a cow seal on the ice, one of them a good size with very thick blubber. Shortly after 1.30 p.m., Abbott returned, having cut three fingers of his right hand almost to the bone as he was stabbing the second beast. The scene inside the cave, as described by Levick, resembled a Victorian operating theatre:

My hands were filthy and soaked with blubber from the stove, and my fingers stiff with cold, besides which we only had the guttering light of a blubber lamp held by Priestley, to aid me. I cleaned off as much blubber as I could from my hands, and dressed the cuts with boracic wool and bandages. I sincerely hope no tendons were cut, but under the circumstances did the best I could, and as the hand was clean and the wounds washed with blood, I thought it better not to poke about in them and make them septic, but to dress them with clean dressings as quickly as possible, which I did . . . His fur mit was nearly full of blood which soon froze into a solid block. I shall feel rotten about it if his tendons are cut, but think it would have been risking serious suppuration if I had attempted enlarging the wounds and picking up the severed ends, even if I had been able to find them in that light, so great was the filth of my hands & whole surroundings.

The following day Levick washed the wounds out once with mercury chloride. 'All three wounds looked a bit puffy but on the whole clean, and there was no pus. I did not attempt any exploration for the lost tendons' end, as I did not think the risk of sepsis justifiable, so redressed the wounds as before. He remains on the sick list and has orders not to use the hand for anything at all.' Three tendons had in fact been severed, denying Abbott thereafter proper use of his right hand. Had his fingers become infected, gangrene and amputation would have been real possibilities.

Levick's decisive and skilful reaction to this crisis, and even more importantly, his anticipation and prevention of minor but debilitating ailments, ensured that all six men (even the hapless Browning) were fit enough at the start of the spring sledging season to embark on their gruelling 230-mile journey to Cape Evans and safety, scheduled by Campbell for the third week in September. Indeed the serious bout of diarrhoea which occurred before the great event might have prevented their setting out had it not been arrested by his careful treatment. This outbreak was the result of ptomaine poisoning from the oven, which

Levick condemned and threw outside. They tried suspending the meat directly from the bamboos, but these also became infected and the outbreak of diarrhoea resumed. One of the eminently sensible conclusions reached by Levick was: 'Those who actually have diarrhoea are best on a liquid diet of nourishing soup which will keep up their strength without giving too much work to their inflamed guts. Those not having diarrhoea had best enjoy a full diet such as they find suits their requirements, as otherwise they cannot start sledging in good condition.'

Psychologically as well as medically, he was forever on the qui vive. Beneath the companionable and often jovial veneer of their daily lives, there were any number of traumas ready to surface. The fate of Scott and his companions, and especially of *Terra Nova*, continued to hover uneasily at the back of their consciousness and their conversation. Long after they had abandoned hope of being picked up, they speculated about the cause. In a melancholy entry written in mid-May, months after they moved into the cave, Levick wrote: 'We are in hopes that the ship may have gone ashore along the coast somewhere near us . . . and that she may be in Granite Harbour or Wood Bay, in either of which cases a relief party might (and probably would) be sent to us as soon as the sea is fairly and permanently frozen over, which would be about the end of June. This prospect seems almost too good to be true.' (It was.) Later on in the same diary entry he returned to the subject, as to a nagging tooth: 'The ship may have foundered with all hands on board . . . in which case we are the only survivors of the whole expedition.' Even as late as July and August they still had expectations of a search party reaching them. As always they had absolutely no notion of what was happening to the tiny knots of people scattered in various pockets around them. They could only speculate – and that way madness lay.

The spectre of mental collapse was genuine, especially for Browning, who succumbed to a rare, and mercifully brief, fit of hysterical depression shortly before they set out on their journey. The final fear, reaching a peak towards the end of their incarceration, was that they would perish on their march over the first major obstacle in their path, the unknown and much-dreaded Drygalski Barrier.

During all these potential crises, Levick kept watch, reacting and anticipating. Just once, on his birthday, 3 July, he allowed himself to express his relief on the medical front: 'We are all up to our weight I think, and though no one is very fat, the party under their dirt and beards look well covered and fit. We are not very pale, in spite of our life of darkness, but have kept a good deal of the bronze of the past season's sledging.'

Maintaining their mental equilibrium was a still more remarkable achievement. In part they alleviated depression and discomfort by concentrating on ordinary pleasures. Food was both occupation and

141

panacea. The preparations for cooking the daily hoosh were made with messianic zeal and thoroughness, experiments as to times of cooking and mixtures of ingredients undertaken with the intellectual curiosity of laboratory technicians, the results analysed and compared as if by a panel of restaurant critics. Gastronomic 'treats' were counted out minutely and democratically. Birthdays and other 'high days' were celebrated by Priestley doling out an extra biscuit or an unscheduled issue of raisins, chocolate and/or sugar. Fortunately, four members of the party had birthdays within the igloo period – Abbott on 10 March, Levick on 3 July, Priestley on 20 July and Campbell on 20 August.* 'I can see', remarked Campbell drily early on, 'that one of Priestley's difficulties in the future is going to be preventing each man from having a birthday once a month.' Almost any excuse would do, and the reward was carefully tailored to fit the occasion. The killing of their sixteenth seal on 5 April warranted an extra biscuit, while the slaughter of no fewer than four emperor penguins on 6 May was marked by an extra biscuit plus a full hoosh. Campbell's wedding anniversary on 10 May was declared a 'fiesta' and celebrated with ten raisins, whereas Levick's mother's birthday on 9 June was a low-key affair, a toast being drunk to her with their Sunday mug of tea. The return of the sun on 10 August ranked second only to Midwinter Day, bringing forth a brain and liver hoosh and sweetened cocoa, plus two biscuits, six lumps of sugar and a stick of chocolate apiece.

Midwinter Day itself, celebrated on 22 June, was anticipated, discussed and enjoyed seemingly out of all proportion to the slender rations on offer. It consisted of a hoosh lovingly prepared by Levick and Priestley of emperor-penguin heart and liver and seal's liver, four biscuits, four sticks of chocolate and twenty-five raisins per man, followed by cocoa 'of the actual strength employed in civilization', four citric acid and two ginger tabloids, and a cigar and plug of tobacco hoarded by Levick for the smokers. There was even a drop of Wincarnis tonic wine for all. Dickason's heartfelt comment was: 'I am enjoying an after breakfast pipe of good tobacco, just before hoosh had our wincarnis. It tasted *marvellous*.' (Priestley, who seems to have been accident-prone, managed to pour his tot into his sleeping bag.) This was meagre fare compared with the feast they had laid into the previous year at Cape Adare, with its 'liberal allowance' of alcohol, its sweets and crackers, and the bran-tub supplied by Lady Scott; yet, declared Priestley, 'had any of us been asked on the night of June 22, 1912, which day we had enjoyed the most there would have been no hesitation about our answers – 1912 every time.'

A meal of such exquisite pleasure rated a prolonged and energetic sing-song. This naval tradition had become an important part of life on

---

* On that day the men gathered around the table in the hut at Cape Adare raised their glasses to the absent leader of the Northern Party.

Inexpressible Island ever since 18 February, when the party found spontaneous relief in song after Levick, Abbott and Browning were reunited with their comrades after their hazardous journey over the piedmont. On other occasions, such as Midwinter Day, it celebrated a particular milestone in their calendar of survival. Saturday evenings were given over to old favourites – 'Rolling Home', or 'Mandalay' – and to new compositions, such as the rather clumsy and labyrinthine ditty penned by Levick to commemorate a ghastly accident in which he spilt and wasted a pint of precious hoosh:

> The whole of the oven came tumbling upon my poor innocent head,
> At the sound of that avalanche tumbling the customers wished they
> were dead,
> They'd hungrily watched the hoosh cooking, and just when they
> thought it was hot,
> With a hoop-la! hoop-la! down came the whole jolly lot.

A particular success, dredged up from memory by one of the 'men', was described by Levick as 'a fine old sea song, with the finest tune to the chorus I have ever heard, and we all sing it often and simply roar out the chorus', as follows:

> Hilly hauly Hilly Hauly-o
> Cheerily boys cheerily
> Bend your backs and give a pull
> Cheerily I say, I say.
> With a long pull and a strong pull
> Haul away together boys
> If every yard we must relay
> Relay boys, relay!

On Sundays, as in pleasanter times at Cape Adare, Campbell read from the New Testament, and hymns and psalms were sung, recollected in the absence of a hymnal with a fair degree of accuracy thanks to the spell spent by the seamen in their home choirs, and to Priestley's Wesleyan chapel childhood. As winter deepened and the men were confined day after day to their bags, sing-songs began to supplement and even replace conversation. Priestley and Browning, gifted with good memories and a good ear for words, took on the main burden of their songs. Ever afterwards Priestley associated certain songs with the unique events of 1912, and like Proust and his *madeleine*, had only to close his eyes to conjure up the pitch blackness of the cave and its distinctive sounds and smells.

Understandably, conversation lost its effervescence over time. Levick wrote: 'Occasionally we think of something worth saying, and say it, in which case the substance of the remark is usually taken up by the party, nosed about and discussed from its centre to its frayed edges.' Priestley, who frequently opted out of the general conversation, preferring to day-dream the tedious hours away, described one 'day of controversies' in which Levick was the prime shaker. He and Priestley opened the proceedings with a discussion about their present chocolate ration and the lamentable amount left behind at Cape Adare; the disputants then moved swiftly on to the likelihood of a fruit cake freezing during spring sledging. Campbell and Levick managed to raise the argument to the higher plane of national ethics and imperial politics, before the tone sank again to an impassioned debate about the best way to consume a single biscuit.

On the messdeck side of the invisible wall there was always plenty to discuss. One Sunday in August, Dickason wrote in his diary: 'I tried to have a sleep during afternoon whilst Rings wanted to have a yarn etc; but I did not manage it, I like to keep my yarning until night as then we want something to talk about.'

When the disputants and chatterers fell silent, day-dreaming was an equal release. Levick wrote sadly of their incessant thoughts of cakes, plum pudding and bread and butter: 'If I could at the present moment buy penny buns for a sovereign apiece, I don't think I should have much money left to spend out of my pay when I got home.' Thoughts of home and future adventures also loomed large. 'We spend much time over making plans for ourselves when we return to civilization, and I am simply full of schemes for myself,' Levick confided to his diary. 'Writing, I mean to take up, and one of my hottest ideas at present is a canoe trip from the Rocky Mountains to the Atlantic, right through Canada, down the Saskatchewan.' He enlisted Campbell's help, since the latter was familiar with the country around Winnipeg and Edmonton and was able to draw the route for him on a roughly sketched map. 'It will make the subject of a good book with fine photographs and should not take more than four months, so that six months half pay would easily see me through it. I write now, to read later, that if I do not do this trip I ought to be led out and shot.* One gets a wider perspective view of life here than one can ever get when one is once back and up to the neck in civilization.' Levick and Campbell also discussed motorbike tours round Britain and abroad in minute detail.

> After hoosh we lie back in our bags and I say, 'Well, where shall we go today?', and Campbell suggests a route which we follow out, needless to say dining sumptuously at the various inns on the way, and ordering the

---

* History does not relate whether Levick ever made good his resolution.

meals with the most minute particulars, wine and all. We have been doing this for weeks, and have nearly exhausted our knowledge of England in the search for fresh roads. He has given me the most glowing accounts of a magnificent refreshment room at Basle, in Switzerland, and we have had many a good meal there together.

When these and other topics had been exhausted, silence descended on the cave, and each man pursued his own skein of reverie. 'I don't suppose that any party of men have reflected more than we have of late, in fact we may almost be said at times to live upon our reflections,' mused Levick. 'We chew upon our mental cuds by the hours, days, and weeks.' Summer days in the English countryside assumed misty contours. 'It is uncommonly cheering to think of the stretches of white dusty road at home at the present time, with green trees and flowers, pretty girls in summer dresses, and all the other things there that make life good, including the motor-bike I'm going to buy when I get back, until one feels inclined to smash through the door of this damned dismal little hole and clear out, only there's this beastly thin Plateau wind nosing round outside. It won't be like this on the Saskatchewan!'

After the evening hoosh had been consumed and the diarists' work was done, Levick read a chapter or two of a book aloud to the others, recumbent in their bags. Their library was meagre and strangely assorted, reflecting the tastes of six disparate readers. He started with Boccaccio's *Decameron*, which he rated 'a most boring production', and indeed it is difficult to see how the six men can have felt much empathy for those sly, wordly and often pornographic parables. *Simon the Jester*, a rather inferior novel, they greatly enjoyed. Their literary mainstay was, however, *David Copperfield*: a merciful total of sixty-four chapters. Levick started to read one of these a day on 28 March, and finally closed the book two months later. Balfour's *Life of Robert Louis Stevenson* then came to their rescue, lasting them for another few weeks.

A picture is conjured up of the five men listening intently in the darkened cave pierced by pinpricks of light, the two cooks resting their poor sore eyes and Levick straining to make out the words in the fitful gloom. It does not seem likely that he would pitch his voice to bring out the drama of the story or alter his accent to suit the characters; his would be a conversational rendering. Still, the power of the writing must on occasion have struck a powerful chord with his listeners. He was not the only performer: Priestley's readings from his diary were much enjoyed from the beginning of June, but were rationed to Sundays, to spin them out as long as possible.

Levick, whose literary bent was to find an outlet in his book on Adélie penguins, started to compose a 'tale of adventure' set 'in the East of the

Mediterranean, where a battleship lies at anchor in Voulah Bay, on the coast of Asia Minor'. The two heroes are an impoverished submariner (representing the ratings) and a moustachioed soldier (the officers); a fig tree provides scenery and a beetle rolling a piece of wood uphill an Aesop element. The story owes its setting to Levick's experiences aboard HMS *Bulwark*, flagship of the Mediterranean Fleet, and their current expedition also puts in an appearance: 'And to think', said the sub,

> that at the present moment, some three dozen officers and men of the Royal Navy, reported to be sane, are blowing on their fingers in the South Polar Regions, and trying to keep their feet warm during several months of complete darkness.' 'All mad' said the Young Soldier 'and I daresay its as cheap to send them there as keep them locked up in an asylum, though how they manage to pass any sort of medical exam before they go, I don't quite see.' 'That's easily accounted for,' said the other, 'because they are examined by the doctors who are going themselves and are therefore mad too – The whole thing's a family concern worked on cooperative principles.

There is a dash of Robert Louis Stevenson there too, absorbed during Levick's weeks of nightly readings. His admiration for the master story-teller grew: 'I have found [his] character studies simply fascinating, and can hardly leave them for the routine of work.' This is Stevenson's description of Falagoa in Samoa: 'We went on further to the end of the bay, where the village sits almost sprayed by waterfalls among its palm-grove, and round under the rocky promontory, by a broken path of rock among the bowers of foliage; a troop of little lads accompanied our progress ... They were unpleasant, cheeky, ugly, urchins.' And this is Levick's version: 'For some time their way led them over parched sandy ground, sparsely covered with grass & prickly pear. After about a mile and a half of this they passed through a dirty little village composed of one stretch of more or less dilapidated dwellings with flat roofs; smelling of stale cheese and sour goats milk, and chiefly occupied by very dirty children with sore eyes, and some cadaverous children which latter were gleaning a scanty subsistence from the gutter.'

At the end of the reading and after 'lights out', the men composed themselves to sleep – and often to dream. At first, as they accustomed themselves to their new diet, they dreamed almost exclusively of food. Priestley recounted a 'dream of frustration' which they all had again and again:

> We would dream that we woke and thought what fools we were to be lying there half-starved when outside there was a shop. We would get

up, struggle into our outdoor clothes and make our way along the passage on our hands and knees as we did in our waking life, barking our shins and shoulders as we went. Outside we would straighten up and there, sure enough, was the shop. In my case it was either a butcher's or a confectioner's shop; to the others one of these or a tobacconist's. But it was early closing day and after one o'clock.'*

Other dreams were made up of the usual kaleidoscope of the day's events and recurrent worries. Priestley recalls a particularly vivid example in which Campbell, Peggotty from *David Copperfield*, vast amounts of food and the wreck of *Terra Nova* were inextricably entwined – recalling Levick's drowning nightmare of many months before.

So the nights and days wore on, much like one another on the surface. By June they had begun to resign themselves to their lot, and – Dickason's private outbursts aside – to appreciate one another. 'I think we have really learnt to make the best of things, because we are all fairly contented, and at least not unhappy, though the squalor and (old standard) discomfort of our surroundings are pretty rough, not to mention the cold. We pull along so well together now, and that makes all the difference in the world.' This state of affairs continued for the next two months, and on 5 August Levick wrote: 'Life much the same as usual.'

Two days later, there was a decisive change, in the weather and in their lives. 'Campbell and I had a good walk on the northern lake and much enjoyed it, as we saw at noon a fine glow, showing that the sun was a very short way below the horizon, and the sight of it seemed like life, hope and all the joys of civilisation returning to us.' Later he described the return of the sun as 'like living again after being dead for six months'. With its return on 10 August, a new sense of urgency stirred. Suddenly it was time to start preparing themselves for the march back to civilisation for which they had pined for so long.

The weeks preceding their departure from the cave were a mirror image of those following their decision to create the igloo. Now, as then, followed a period of anxiety accompanied by a flurry of activity. Anxiety was rooted in the upheaval attendant on their departure – 'we shall have a rotten time getting ready for the sledge journey, and getting away out from this blited [sic] area' – and the unknown hazards of the terrain they would have to cross on their way to Cape Evans. The Drygalski Barrier in particular assumed ogre-like proportions. The 1908 South Magnetic Pole Party had described it as a place in which chasm-like crevasses alternated with

---

* Quoted in the Scott Memorial Lecture delivered by Sir Raymond Priestley at the Royal Geographical Society in June 1962.

immense seracs* – 'as though', in Professor David's analogy, 'a stormy sea had suddenly been frozen solid'. It would be a cripplingly difficult obstacle course for men debilitated by sickness and starvation. 'Personally', wrote Levick on 14 August, 'I am looking forward to the sledge journey before us with mixed feelings, and I think this applies to all of us: relief at getting away from this dismal squalid life, and a little reluctance at the idea of the bad time we are probably in for, crossing the Drygalski Barrier. We all talk a good deal about this. It seems to be always blowing there except in Midsummer, and clouds of drift are generally to be seen whirling over it, and miles out to sea.' He added ominously: 'we have all done enough spring sledging to know it isn't all beer and skittles, and enough travel on the sea ice to know its uncertainties.'

After their months of inactivity, there seemed almost too much to be done. First they had to get themselves fit, although Levick felt that they were in astonishingly good shape in the circumstances: 'I don't want to . . . say that we are in good training, because we aren't, but our healthy state after all this forced inactivity and cramped, squalid quarters I can only regard as simply wonderful.' They started to take walks outside as soon as they were able to leave the cave during daylight hours, supplementing these from the beginning of September by a programme of Swedish exercises, with which Abbott was extremely familiar and which Levick had rather desultorily promoted earlier in the cave ('I hope I can keep this up, but one never does!'), aimed at strengthening their stomach and wasted leg muscles.† Priestley noted with surprise that the exercises managed to iron out the 'igloo back' curvature from their spines.

Then there was the question of assembling the sledging rations, which were to be positively gargantuan compared with their present portions: each man was to have two mugs of meat per day and one mug of blubber. They allowed enough for an eight-week journey, for which eight bags of meat would be required, each one containing forty-two mugs' worth, or one week's meat for three men. (The party was to be split in two as before, with one sledge and one tent each.) On 11 September they were still short of meat, but by the 20th Levick had 'finished the seventh bag of sealmeat and altogether cut up 38 mugfuls', and a lucky kill of five emperor penguins on the 28th relieved them of immediate worry. All this food, plus their hard-won geological specimens – which they had the greatest difficulty in locating and bringing to the surface, buried as they had been for months in drift – had to be loaded onto their two sledges. Before this could be done, the sledges themselves had to be dug out, scraped down

---

* Pinnacles of ice formed at the intersection of crevasses.

† Similar, perhaps, to Vladimir and Estragon's contrapuntal conversation in *Waiting for Godot*: 'We could do our exercises. / Our movements. / Our elevations. / Our relaxations. / Our elongations. / Our relaxations. / To warm us up. / To calm us down. / Off we go.'

and the runners waxed. The iron-runner sledge was disinterred on 13 August, the other on 21 September. A round of repairs and refinements to clothing, sleeping bags and sledging gear followed.

Vital question marks still hung threateningly over their departure. When would it be safe to set out? Would they be well enough? And would they make it across the Drygalski?

Campbell was determined to leave as early as possible. He had already decided on 1 June the route they must take, repeating this on 13 July: 'I don't think this bay will ever be safe to travel on, so we shall have to take the Drygalski Tongue route and march later.' Levick concurred with this analysis, the main point being that the incessant wind prevented the sea ice around the Drygalski from freezing over and thus creating a safe route for sledges; instead they would have to cross the Barrier overland – a much more hazardous operation. Campbell fixed 22 September as the departure date; Levick and Priestley would have preferred the end of the first week in October, 'seeing no reason for starting earlier, and the temperature will have risen by then'. More importantly, the winds would probably have lost some of their bite and fury.

For many months it had been a moot point as to what condition Browning would be in when the moment for departure arrived. What was not anticipated was that the whole party would succumb to a 'nasty little epidemic' of diarrhoea, caused (in spite of all Levick's vigilance) by infected meat, which laid them all low during the first ten days of September, and flared up again a fortnight later. It could not have come at a worse time. Dickason was especially badly affected, and even the normally indestructible Priestley was left feeling weakened and depressed. On the 10th Levick reported a crisis: 'Poor ———— broke down this morning: said he couldn't eat his hoosh and started to lose his head, and generally chuck his hand in. Campbell and I both had a go at him and rowed him and then bucked him up generally. He said he was feeling rotten and wouldn't be able to march with us down the coast, and a lot of rot like that, but we talked him out of it, and he is comparatively cheerful again tonight.'* The following day he noted: 'Browning in rather a bad way I am afraid. I had a yarn with him alone this morning. I am afraid he is getting chronic inflammation of the entestines [sic].' It was a long fortnight later before Priestley was able to write in his diary: 'Everybody seems to be recovering from the last epidemic.'

As for the Drygalski Barrier, there was nothing for it but to go and see for themselves. And go they did. By 29 September their bags were packed, their erstwhile home abandoned, a final photograph taken in their tatterdemalion clothes. They had already left the equivalent of a note for

---

* The individual in question could have been Dickason, but in the light of later events most probably Browning.

the milkman – a missive fixed to a bamboo at the depot for any would-be rescuers. On the last day of the month they changed into an assortment of newish, cleanish clothes which they had been hoarding during all their months in the igloo. Then they were off.

# 6

# The Long Haul to Cape Evans

## 30 September–7 November 1912

The day of departure, 30 September 1912, long agonised over and frequently postponed, dawned calm and clear. The men's spirits rose as they cast lots for the spare sweaters, mitts and underwear which Campbell had stowed away since their disembarkation from the *Terra Nova* nearly nine months earlier. 'To keep them clean', he wrote rather touchingly, 'we only changed into them just before leaving the igloo.' When Priestley took his trousers off, they stood up on their own. Levick was also in grateful possession of two pairs of fairly reputable finnesko.

However, behind the seemingly cheerful grins of the official photograph of the Northern Party on the point of departure – captured for posterity whatever the outcome of the journey – lay the fear that in their weakened state this final adventure was likely to prove at least as dangerous as anything that had gone before. The date itself raised a serious question mark over the success of the whole enterprise. Campbell had been set on leaving on 22 September, Levick and Priestley strongly favoured holding out until 7 October. Their argument for postponement had been clear and logical, based on their own experience of spring and summer sledging at Cape Adare. During spring sledging (roughly speaking, August and September) temperatures more often than not were likely to be sub-zero and to be accompanied by drift, blizzards and ferocious winds. It was not weather to mess with, as another member of the *Terra Nova* expedition graphically described: 'as the wind grew stronger the layer of whirling snow would get thicker till in a full blizzard it would be 100 feet thick and so dense that visibility would be reduced to a single metre's distance'. Days spent marching at that season, although plagued by frostbite and snow blindness, would be just about bearable. Days confined to the tent, and every single night, would be refined torture, while setting out in the mornings would always involve a miserably long-drawn-out and painful routine. Debenham's view was: 'Whether the actual sledge-hauling is pleasant depends almost entirely on the weather, which is almost the only variable in the Antarctic. Mere cold does not matter very much – it is the amount of wind with it that counts, and also whether you are facing it or not.' Priestley did not mince his words: 'I know of no other experience that will take as much out of a body of men in as short a time.' As October advanced, however, and spring shaded into summer, temperatures would be on the rise; the weather, although still to be treated with the respect due to an unpredictable beast, would no longer be in complete control. Given a decent travelling surface, journeys might even be pleasurable.

Since Campbell had shared Priestley's experiences the previous year and must have drawn some of the same conclusions, the question arises: why was he so anxious to set out on the 230-mile journey while the continent had not yet emerged from the grip of winter, especially since the two senior members of his party had several times expressed their reservations? There was no absolute urgency about the date of their arrival at Cape Evans – indeed, they had no idea if they would find the station manned at all. Although Campbell himself gives no clue as to his motivation, the explanation must relate to life in the igloo. Perhaps he felt that the latest epidemic of diarrhoea had proved so demoralising that decisive action was called for; perhaps he feared that the member most at risk, Browning, would not survive a further spell of incarceration; perhaps he himself was driven by a desperate desire to break free.

Whatever the reasoning behind Campbell's decision, their departure – not in fact on 22 September, nor on 7 October, but midway between the two – exposed the whole party to considerable difficulties, and Browning to a very real threat of death. With hindsight, the two procrastinators, Levick and Priestley, can be said to have had the better instinct. During their first week out, the party's progress was agonisingly slow – a mere 32 miles. During their second week, from 7 October, they achieved 68 miles. Arguably, if they had delayed their departure by that one week, they might have doubled their mileage at the time when physically and psychologically they needed most to make good progress.

Hour after hour the two groups of sledgers – Campbell, Priestley and Dickason pulling the 12-foot wooden-runner sledge, Levick, Abbott and Browning the 10-foot iron-runner version – stumbled through the heavy drift, unable to see more than a few feet ahead. At times it was so bad that they were steering blind, reliant on Campbell's compass to guide them. Dickason and Browning were both too weak and too ill to pull at all at first, so each team was down to two men. Antarctic snow – not the soft, flaky variety known to us, but hard and granular, more akin to hailstones – stung their faces and compounded the misery of frostbite. When a day of howling wind and thick drift drove them back to their tents, the enforced inactivity and biting cold made life intolerable.

Dickason, and especially Browning, were in a private hell of their own. Dickason was suffering the final throes of the severe outbreak of diarrhoea that had affected the whole party.* Browning was of course in a different category entirely, chronically weakened and unable to walk for any distance, let alone lend a hand at hauling. His enforced rests became more and more frequent, and he was miserably conscious of jeopardising the progress of his stronger, fitter companions. Priestley revealed that Browning's inability to do his share of the work preyed constantly on the sick man's mind; he was, in fact, well on the way to fulfilling his own prophecy that he was feeling rotten and wouldn't be able to march down the coast.

Levick was well aware of the crisis looming for Browning. On the showing of the first few days, his condition would deteriorate inexorably during the journey. If the weather confined them to their tents for any length of time, if the terrain proved to be of the sandpaper variety dreaded by sledging parties, if any number of unknowns materialised, the progressive damage to his organs might well be irreversible – if he survived at all.

The physical stress that the whole party experienced day by day was compounded in their minds by their absolute ignorance of what was happening to the other members of the expedition at loose on the ice cap. The fate of the Polar Party was of paramount interest, of course, but vital too was the fate of the main support group and of their instrument of delivery, *Terra Nova*. The Northern Party had experienced the wearing stresses of uncertainty before, but had been able to carry out their fall back plan to build themselves a winter refuge. Now there was no fall back. If Cape Evans were deserted (always supposing they made it that far), if its store of food was depleted or non-existent, and if there were no contingency plans outlined for their rescue, they would not survive.

The first stretch of their journey took them from Inexpressible Island to Relief Inlet, on the northern side of the Drygalski Ice Tongue, the farthest point reached by Professor David in 1908. Sledging southwards from there to Cape Evans the Northern Party's route would more or less march with his. So as they brushed the filthy igloo ice off their boots for the last time, they were heading into the unknown. Their shrunken world of the previous seven months must have seemed almost safe, almost acceptable, as they left it.

---

* Antony Beevor's chronicle of cruelty, *Stalingrad* (Viking, 1998), described how, in Russian labour camps after Germany's surrender in 1945, 'a combination of exhaustion, stress and cold greatly upset the metabolism of its victims'. This meant that their bodies could only absorb a fraction of what they ate – 'an accelerated process of starvation'. He continues: 'Severe malnutrition reduced a patient's ability to survive infectious diseases, such as hepatitis and dysentery.'

The tensions of early October were reflected in the unusual brevity of the diary entries. Levick's record for the first full day of the march on 1 October was typically understated, but the anxiety is palpable: 'Under way 7.30: turned out 5.30, and did a very hard day's work as the going was very bad & we often had to relay. At 6 p.m. we camped. Browning and Dickason both very bad diarrhoea all day, & frequently taken ill en route. Browning too weak to pull much.'

In spite of their misgivings, breaking free from their underground cell lifted their spirits. Priestley wrote: 'I have never looked forward before or since to spring sledging, and yet we were as pleased as anything to be away from the cave.' A similar hint of euphoria creeps into Levick's account: 'Though we were all really worn out, it is simply wonderful that we could do a day's work like that after our recent life.' They also enjoyed the full sledging diet: as well as meat and blubber, they were allowed a mug of cocoa each, three biscuits, one stick of chocolate, eight lumps of sugar, and – joy of joys – a little pemmican to add to the hoosh. For their lunchtime snacks (which they ate in the lee of the sledges, often with drift blowing straight over them) they hit upon a *nouvelle* delicacy, strips of raw penguin meat, 'the finest possible stuff to sledge on', and beneficial for Browning to boot.

That first day out, 1 October, was attended by a deceptive and all-too-brief period of calm, the sort described by the composer Peter Maxwell Davies as 'the mightiest, gentlest, longest whisper ever. It was a sound which seemed almost quieter than the silence which surrounded it'.* To men used to the incessant howl of the blizzard, it seemed like a benediction.

The following day, sledging across infuriatingly treacly granular snow 'whose action', complained Priestley, 'may be likened to that of a fly-paper on a fly attempting to use it as a promenade', they were brought up sharply by a formidable crevasse, at first sight unfordable. They were fortunate indeed to find a mighty snow bridge, measuring 175 paces from one side of the abyss to the other, which looked strong enough to bear the weight of their laden sledges. Hesitantly, step by step, Campbell, Priestley, Abbott and Dickason crossed the crevasse, followed by Levick in charge of Browning; otherwise they would have been forced to walk along the crack for an unknown distance over dubious ice. Campbell was all for pausing to make a thorough scientific examination, 'as from its width it had more the appearance of an inlet of the sea ending in a wide crevasse', but since the gale was rising and the drifting snow impenetrably thick, caution triumphed over curiosity.

---

* Maxwell Davies spent a month in Antarctica in December 1997 and January 1998 after being commissioned by the British Antarctic Survey to write an *Antarctic Symphony*.

Browning was again too weak and ill to pull. Levick made him walk by the sledge, and dosed him that evening with chlorodyne*. The next day the weather and Browning conspired to make the total tally a paltry couple of miles; the one following they achieved no mileage at all. Campbell's few lines for 4 October are especially tight-lipped: 'Blowing hard with blinding drift. We delayed breakfast until 9 hoping it would clear but as there was no improvement in the weather we turned in again, as we were not marching. We went on half ration of biscuit. Very cold.' No sing-song that day.

The day of reckoning came on 7 October when, having reached and crossed the milestone of Relief Inlet, they were faced with the dreaded Drygalski Barrier. Imagine their incredulity therefore when the gigantic tongue, protruding 30 miles out into the Ross Sea, proved to be a negligible adversary. 'We found a gentler declivity of snowdrift down onto the sea ice of the Inlet, and got the sledges down to and across this to the other side', where another providential drift enabled them to pull the sledges up onto the tremendous ice cliff ('tough work', noted Levick laconically). As they started across the flat surface they managed to avoid the barrancas† which had plagued Professor David's party, and camped triumphantly that night a fair distance across. The monster had been faced down, and their igloo life was also firmly behind them: 'The past winter has already begun to seem like a bad dream, & we are again ordinary mortals.' Even though paradoxically every step took them further away from England, they were going home.

Thereafter the almost tangible sense of relief is evident in the much fuller diary entries which follow. The animal kingdom was enjoyed again for its behaviour rather than its blubber, and Priestley, Campbell and Levick each recorded the same tragi-comic incident. This is Levick's account. 'We saw a cow Weddell, evidently in calf, come up through a hole in the tide crack. She lay lazily on the ice by the hole, & appeared to be going to sleep when another seal came half out of the same hole and either from wanton savagery, or annoyance at finding the other in the way, bit her savagely in the belly, & then slid back into the water.'

They were all too soon to be given a salutary reminder that man-hauling in Antarctica holds out few moments of light relief. Over-confidence can swiftly lead to disaster in this treacherous land where, Levick complained, 'the light is so flat that you seem to be walking into an abyss of white all the time, and cannot see any unevenness in the snow or even where the horizon line of the Barrier joins the sky, so that you don't know you are coming to a hollow or projection till you put your foot into it or trip over it.' On 8 October, just after their successful climb up onto the ice tongue,

---

* An anti-diarrhetic containing opium.

† Deep ravines with precipitously sloping sides.

as they ran down one of a series of undulations, 'Campbell's sledge was . . . about 50 yards in advance of mine, when I saw Priestley suddenly throw himself flat on the ground, to stop the sledge, and they all brought her up with a jerk. On going up, we found that they had walked to within 2 yards of a barranca with a sheer drop of at least thirty feet, and it was quite by good luck that Campbell saw it in time, before he walked over it.' If they had plunged over the edge someone would almost certainly have broken a limb, which would probably have spelled the end for the whole party. After this narrow shave they hauled themselves laboriously back up the slope and around the obstacle, camping that night some six miles from the edge of the Barrier and surrounded by a minefield of barrancas which they would have to tackle the following day. To cap it all, Browning and Dickason were again unwell, and Campbell's group also seemed listless and out of sorts, not putting 'nearly their usual lively buck into pulling'.

The barrancas were as bad as anticipated. Their route took them over a succession of ice waves rearing up to 50 feet in height, with their broken crests or sheer cliff faces pointing southwards; in other places steep gorges yawned at their feet. After two unpleasant, gruelling days of dogged hauling in a stiff breeze and thick drift they neared the edge of the ice tongue, where at last they glimpsed sea ice. Most cheering of all, Mount Erebus – the scene of their departure twenty-one months earlier – was visible in the far distance, crowned by its trademark plume of steam. 'We felt then', wrote Priestley, 'that we were really within measurable distance of home and friends. Right under the shadow of that mighty cone lay the winter quarters of the Polar Party, and there, whether the party were there or not, would be a record that we could read, and which would tell us clearly what had happened to our comrades.'

The Drygalski smiled on their departure as unexpectedly as it had upon their arrival. An hour's hard pulling on 10 October brought them to a place where by another stroke of good luck a gradual slope took them right down onto sea ice. This called for serious celebration, and so they allowed themselves an extra biscuit each, and a stick of chocolate.

They were 60 miles down, with 170 to go.

The next stage of their seemingly interminable journey was across the Geikie Inlet and up onto and across a lesser ice-tongue barrier, the Nordenskjöld. It was the first time they had travelled any distance on sea ice since they had left Cape Adare. Now the going was to prove considerably tougher.

The day after their uneventful descent from the Drygalski, 11 October, was something of an anticlimax too, but an unpleasant one: it came on to blizzard, the temperature plummeted, and they were forced back into their tents. Only the chance arrival on their doorstep of a lone emperor penguin helped to relieve the monotony and allay their dietary worries. 'Campbell killed it,' wrote Levick, 'and has presented our tent with half its meat. I must return the compliment as soon as possible.'* The following day, being cold but clear, they determined to push on as far and as fast as possible. The two sledges were hastily converted into a double-decker, and in spite of stumbling almost immediately on pack ice with pressure ridges up to nine feet high and banks of snow several feet thick, they made good progress, pulling for some ten hours with just a few 'easies'. But although they were relieved to be on the march again, it was appalling stuff to contend with. Priestley wrote: 'We were frequently floundering for several yards together up to the sockets of our thighs in snow, while the latter was hard and cloggy with a thick crust, and every step was like drawing a tooth.' Often they had to relay, which cost them much in time and temper.

This depressing and debilitating hauling went on day after day. Levick wrote on 14 October: 'We seem to have spent the greater part of the day hoiking the sledge through deep drifts of soft snow over pressure ridges, up to our knees in snow . . . it was hard to find anything far enough ahead to steer by.' It got worse. On the afternoon of the 15th they 'got hung up in a perfect tangle of pressure ice, heaped up in all directions, with a profusion of sharp snags and projections hidden in a smother of soft feathery snow, which made the going very bad indeed'. The following day they ground along as before, achieving just $2\frac{1}{2}$ miles before camping in exhaustion. The day after was so bad for light, wind and snow that they gave up altogether and retired to their tents.

This marked rock bottom for the party. They were suffering from painful snow-blindness, and were all feeling 'so wretchedly stale' and 'most damnably slack' that Levick issued a tot of brandy all round. Partly, no doubt, their want of fitness was psychological – they had struggled so hard and so long to achieve so little. During that week they had managed a mere 41 miles – an average of under 6 miles a day, no better than their tussle with the Drygalski. Far more serious was the rapid depletion of their rations. They had set out with food enough to last them twenty-eight days. Fourteen days later, on 13 October, Levick had written: 'We have just 14 days half rations left.' They were well short of completing even half the journey to Cape Evans. Apart from the solitary emperor penguin they had not managed to bag any more meat, and some of the remaining joints were going bad through exposure to the sun. Campbell complained of cramp, stomach pains and nausea. If they continued to eat infected meat an ensuing attack of ptomaine poisoning might well prove fatal, not only to Browning. Levick worried away at their predicament: 'provisions are going low', 'down to a pretty small allowance of meat', 'curious that we have so far seen no seals since Relief Inlet'. (For curious, read disastrous.)

---

* He never got the chance.

Then, as seems to have been a feature of this switchback-ride of a journey, their luck changed. A day's enforced rest and a fine morning spurred their departure on 18 October, and although they had to relay for most of the day, they were finally quit of the 'infernal' pack ice. On camping that night, they could make out a seemingly smooth route through to the cliffs rising dauntingly some two miles ahead. The following day they managed to kill a young bull seal; although it was clearly diseased, with a cyst in its liver the size of a large grape, Levick passed it as fit to eat. Even so, 'we have only seven days chocolate & about eight days biscuit, on half rations, left, so as we are not half way yet, shall have to finish the journey on seal meat I suppose'. This, from the dedicated professional who knew only too well that seal meat was poison to Browning, was not the throw-away line it appears.

As they approached the Nordenskjöld Ice Tongue, they were greeted by a succession of mirages, which made it change shape before their eyes, forming and reforming into a monstrous, misshapen interpretation of some celestial city. However beautiful the 'dancing evolutions' described by Priestley, they reduced the men almost to madness as they 'tramped and tramped away without coming appreciably nearer' to the cliff which they hoped would prove the last major obstacle on their route. The gloom which seems to have settled on the men may be gauged from Levick's entry of 20 October – the day they finally ascended the ice barrier and which should therefore have been one of celebration. The tone is dead-beat, the report of a man at the end of his tether:

It took us a whole days sledging to reach the Nordenskjöld, on which we are now camped. The surface was very trying all the way, though there was little pressure ice. The monotony of hauling these damned sledges hour after hour, is making us all completely fed up. We reached the Barrier at 4.10 p.m. & hauled the two sledges & gear up onto the top, where we camped. There was a snow slope up the face of the Barrier when we reached it, and this was fortunate for us, as the cliff is about 40 feet high, and there was no other place up which we could haul the sledges, for 5 miles each way.

'It is distinctly colder up here than on the sea ice,' he concluded mournfully.

Morale was ebbing fast. Even Levick, a tower of strength in anticipating and treating the ills of his companions, was becoming waspish in his asides: 'Campbell suffering from "heartburn" for which I treated him', and later, 'Campbell a bit upset again: probably a bit of chill with dyspepsia. Have advised him to leave the solid part of his hoosh, and given him medicine, but doubt the first part of the treatment will be carried out.' His assiduous care of Browning also waned somewhat at this time. To Priestley, the pull across the Nordenskjöld remained all too vivid: 'Our tempers had stood an almost unparalleled strain during the past winter, and stood it sucessfully; we knew each other more thoroughly than most men ever know their companions, and yet we found it hard to converse with any freedom on the march during those days.'

The general 'slackness' of the party may well have raised the possibility in Levick's mind of that other polar killer – scurvy. Was their lack of condition really just the inevitable result of unaccustomed physical exertion on an inadequate diet, or could it be the start of something more sinister? James Lind's description of the early symptoms of the disease certainly tallied with some of those experienced by the Northern Party during their march. 'The first indication of the approach of this disease is generally a change of colour in the face, from the natural and usual look, to a pale and bloated complexion; with a listlessness to action, or an aversion to any sort of exercise. Their former aversion to motion degenerates soon into an universal lassitude.' Since they were not carrying any anti-scorbutic remedies, they could only hope, and continue their debilitating journey. It came as a relief when, the exhausting climb completed, the short journey across the Nordenskjöld on 21 October proved to be smooth all the way, with no crevasses or barrancas, and in the afternoon they were lucky enough to find a reasonably gentle slope leading down onto sea ice. As they departed this second ice tongue, they cached some of their possessions, and as a reminder of their passing Campbell scratched a sentence on an empty oil can: 'Party left here 21/10/12; all well, making for Cape Evans'. A skua passed them that evening, flying low, headed in the same direction. A bird of good omen, perhaps.

The following day took them into Tripp Bay. Overhead it was dismally cold and overcast, underfoot the surface was exasperatingly heavy, pressure ice and soft snow dragging at their legs. In their weakened state the effort required to pull the sledge – converted once more into a double-decker – was exhausting, and a falling-off in the number of haulers (Campbell as well as Browning) placed an intolerable burden on the rest. Levick, who was stationed at the front for three days in a row and had to keep alert for crevasses and other hazards, was also suffering from chronic and painful snow-blindness. Even the sudden sighting and slaughter of a solitary seal, which provided a 'glorious hoosh' of liver, kidney and brain, was a mixed blessing, proving far too rich for the two invalids, especially as the party was down to just two biscuits per man per day. Although Levick started to dose them all, except Browning, with the purgative calomel to counteract their now almost exclusively carnivorous diet, Campbell continued to feel slack and sick.

They were fast running out of carbohydrate, but at least their dwindling supply of meat was no longer a problem. Having crossed the bay beyond the Nordenskjöld, they made their way slowly but steadily due south, as far as possible hugging the shore, where the going was easier, and passing many tabular Barrier icebergs, the 'Dreadnoughts of the South', which they had not seen since their travels around Robertson Bay. As they neared Tripp Island on 24 October, they came upon a clutch of twenty-two Weddell seals, mostly cows suckling calves, and some in calf. They killed a bull, but did not disturb any of the mothers and infants, anticipating that they would find a reliable supply of fresh meat from then on.

The gradual improvement in the weather and the dramatic change of scenery was cheering, and Priestley even managed a brief return to the scientific preoccupations of previous sledging journeys. On the 25th, as they were camped opposite Tripp Island, the geologist seized the chance to ski over and spend the morning exploring and collecting specimens, while the others started off towards a further group of islands, which they reached the following day. Levick was clearly a touch envious of Priestley's brief liberation, writing tartly as they set off again: 'Owing to delay over geologising at Tripp Island, we have only done 7 miles.' They managed, however, to reach Depot Island later on that day.

The lack of biscuit had exacerbated Browning's condition, which for days had been deteriorating with shocking speed, although he was trying to keep up his spirits with his usual pluck. They were still only halfway to Cape Evans, and by 26 October Levick was seriously alarmed. His patient was 'complaining of feeling sick, and . . . has complained a good deal of pain in the small of the back lately. I can't help being reminded of Addison's disease, but hope it isn't.'

Levick was undoubtedly familiar with *Quain's Dictionary of Medicine*, the regularly updated medical bible of the period. There the symptoms of Addison's Disease cited include extreme muscular weakness, nausea and diarrhoea. (Another possible symptom, the darkening of normal pigmentation – giving it the colloquial name of 'Bronzed Skin Disease' – would have been difficult to detect beneath the Northern Party's sledging sunburn and ingrained dirt.) He was in fact probably alarmed by a distinctive feature of another strain of the disease, in which bronzing does not occur. Quain explains how 'blows on the back or strains from laborious occupation' lead to 'extensive tubercular disease of suprarenal capsules', which might account for Browning's back pains. As the disease progresses, the pulse might be expected to weaken and attacks of vomiting and/or diarrhoea become frequent, then uncontrollable. After suffering convulsions, the patient would become delirious or pass from coma into death.* Although

---

* In the midst of his anxiety, Levick might have recalled with a wry inward smile Quain's recommended treatment for Addison's Disease – that 'the patient should adopt a quiet life and retire from any work that makes any demands on his physical or mental powers. He

Levick might have been encouraged by one sentence in the dictionary – 'this is a rare disease and is probably diagnosed erroneously more often than it is overlooked' – he was worried enough to hold a crisis meeting with Campbell. The latter suggested that Levick and Browning should remain at Granite Harbour (their next port of call) with all the gear while the rest pushed on with a light sledge to get provisions from the depot at Butter Point. However, 'Levick thought it best to bring him on as if it was organic the sooner he could be laid up in a hut the better. So we shall push on, putting him on the sledge when he gets tired, and to keep his strength up give him one extra biscuit per day.' The doctor, mindful of the needs of the sledge-pullers, decided to reduce this to one extra every other day; even so, they only had four or five days' biscuit left.

Depot Island was named for the geological specimens amassed by Professor David during the first half of his 1908–09 journey, and the Northern Party had camped within sight of the six-foot bamboo marking it. ('If only it were biscuits instead of stones!') Priestley and Campbell dutifully collected the specimens, and they were packed between the two decks of the double-decker sledge, where they served a useful function as extra ballast. David's specimens were also tangible reminders to the Northern Party of those earlier polar adventurers on their own route to safety. Indeed, although Browning's health was at crisis point, the fusion of David's journey past and their own journey present led them for the first time to contemplate the possibility of a journey yet to come. Priestley confided to his diary: 'It is almost incredible to think that probably we shall be in New Zealand within three months from now.' It was another milestone reached: 34 miles in 5 days, but still only a painfully slow average of under 7 miles a day.

Then their luck took a turn for the better. On 27 October, they not only joined hands metaphorically with Professor David, but also came upon a smooth patch of ice. 'At last,' wrote Levick exultantly, 'after being 27 days out, we struck a good surface and in many places we have been hauling over blue ice. The luxury of walking along at nearly three miles an hour, and only a steady pull in the traces instead of the incessant toil of the past few weeks has been a great treat.' They achieved twelve miles – it was the best marching day since they started.

Their route now began to slant south-east down to Butter Point, after which it would swing across almost due east to Ross Island and Cape Evans. They fancied they could see Mount Erebus signalling to them with

---

should live in the country in a sunny or bracing place protected from cold and east wind and not subject to rapid alterations of temperature. When the general condition is good, gentle exercise may be allowed, but fatigue, worry, and strain must be carefully avoided. Any faintness should be the signal for complete rest in the horizontal position for some days. The Diet should be simple and nutritious . . . Ice may be sucked before food . . . and iced champagne may be employed as a stimulant.' No problems there, then.

21. A sledging halt. The 10-foot iron-runner sledge which gave Levick so much cause for complaint is on the left, the superior 12-foot wooden-runner version claimed by Campbell's team on the right. As was a feature of Scott's expeditions, taking sights and collecting specimens continued as the men, exhausted and emaciated, struggled back to Cape Evans.

its live fumeroles (probably just clouds or drifts of blizzard). Where possible they continued to follow the shoreline to avoid the pack ice further out to sea. Surfaces varied between smooth blue ice and areas of pressure, which at times were so deeply ridged that the men had to hack out a path with their ice axes. Granite Harbour they crossed with little difficulty, however, and camped (as they thought) well past Cape Roberts, which guarded the harbour's southern side, 'almost in a bee line for Dunlop Island'.

As the men continued their march, Levick's diary entries grew longer and more detailed. He was beginning to enjoy himself. Although tired, he was feeling fit. The doctor in him was temporarily on leave, the naturalist on duty. 'We passed hundreds of seals with young, which are very thick here in the harbour, and a few skuas were about.' 'Several times when I woke last night I could hear the seal kids bleating like lambs near the tent, and Campbell, who was out, saw the midnight sun for the first time.' 'The view we got of the harbour, with mountains and glaciers at the back, was very fine.' Priestley was now making up for lost time, collecting geological specimens everywhere he could, as indeed Scott would have expected. In a faint echo of the Polar Party's dogged insistence on dragging their precious loads of rocks back with them to their last resting place, Priestley continued to pick up and pack whatever he found of value or interest, and there was not a murmur of dissent from any of the men who had to put their backs into hauling his trophies for eventual dispatch to London.

The men's newly rediscovered interest in nature and science did not preclude the familiar, numbingly tiresome daily routine from unrolling as before. As they climbed into their sleeping bags on 28 October another day stretched ahead with its anticipated ration of tribulations and small satisfactions. But 29 October was a day unlike any other. Levick's lengthy entry stands out for the sheer excitement he communicates.

A wonderful day. We turned out at 4.40 a.m. and got away about seven. Made fine pace for 3 miles, when we arrived at a point of land, south of the piedmont leading from what we have supposed to be Cape Roberts. Then we sighted the bamboo depot mark, and in great excitement pulled the sledge in and found a depot left by a party consisting of Griffith Taylor, Debenham, Gran and Forde [the Second Western Party], last February.* In the depot was a case and a half of biscuit, and small bags containing butter, cocoa, tea, sugar and raisins, some lard and salt . . . We have had such a blow out today, as we haven't had for a year. We pitched camp, had an enormous feed of hoosh, cocoa (very sweet) and raisins, with lashings of biscuit and butter. I sat for a long time after this little lunch, with a hunk of butter in one hand and biscuit in the other, biting off alternately, first a mouthful of butter, then a piece of biscuit, and it was a grand treat, being the first fat of any sort excepting blubber we have had for ten months. After this Abbott, Browning & I went out and killed and butchered a bull Weddell seal for meat to take us in to Cape Evans, and then we retired to our bags and ate more biscuit, and I read Robert Browning, as Taylor had left a copy at the depot. At 6 p.m. we turned out and had another enormous meal of the same kind, excepting that we had tea instead of cocoa, and tea of the proper strength too, and not just coloured water. Now we are turning in again and have decided to eat all the rest of the sugar (about

---

* On 5 February 1912 Taylor wrote: 'We made a depôt on the highest point of the Cape and fixed a flag alongside, with the letter [to Pennell] in a little matchbox . . . We took nothing but what we stood up in, and our notes and instruments.' The depot contained one week's provisions – more than enough for a 'blow out' for six starving men.

26 lumps each) instead of keeping it, so as not to be hungry during the night.

Replete and, in Campbell's phrase, 'quite torpid with food', they were able to turn their minds to the 'stupendous news' contained in Taylor's letter to Pennell, signed by all the Western Party and fastened to the bamboo. This disclosed that, since adverse weather from 20 to 27 July had prevented the ship from picking up the party, they had decided to carry on down to Butter Point. In his diary, Priestley expressed the general relief: 'This is most satisfactory news, for it means that we had had nothing to do with the trouble to the ship, and I think Captain Scott must have reached the Pole, made up the coast to fetch us, and been blown north by the autumn gales. We shall know more when we reach Cape Evans, but this is enough to set us all smiling at present.' Levick was busily embroidering a more elaborate and completely erroneous fantasy:

We deduce . . . that the ship was hanging about for nearly a month, trying to pick the party up, after landing us at Evans Coves, and then being short of coal, decided to wait for Capt. Scott and the Southern Party, and to take them off on their return from the Pole, picking us up at Evans Coves on the way to New Zealand: that something happened to the ship after they picked the Southern Party up, say they broke their propellor or burst a steam pipe, and that in the heavy weather we got at the beginning of March, they got blown north, and had to retreat to New Zealand, under sail, being unable to head up against the wind to take us off before the Ross Sea froze over in the autumn. If this is correct, we are alone in the Antarctic, and will be fetched away from Cape Evans in 2 months time by a relief ship.

(The last sentence relied for its conclusion on two giant presuppositions: that money would be available to fund a relief ship, and that they had not already been given up for dead, in which case Britain would be mourning them, not searching for them.)

Their bellies and their imaginations sated, the men's thoughts turned turned to the days ahead. 'We gather now, that the old rough chart we have had [Campbell's out-of-date Admiralty chart, with very few place names marked on it] was very inaccurate and that we are probably at Cape Roberts, and 39 miles from Butter Point. We shall be off early in the morning.' In the mean time, as entertainment following their *grande bouffe*, they witnessed a fearsome gladiatorial bout between two bull Weddells, who 'fought terribly and inflicted very severe wounds about the breast and abdomen, each being dreadfully torn about and bleeding profusely, when they stopped, probably from sheer exhaustion', and Levick tried his hand at a new form of marksmanship. 'We nearly had a skua for hoosh too, as I threw an ice axe at one and hit it, but it recovered from the shock and flew away before I got it.'

The orgy of food they had enjoyed that day was the first of many to come, for they were now entering the land of plenty. 'In a journal left by Taylor', wrote Levick gleefully, 'we learn that Capt. Scott had left a large depot on Dunlop Island, 11 miles south of us (which they probably picked up on their way back but we ought to find something) and that they left a small depot at Cape Bernacchi, and another at Butter Point, so without a doubt we are in great riches now after our late circumstances.' So it proved. They ate their way down the coast of Victoria Land, grazing on biscuit and Cerebos salt as they went ('I have been eating it literally by the teaspoonful'), and although when they reached Dunlop Island on 31 October they saw no signs of the depot, when they reached Cape Bernacchi on 1 November, there was plunder galore: 'Antarctic' sledging biscuits, pemmican, sugar, cocoa, tea and raisins. They managed to restrain themselves for another mile before pitching camp and tucking into 'the Royalest feed we have had for a year'. 'I am not ashamed to say', added Levick, 'that I can't stoop properly to pick anything off the ground. This will sound brutal to the ordinary individual, but to those who have to sledge it won't, as only they understand.' He was already anticipating the next feast: 'We are now only 9 miles or so from Butter Point, where we believe there is another depot of food left there by Shackleton's people, but we probably shan't touch this.' Of course not.

Although the novelty foods were the greatest luxury, they did not have the nutritional values of the humble biscuit. By 1 November they were already visibly less emaciated, and the change of diet undoubtedly saved Browning's life. He became stronger by the day and was able to help with the hauling, which did much to raise his morale. The sudden reappearance of biscuits into their diet had an unfortunate side-effect. Priestley's mouth, covered with painful sores and blood blisters, and his tongue both swelled to grotesque proportions; he could not eat without chewing on one or the other and his speech was reduced to an incomprehensible mumble.

As his concern about Browning subsided, Levick was able to enjoy a good grumble. The first criticism concerned footwear.

The salt fleck ice makes one's finnesco in a bad mess, and yesterday my sennegras was in a sticky mess when I took it out at night, and very wet . . . My first pair of finnesco were white fur, and [my] second pair brown, which is much better as the darker colour absorbs heat from the sun and the difference in warmth is remarkable, even when the sun is very low. One good effect of this is that it gives some of the sweat a chance to evaporate during the march. I have noticed the white finnesco to be very bad in this respect and it is a fact worth noting in future.

Next in line of fire was the biscuit.

The biscuit we have had lately has been far too much baked. This applies both to our own last case, and to those we found at Taylor's depot. Now that we have plenty, of course it is not so serious, but before, when we were very short, and treasuring every crumb, it was a serious matter, as the dark brown outer part has practically lost its nourishing properties. The manufacturers should be carefully warned of this with regard to polar expeditions, and each case examined by a doctor before it is packed at home.

He was also, one suspects, somewhat riled that none of the depot-layers had thought to include an absolutely vital commodity: 'One thing only we all hope for but cannot count on, and that is baccy', although 'there are probably plenty of cigarettes and cigar ends lying about, and they'll fill the gap all right.'

During that halcyon week from 27 October to 2 November, fuelled by hope and extra rations, they cruised along at an average of nearly 11 miles a day to achieve a very creditable 75 miles, shrugging off a difficult day on the 'exposed and pressure-screwed strip of sea ice between Cape Roberts and Dunlop Island'. After Butter Point they proposed to turn eastwards and travel straight across the McMurdo Sound for 30 miles, ending up at Cape Evans, where they would expect to find provisions aplenty, enough to last them, if Levick's earlier surmises had been correct, until they were picked up by a relief ship a couple of months later.

Nothing turned out as planned. 'The plot has thickened greatly, and we are in a state of perplexity as to what has happened.' The astonishing news, contained in a letter left for Campbell at Butter Point and dated 9 April 1912, was that Atkinson had tried desperately to reach them that autumn, but had been defeated by the weather. This note spawned yet more fantastical theories: 'What it all means, we are at a loss to know, but I suppose they may have known that something had happened to the ship . . . and that they had made a sailing back to New Zealand and left a party behind here to try and reach us in the autumn.' The plot, having thickened, became positively impenetrable: 'then there is the fact to account for, that they didn't come to meet us this spring [i.e., when the Northern Party themselves were setting out], and to fit this we can only suppose one of two things – either, that not having got to us in the autumn they think we are certain to be dead, or else that Atkinson's party met with an accident and died themselves on their way back to the hut at Cape Evans last autumn.'

Campbell especially was in a state of high anxiety, and so they set off straight away, camping some three miles out from Butter Point. Levick wrote: 'Tomorrow we have about 23 miles to march to cross over to Cape Evans and with our heavy sledge it will just about take the last kick out of us, but we feel most anxious about things in general and are burning to get in and find out what has happened.' In these uncertain times they were not after all able to leave the depot unraided, and Levick recorded that evening 'another extraordinary meal on the luxuries we found. I ate about half a pound of butter, a lot of gooseberry jam, biscuit, raisins and figs, and we had very strong and sweet cocoa, with "Trumilk" in it, and then each a tot of the medical brandy . . . I didn't mention that we also had a pemmican hoosh.'

True to form, Antarctica was not prepared to let them lightly off the hook. On 3 November they had 'a rather annoying day' which involved the demolition of their iron-runner sledge. At midday, just as they had got over a ridge of 'bothersome pressure', all the struts of the port runner started out of their stops, and the iron brackets broke away. Abandoning the sledge, which they hoisted on end to mark the gear they had been forced to leave behind, they carried on across the sea ice of the sound, making straight for Cape Evans. 'I was leading, as usual, on the traces', recounted Levick, 'and we had just crossed a ridge of pressure ice and come suddenly out onto a smooth field, when I had a distinct sensation that there was something wrong somewhere, and then I noticed that the ice we were on was much darker and duller than usual and moments later Campbell sang out from behind to me to wheel round, and we were round in a moment, and doubling back on our tracks.' Regaining the safety of the pressure ridge, they realised that the sea ice was newly formed and totally incapable of supporting them and their single sledge. The only solution was to head in a more southerly direction, away from their destination, towards the safety of the Barrier, and turn eastwards again towards Cape Evans at a lower point as soon as the ice was safe. To their intense frustration, the surface seemed to be rotten throughout: 'There has evidently been a big break out of the ice in the Sound, quite lately: probably an abnormal state of things, as neither Shackleton's or Capt. Scott's parties experienced it in former years, when the ice was fast till the summer.'

There was nothing for it but to track backwards in a south-westerly direction, away from their goal, and camp where the ice would support them. Having lost so much time, they decided to split forces. Campbell, Levick and Browning would return to Butter Point the following day to pick up extra rations, while Priestley, Abbott and Dickason made their way back to the incapacitated sledge to see if it could be refitted with iron runners. To crown it all, one of Levick's last pair of finnesco had developed a great tear in the heel and was worn through under the ball of the foot. Abbott volunteered to carry out running repairs for him.

The following morning the first contingent reached Butter Point and left loaded with supplies, Levick carrying 46lbs of biscuit, Campbell 42lbs of pemmican, and the still-convalescent Browning 15lbs of oddments. They did not rejoin the others until 4.40 p.m. 'This was the first really unwise thing we have done since we left Evans Coves. To walk 9 miles from our encampment on sea ice and not take sleeping bags with us was wrong.' (Levick may have been recalling that memorable day in March and the near-miss he, Abbott and Browning had experienced when they had had to abandon their tent and sleeping bags just before they moved into the igloo.) All was well this time, however: 'we are back all right, and the weather fine all day'.

Another cheering development, noted by Campbell, was the marked improvement in Browning's condition: 'A week ago he could walk by the sledge on a march of 8 or 10 miles, tonight, though tired, he is none the worse for his 18 mile walk.' Levick was also pleased with his patient – 'I can only regard him now as off the sick list. He looks well and has filled out again and is in every way a normal man once more' – although he continued to keep an eye on what he ate. They had now abandoned seal meat and blubber entirely, and ate only a moderate amount of pemmican, 'so that we are nearly off meat altogether thank God. We have had enough to last us a good while.'

Priestley's group, meanwhile, had managed to exchange the wooden runners for the iron ones. Replenished thus with food and an improved means of transport, their new plan was to head back along the coast to Hut Point, from where they would have a short and easy march north to Cape Evans. The men were in a surprisingly relaxed, even lackadaisical state of mind. 'The fact is', wrote Levick, 'anxious as we are for news, we aren't in such a hurry as we were.' Even so, they rose on 5 November at 3.30 a.m. ('if we are getting plenty to eat, no-one can say we aren't working for it'), packed all the geological specimens they could find, which included Taylor's and Debenham's from Cape Roberts as well as those amassed by Priestley, and covered some 24 miles before they struck bad surfaces yet again, 10 miles from the safety of the Barrier and had to retrace their steps and seek out another way. Considerable excitement was generated by the sighting of three figures approaching them from the direction of Hut Point – 'but we found after semaphoring to them for fifteen minutes, that they were Emperor Penguins'.

During the course of that one morning they were bemused to encounter three entirely different types of ice: thick ice covered with snow, evidently

168

formed the previous autumn; thinner but still safe ice, salt-flecked and fairly dark; and very dark and smooth ice, thin and clearly unsafe, evidently the most recently formed of the three. Levick noticed that the three types were frequently separated by pressure ridges but often also sealed together by clean-cut edges; the ice stretched out for miles in great rectangular fields. 'Sometimes, however, we found the two thinner types in small strips, and often had to dash across the third variety at full speed, and were glad enough to get to the other side.' Their nerve and their luck held throughout the morning, but then they ran out of safe ice, and had to resort to hopping onto the Barrier to do battle with the sastrugi there before venturing down onto sea ice once more. By now their laid-back mood had been replaced by a fierce determination to reach Hut Point without delay. After a quick break for hoosh at 6 p.m. they carried on sledging until 1 a.m. the following morning, knocked off for four hours, then turned out again and continued on their relentless way.

The frustration continued. They had got within a mile of Hut Point when the starboard runner of the sledge cobbled together by Priestley's team collapsed. Levick's team broke for hoosh while Campbell, Priestley and Dickason walked on to the hut built by Scott's *Discovery* team. They returned in the late afternoon with a borrowed sledge and another instalment of news – this time factually reliable, although still tantalisingly incomplete – to the effect that 'Wright and 8 men with the mules which the ship brought this year, and Atkinson with Dimitri and Cherry-Garrard, have gone off to search for the bodies'. Pondering over this missive (left by Atkinson for Pennell), the Northern Party could only guess at 'the bad calamity that must have happened to the Pole Party last year. It seems certain that Capt. Scott, Teddy Evans and Bill were of the party, but who else we don't know yet.' They were fairly sure that Atkinson, Nelson, Cherry-Garrard and Debenham would be at Cape Evans, but what had happened to the others, and to the ship, they had no idea.

It seems extraordinary to relate, in the light of this devastating and completely unexpected news, that Levick should still have been thinking of his dinner, but in the next breath he recorded: 'Campbell brought a little food away with him from the hut, including a few old rock cakes and some butter, which were a great treat, and 6 onions, and also some baccy: most precious of all things.' It was perhaps too cataclysmic an event to have sunk in at first; or else a measure of the way in which the party had become so focused on their own survival that the death of the principals in the whole expedition had become unreal to them. Truth to tell, they had been away from the rest of the expedition for so long that even the colossi they had come to love and admire – Wilson, Bowers and Oates – had begun to fade in their minds. Scott himself they hardly knew. Priestley later made the point that he had joined the expedition 'very late . . . and within two months I said "Goodbye" to him and his comrades of the Southern Party and never saw them again'. There was also the fact that no one – not in Antarctica, not in New Zealand, not in London – expected the Polar Party to perish. The tragedy took a long time to sink in.

They were, however, fast re-entering the real world. On 7 November, before they set out on the last lap to Cape Evans, Levick had a talk with Campbell after breakfast about future plans. 'He is left head of the expedition apparently, and I second in command.'

That evening came the long-anticipated reunion with their erstwhile companions, although in the event the return of the missing, presumed dead proved something of an anti-climax. They arrived at Cape Evans at about 3.30 p.m., and found the stove alight, but no one at home. 'Presently', however, 'in came Debenham and Mr Archer the cook, and they were mightily glad to see us, having I believe given us up for lost. They turned absolutely pale at first, and couldn't speak a word for a few moments, and I believe they thought we were ghosts.' They were the only two occupants of the hut, since all the others remaining in Antarctica – Atkinson, Wright, Cherry-Garrard, Nelson, Gran, Crean, Hooper, Williamson, Keohane and Dimitri – were out searching for the bodies of Scott and his companions.

At last the Northern Party were able to unpick the tantalising fabric of half-truths they had been weaving for so many months. First of all they learned the dreadful disintegration of the expedition's grand design. The only relief came from discovering that the polar team had not, as they had begun to fear, consisted of two units of four men each, which would have meant eight men lost – they had of course no inkling that Scott had at the last moment asked Oates to make the numbers up to five. They were told that neither horses nor dogs had been of any use up the Beardmore Glacier, so that man-hauling had been the only way. They heard how, when last seen by the supporting party, the Southern Party were 150 miles from the Pole, with Scott, Taff Evans and Wilson going well but Bowers and Oates weakening a little and looking puffy about the face, and how Lieutenant Evans had only escaped death by scurvy through the selfless loyalty of Lashly and Crean and been invalided back to New Zealand. They learnt how the Cape Crozier party had also nearly perished, and found out at last what had caused their own seeming desertion by the *Terra Nova*: 'The ship had made many attempts to reach us last autumn, but had not been able to do so, though once they got within 30 miles of us, but they met with bad weather, and ran great risk from the pack, having once got frozen in for two days. When they finally left here they arranged to come and let them know here if they picked us up after all, but entertained very small hope of doing so.' So *that* was the simple explanation behind all their agonised conjectures.

What does not seem to have been revealed at this time was the decision made on Midwinter Day to go and hunt for the bodies of the Southern Party instead of the possibly-still-alive members of the Northern Party. It had been an acute moral dilemma for a group of honourable men to face as they made their decision on Midwinter Day 1912, seated round the table at Cape Evans. Atkinson had called for silence after they had consumed their asparagus, roast beef, ice cream and plum pudding, drunk numerous toasts and been splendidly entertained by Gran, patched and painted as a clown. 'He spoke clearly and modestly,' wrote Gran, 'and everyone had a chance to express an opinion.' Atkinson had given them a simple choice:

> Two alternatives lay before us. One was to go south and try to discover the fate of Captain Scott's party . . . On general grounds it was of great importance not to leave the record of the Expedition incomplete, with one of its most striking chapters a blank. The other alternative was to go west and north to relieve Campbell and his party, always supposing they had survived the winter.

Put to the vote, the unanimous decision was to go south in search of Scott and his companions.* It would have been a difficult subject to broach with the Northern Party themselves – effectively a group of men who had been dismissed as less important than a set of corpses. It seems that those who made the decision did not like to dwell on it. Debenham wrote: 'I always stuck to it that there was ice along the coast northwards but after the first never spoke of it except to Charles as it made Atch uneasy and feel that we were not doing right in going to the south.'

Many hours of sadness and good cheer passed before the momentous events that had taken place during their absence finally sank in. 'It is hard to realise our comfort and safety now, and we can scarcely satisfy our appetites, however much we eat of all the good things.' It was fortunate that one member of their depleted company was Archer, the ship's cook requisitioned by the shore party, a splendid character who, according to Gran, 'managed to make life into a great joke'. He, wrote Campbell gratefully, 'provided a sumptuous dinner, and we sailed into it in a way that made Debenham hold his breath'. Levick luxuriated in his first bath for ten months and noted: 'All the hair on my face has turned bright red.' On that first evening it was enough to relish their present good fortune and the company of their friends. That night they slept in a house (of a kind) for the first time in 304 days.

---

* There was in fact one dissenting voice – almost certainly that of Cherry-Garrard, who was to write in *The Worst Journey*: 'just then it seemed to me unthinkable that we should leave live men to search for those who were dead'.

# 7

# The Return

## 7 November 1912–14 June 1913

The Northern Party walked into the hut at Cape Evans on 7 November 1912 as skeletons. 'We were entirely free from fat, and, indeed, were so lean that our legs and arms were corrugated,' wrote Priestley. By the time the search party returned three weeks later with their sad burden of letters, diaries and personal effects, the Northern Party weighed more than when they had left for Cape Adare. Campbell and Priestley had gained nearly three stone in six days, while 'Levick', commented Gran, 'is the spit image of Henry VIII.' Only Archer and Debenham had seen them in their corrugated period. The others must have found it difficult to make the leap of imagination between the men and their story. Indeed, they looked so well and talked down their adventure to such an extent that it was hard to believe their life had been anything out of the ordinary. Cherry-Garrard wrote: 'All the Northern Party look very fat and fit, and they are most cheerful about the time they have had, and make light of all the anxious days they must have spent and their hard times.' Debenham's description of their journey back and their previous existence was typical: 'They started south on the 30th September and after the first week had a good trip down and once they reached our dêpot at C. Roberts they were in splendid fettle . . . They had a most successful autumn sledging, found far better fossil woods etc. than we did at Granite Harbour and now they are thro' it safely they would not have missed it for worlds.' Gran summed up their igloo life in another echo of *Waiting for Godot*: 'But nothing much had befallen them.' It was not until *Terra Nova* stopped off briefly at Evans Coves on her final journey back to New Zealand that those who visited the cave realised the full extent of the privations and miseries they had endured.

The relief felt by the first contingent of the search party – Atkinson, Cherry-Garrard and Dimitri – when they reached Hut Point on 25 November and read Campbell's letter was too indescribable for many words. Cherry-Garrard wrote simply: 'It is the happiest day for nearly a year – almost the only happy one.' Three days later the mule party arrived. By then Campbell was himself at Hut Point with Atkinson and a dog team, and had climbed up to a vantage point overlooking the Barrier, where to his relief he spotted the last of his charges safely encamped. Gran was one of the muleteers. 'We saw men coming towards us and recognized all but one. Suddenly Williamson, who had pushed on ahead with his wonderful "Gulab"* shouted, "It's Lieutenant Campbell!" A thunderous hurrah greeted this happy news, and we hurried to cover the last lap in towards land. We grasped the hand of the chief of the northern party to assure ourselves it was no ghost we had seen. Campbell it was, and bouncing with health too.'

He may have been bouncing with health then, but three weeks earlier it had been a different story. Not only were the Northern Party dangerously thin, but they had developed symptoms suspiciously like those of scurvy. Campbell wrote on 8 November: 'I find our party are not so fit as I thought; most of us had developed swollen ankles and legs (oedema) and when the flesh is pressed in the holes remain there.'† 'I don't like these symptoms,' wrote Levick. As well as oedema, Levick was suffering from cramps in his calves and pains in his shins and shoulder. When he inspected Campbell's gums, however (which had worried him back in the igloo), they were quite clear. As a precaution he recommended that a seal should be killed and eaten by the whole party, adding hastily, to avoid alarming Campbell, that there was 'not the least reason for him to be anxious on the score of scurvy'.

Levick's perplexity continued. He noted that it was only a fortnight earlier that they had been eating large quantities of seal meat, 'so I should be very surprised if we got scurvy, but there is the possibility'. In his last diary entry, on 14 November, he continued to labour the point. He had been talking it over with Debenham, and had discovered that Wilson, Bowers and Cherry-Garrard had all suffered from oedema of the legs and feet after their Cape Crozier journey, and that Scott had mentioned during a lecture on scurvy the previous year that his 'Furthest South' party in 1902 had been afflicted likewise. In both cases the symptoms had started a few days after their return to base. 'This is curious and interesting', wrote Levick, 'and is a parallel case to ours. As the condition does not come on till some time after the men return, I can find no satisfactory explanation, but it sets my mind at rest on the subject of scurvy.' He continued, with a

---

* A mule with a badly chafed neck and a stout heart. By that time only five of the original seven remained, and two more had to be destroyed shortly afterwards.

† That did not prevent Campbell from organising one of his hallowed weekly rituals: 'Debenham had been very short handed with only Archer to help him so we had a good Saturday clear up and scrub.'

hint of professional self-satisfaction: 'I am glad, as it would certainly have upset all my well formed opinions on the subject, had we shown any symptoms now. One thing seems to me to be quite plain, and that is that a party will not contract scurvy who feed on fresh meat, no matter how squalid and depressing their surroundings may be.'

For his part, Priestley put their condition down to general debility, brought on by prolonged overwork and overstrain. There would not have been much point in Levick consulting Atkinson when he returned with the search party, for he was of the school that attributed scurvy solely to food contamination. Although Atkinson knew for a fact that Teddy Evans had nearly died of the disease, when he had examined the Polar Party in their tent before it was collapsed over the corpses, he could find no evidence of it. Later analysts have included scurvy among their symptoms. In retrospect, then, it seems doubly fortunate that it was Levick rather than Atkinson who had been chosen for the Northern Party. In the near-blackness of the igloo, he had battled to keep surfaces and utensils clean and kept as close a look-out as possible for signs of contamination in meat (as Atkinson would have done). But he had simultaneously constructed a carefully balanced diet, of which fresh meat was a major component. Now he immediately organised a special issue of fresh meat, even though he did not believe scurvy to be the problem. He was possessed of that precious thing in a doctor – an open mind.

All the men of the Northern Party had been disappointed to have arrived just too late to swell the ranks of the search party, and Campbell wrote as much in letters that he left at Hut Point. Cherry-Garrard's reaction was one of admiration tinged with disbelief: 'If I had lived through ten months such as those men had just endured, wild horses would not have dragged me out sledging again.' They did go out sledging again – but at first only as far as Hut Point. Levick, Abbott and Dickason set off on 11 November to leave Campbell's letter for the search party, to collect the depot they had left there, mend their broken sledge and return the one they had borrowed. They met with a blizzard, so camped in Shackleton's old hut, where they cooked their hoosh on a primus stove, 'having contracted an unreasoning dislike to blubber as a fuel'.

Mission accomplished, Levick roused the two men when he awoke at 3.30 a.m., and they embarked on the return journey ('I saw Dickason look suspiciously through the window & try to see where the sun was but he did not ask any questions'). They got back to Cape Evans at 8.15 p.m. 'Found a feed of rock cakes and tea waiting for us, and I had just dispatched mine, and was expecting dinner to be laid, when one of the men came in to ask me what time I made it by my [actually Debenham's] watch. I said "a quarter to nine". It turned out that it was just five p.m.! Somehow or other Debenham's watch had dropped four hours or gained eight, and instead of turning out at 3.30 a.m. as I thought we had, we had turned out at 11 o'clock last night!' Levick confided to his diary: 'Was a bit of a juggins not to notice the position of the sun today, but wasn't needing it for navigation, and simply never thought of the north at all.' Campbell would undoubtedly have been both unsurprised and profoundly irritated by this degree of incompetence; luckily he was not of the party. Typically, Levick managed to see the bright side of their 22-hour day: 'And it was well we had done so, as an hour after we arrived, a blizzard started from the S.E., and is now in full swing, and we have got in just nicely for it.'

On an earlier trip the admirable Pennell had deposited all the Northern Party's spare clothes at Cape Evans, so they were again well supplied. Their only lack was boots, but Campbell managed to find each man a new pair. They were torture. During his trip to Hut Point, Levick complained: 'We all wore new ski boots, and felt footsore,' and with a sigh of relief on the 13th: 'We wore finnesco today. More comfortable than new ski boots.'

For the next three weeks, as they waited anxiously for news of the dead men, the Northern Party busied themselves with writing up their diaries and translating the black and greasy igloo scrawls into recognisable English. Campbell and Levick rewrote theirs as fair copies, and Priestley typed his on the absent Cherry-Garrard's editorial machine. Levick, with much trepidation, developed his and Priestley's photographs, and was relieved and delighted by their overall quality. It was a most pleasurable occupation. He wrote on 8 November: 'In great comfort, and at the Hut all day. I have been busy developing some of my negatives.' The photographs of the famous fossil had a curious history: they had been developed from plates left by Mawson at Butter Point in 1908, to which Levick had helped himself when they dropped the Western Party off there in 1911. 'I took the photographs in January 1912, and only developed them yesterday, Nov. 9 1912, 10 months after they were taken, and they are flawless & clear.' Butter does not melt in the Antarctic, nor do photographic plates decay.

The return of the search party marked the beginning of the end of Scott's last expedition. At first the travellers' respective tales continued over many days and far into the night. The Northern Party regaled the hut with a watered-down version of their adventures, and learned the dreadful details of the discovery of the bodies of Scott, Wilson and Bowers. Levick transcribed a passage of vivid first-hand intensity from Gran's recital:

The Owner, Wilson and Birdie. All ghastly. I will never forget it as long as I live. A horrible nightmare could not have shown more horror than this 'Campo Santo'. In a tent – snow-covered till up above the door, we found the three bodies. The Owner in the middle, half out of his bag. Birdie on his right and Uncle Bill on his left, lying headways to the door. The frost had made the skin yellow and transparent, and I have never seen anything worse in my life. The Owner seems to have struggled hard in the moment of death, whilst the two others seemed to have gone off in a kind of sleep . . . The sun shines lovely over this place of death.

Because of their enforced separation from the main group, the Northern Party were not feeling the same intensity of personal loss as the others. Atkinson was mourning his friend Oates, Cherry-Garrard Bowers, and everybody Uncle Bill. But the gallantry with which all had met their deaths was a comfort and an inspiration, and although Scott had attracted their loyalty and respect rather than their love, his final letters and his 'Message to Public' set him on a pinnacle for all of them.

For the Northern Party the person who had emerged most surprisingly from the shadows during their absence was Atkinson. Abbott, who had shared many a watch with him on the voyage out, had liked him 'immensely', and the officers had appreciated him as part of the 'solid, dependable and somewhat humorous' Soldier/Atch double act; now they saw him transformed into *Fidus Achates*, an effortlessly democratic leader who had somehow pulled together the remnants of the expedition under the most harrowing circumstances. By request and example alone, he had got the best out of the six officers and seven men remaining at Cape Evans throughout the winter of 1912. He had run a far more egalitarian ship than Scott, involving the ratings in the daily chores and evening entertainments, opening up the winter lectures to cover non-scientific topics, consulting veterans Lashly and Crean before making important decisions, and putting to a vote of the whole hut the crucial choice between searching for the dead Polar Party or the possibly alive Northern Party. His brand of leadership inspired admiration and deep loyalty. During the desperate attempt he had made in April 1911 with Wright, Williamson and Keohane to reach the Northern Party, he had realised that Wright was dead against the hazardous and hopeless journey: 'Not until after I told him that we should have to turn back, did he tell me how thankful he was at the decision. He had come on this trip fully believing that there was every probability of the party being lost, but had never demurred and never offered a contrary opinion, and one cannot be thankful enough to such men.' Wright for his part felt that 'We all respected him, felt for him, pitch-forked into a difficult situation and more than that, I think I can say we loved him.'

The two doctors were coincidentally in the right place at the right time – Levick to watch over the health of his small group through the grim polar winter, Atkinson to raise the spirits of the deeply demoralised survivors. The main party had carried a heavy burden throughout the winter of 1912: the leader of the expedition was lost, the second-in-command incapacitated and absent, the third-in-command probably dead also, and at least one person suffering from physical and mental collapse. The men of the Admiralty had been wiser than they could have guessed in releasing Atkinson and Levick into Scott's service.

On their return to Cape Evans, the Northern Party became absorbed into the larger group once more. Campbell and Atkinson applied themselves to the task of organising an orderly retreat from Antarctica; Priestley and Debenham forged a new alliance of common interests that would lead eventually to the foundation of the Scott Polar Research Institute in Cambridge; Levick resumed his bonhomous anonymity, and Abbott, Browning and Dickason rejoined the ranks on the messdeck side of the hut. But Priestley recorded that it was a standing jest that the six remained as thick as thieves. They had, after all, spent twenty months in each other's exclusive company.

There was one last adventure to come. As Cherry-Garrard was emerging from Hut Point, wreathed in smiles at the news of the Northern Party's survival, Debenham and Priestley were planning an ascent of Mount Erebus. The 13,200-foot volcano had been climbed in March 1908 by David, Mawson and Mackay, with three others as a support group. It had been an important 'first' and had yielded significant geological and meteorological information. Priestley wanted to have further results to show to his mentor in Sydney.

Professor David had conjured up a vivid picture of his own group's unorthodox departure: 'we filed off in a procession more bizarre than beautiful. Some of us with our sleeping bags hanging straight down our backs, with the foot of the bag curled upwards and outwards, resembled the scorpion men of the Assyrian sculptures: others marched with their household goods done up in the form of huge sausages; yet another presented Sindbad, with the place of the 'Old Man of the Sea' taken by a huge brown bag, stuffed with all our cooking utensils; this bag had a knack of suddenly slipping off his shoulders, and bow-stringing him around his neck.'

The second conquest of Erebus by Priestley, Debenham and Dickason was delayed by bad weather and the unexpectedly early return of the search party. When it finally got going on 4 December, Gran, Hooper and Abbott volunteered to swell the numbers. For the next two days they were snowbound, but by the 8th they had climbed to 8,000 feet. Debenham wrote that they had been enjoying the most extensive views that he for one had ever seen – 'range upon range, peak after peak and glaciers innumerable'. Two days later four of the party were encamped in the extinct lower crater at 11,000 feet, while Debenham remained 2,000 feet

22. The symmetrical cone and distinctive fumeroles of Mount Erebus had acted as a beacon of hope to the Northern Party. In one last Antarctic adventure, Priestley led a party to climb the active volcano; Tryggve Gran was lucky to survive when the upper crater suddenly erupted.

below to continue his geological surveys with Dickason for company.* The others climbed upwards through scenery of Alpine loveliness, with stupendous mountain views westwards. Smoke billowed dramatically from the live crater, the air smelled strongly of sulphur and the snow was tainted green.

They reached the summit and peered into the steep and steaming innards of the crater, before building a cairn to make their mark. Abbott and the frostbitten Hooper started their descent, but an oversight by Priestley nearly cost Gran dear. He had left a roll of film at the summit by mistake, instead of his written record of their ascent, and the ever-willing

---

* Thrown together with two of the Northern Party 'men' on this trip, Debenham noted: 'Dickason and Abbott are fine fellows and the over rigid discipline of Cape Adare has done them no harm, they compare excellently with our men who have been a little spoilt the last year.'

Norwegian went to make the substitution. 'Suddenly', Gran wrote, 'I heard a gurgling sound and, before I had time to think, the ground beneath me began to tremble. From the crater up rushed a gigantic cloud of smoke. There was a clap of thunder, and the next second I was enveloped in blackness. Close by I spotted a patch of snow; I plunged into it and buried my head to save myself from choking.' Large lumps of burning pumice were ejected in a stream around him 'in shape like the halves of volcanic bombs, and with bunches of long, drawn-out, hair-like shreds of glass in their interior.' He staggered hastily down, to meet Priestley climbing anxiously up, and 'together we made for our camp. We were both played out, and there was a moment when I thought we would never make it. At the end we were almost crawling.' As a geologist, Priestley was envious: although Gran suffered a nasty bout of sulphur poisoning, he had had a unique opportunity of witnessing Erebus in a state of eruption: an extraordinary juxtaposition of fire and ice. For Gran to have died in Antarctica as a result of volcanic activity would have been as strange a fate as for Ponting to have been eaten by a killer whale.

After this last escapade, the crater party met up at Cape Royds with Campbell, Atkinson, Wright, Cherry-Garrard, Archer and Williamson, who had been surveying, geologising and studying penguins while eating their way through the delectable provisions depoted by Shackleton two years earlier, including ptarmigan, sardines, tomato sauce, tinned soups and bottled fruits. Life at Cape Royds, wrote Cherry-Garrard, was very pleasant: 'With bright sunlight, a lop on the sea which splashed and gurgled under the ice-foot, the beautiful mountains all round us, and the penguins nesting at our door, this was better than the Beardmore Glacier, where we had expected to be at this date. What, then, must it have been to the six men who were just returned from the very Gate of Hell?'

The two groups returned together to Cape Evans to await *Terra Nova*, Gran and Dickason plunging into a crevasse on the way, which left them dangling companionably side by side between two sheer walls of blue ice. Back at base, reported Gran with fascination, Levick was fatter than ever.

The façade of cheerfulness was maintained fairly effortlessly through a blessed period of calm weather and sunshine in the run up to Christmas. Gran built himself a ski ramp and practised his jumps, and joined the penguins for a dip in McMurdo Sound which chilled him to the marrow. Although all were making the most of the time remaining and there was plenty of work for the scientists to get through, the expedition by then was, like Oscar Wilde's Bunbury, 'quite exploded'. They just wanted to go home.

The year 1912 ended appropriately with a hurricane. Although all were in good physical shape, and the Northern Party appeared to have recovered completely from the effects of exhaustion and malnutrition, mental cracks had begun to appear. Gran sounded a warning note as they waited for the ship, delayed on so many previous occasions: 'One more year here in the south would bring the most serious consequences. I am personally in good shape, but the same cannot be said for several of the others.' Cherry-Garrard was already suffering from heart strain and from the depressive illness that followed what he would always see as his great betrayal of the Polar Party. Abbott was also beginning to give cause for concern.

Cherry was not alone in feeling oppressed, not only by the deaths of the Polar Party and the 'what ifs' that would forever cling to them, but by the reaction they could expect to face when they returned to Britain. They were already anticipating the criticisms listed by Lord Curzon, President of the Royal Geographical Society, in his memorial address (printed in the Society's journal on black-bordered paper): 'It is easy to be wise after the event, and to say that the addition of a fifth man to the party of four that was originally intended for the Pole, the postponement of the start for a whole month, because of the collapse of the ponies – but for which postponement Scott and Amundsen might actually have met and shaken hands at the Pole – and above all the decision of Scott to rely upon human haulage in preference to dogs, were contributory or ulterior causes of the disaster.' Those charges were just the beginning of a barrage of criticism which continued for half a century, and attained mountainous proportions with the publication of Roland Huntford's book tilting Scott against Amundsen in 1979.

Three months earlier, the day after the Northern Party had returned to base, Debenham had taken Campbell on the equivalent of the ship's 'rounds', and the new leader had been relieved at the quantity of gear and provisions remaining. Already at the back of his mind had been forming the possibility (implanted by experience) that *Terra Nova* might again be prevented from picking them up in January, and that they might have to spend yet another winter in Antarctica. He had written after his tour of inspection: 'If we are down for another there should be no lack.' Now, as January passed its halfway point, this very real possibility had to be faced. The degree of anxiety and expectation was flagged up by the predictable appearance of a mirage. The Northern Party had earlier sighted *Terra Nova* several times at Evans Coves and wasted their semaphore skills on a group of emperor penguins; the men waiting in vain for the Polar Party's return had been convinced of their imminent arrival. 'I wonder', mused Gran now, 'how many ships we shall see before she really comes.'

On 17 January, Campbell gave the order – especially emotive for the Northern Party – to start killing seals. Gran and Debenham set off together after breakfast. Debenham recorded: 'We were just about to disappear over a hill when Gran turned to have a last look towards the north. His shout quite deafened me and then we both dashed for the hut with the news, all of us becoming complete schoolboys until, as the ship drew near, we prepared to give our tragic news to our shipmates.' Gran carrolled in his diary: 'Terra Nova in sight! Hurrah! Hurrah! Great jubilation. Hurrah!'

The immaculate officers and crew lining the equally immaculate decks of the ship gazed anxiously down, trying to spot a Northern Party face among the grimy, bearded crowd thronging the ice foot. Teddy Evans, in charge of the ship and newly promoted as the youngest Commander in the Royal Navy, described the scene:

> Glasses were levelled on the beach, and soon we discerned little men running hither and thither in wild excitement . . . The shore party gave three cheers, which we on board replied to, and espying Campbell I was overjoyed, for I feared more on his behalf than on the others, owing to the small amount of provisions he had left him at Evans Coves. I shouted out, 'Campbell, is every one well,' and after a moment's hesitation he replied, 'The Southern Party reached the South Pole on the 17th January, last year, but were all lost on the return journey – we have their records.' It was a moment of hush and overwhelming sorrow – a great stillness ran through the ship's little company and through the party on shore.

It was a hint of the grief that would overwhelm much of the British Empire in the months to come.

The trappings of triumph were instantly dismantled. Union Jacks and ensigns were lowered to half-mast, the wardroom was stripped of its bunting, champagne, chocolates and cigars. Five bundles of individually packeted letters were discreetly removed from sight. The ship's party already knew that Amundsen had been first to the Pole, but before Campbell shouted out the devastating and unexpected news across the water, Evans had simply been concerned at how best to greet the Polar Party knowing that Amundsen had beaten them to it – 'it was something like having to congratulate a dear friend on winning second prize in a great hard won race – which is exactly what it was. But it was not even to be that . . .'

The cheers and laughter of the shore party must have jarred on the others at first. But it was hilarity brought on by relief; they had done their grieving long before. Now their eyes were turned towards New Zealand, their thoughts to home and the future. Gran wrote that first night on board: 'The gramophone is playing a wonderful tune – "Eternal Waltz". How I long to dance, dance, dance again after all these years. This waltz is the first breath of real life. Goodness, how good life seems tonight.' The next day was his twenty-fourth birthday.*

An orderly retreat from Antarctica was instinctive to Campbell, Evans and Pennell. There was still work to be done. The remaining mules were shot; the hut was cleared and tidied for future incumbents. A heavy nine-foot wooden cross, carved *in situ* by Davies, was carried, in the manner of pall-bearers, by seven members of the search party and the ship's carpenter. This they erected after a short and muted ceremony on Observation Hill, a distinctive landmark at the southern end of Ross Island commanding the view over the Great Ice Barrier, and a beacon to incoming travellers. They inscribed it, at Cherry-Garrard's suggestion, with Tennyson's lines: 'To strive, to seek, to find, and not to yield.'

The dead honoured, the living were embarked on 19 January, including the surviving dogs, which had been earmarked for adoption by expedition members. Levick took Gossoy, Browning Master Cook. All that remained was to pick up the various depots of geological specimens, their own and those left behind by Shackleton's expedition. Gran and six ratings set off on skis to secure the depot of fossils and corals left by the Western Party at Geology Point, 17 miles distant at the end of Granite Harbour. At one point they made use of one of Campbell's kayaks to cross a broad open channel. 'It only took ten minutes to rig up and launch the "boat". It floated like a duck; its builder Abbott was the first to try it. We gave him a ski for an oar, and when he had crossed we hauled it back with a line. Thus we managed to cross the gap in a relatively short time. This "boat" was a splendid idea.'

Forging through heavy pack with the party all safely aboard, *Terra Nova* set her prow towards the north, anchoring off Evans Coves on 25 January. Priestley led a group to pick up the Northern Party's geological depot, and at 4 a.m. on the 26th, a deputation paid a visit of respect and curiosity to the igloo on Inexpressible Island. The report by Evans and Pennell in *The Last Expedition*, based on Evans' diary, stands out from the matter-of-fact tone of the rest of their writing:

> The visit to the igloo revealed in itself a story of hardship that brought home to us what Campbell never would have told. There was only one place in this smoke-begrimed cavern where a short man could stand upright. In odd corners were discarded clothes saturated with blubber and absolutely black. The weight of these garments was extraordinary, and we experienced strange sensations as we examined the cheerless

---

* He noted, in passing: 'The world news is that the Serbs, Bulgars, and Montenegrans have thrashed the Turks.'

hole that had been the only home of six of our hardiest men. No cell prisoners ever lived through such discomfort.'*

Most of *Terra Nova*'s crew bagged mementos of their visit; that inveterate magpie, Wilfrid Bruce, took away with him the bamboo with which they had stirred their daily hoosh. Cherry-Garrard was not one of the tourists, but wished he had been: 'I wish I had seen that igloo: with its black and blubber and beastliness. Those who saw it came back with faces of amazement and admiration.'

Their last action on land was to leave a depot of provisions at the head of Terra Nova Bay, enough for half a dozen desperate men to make it to the next significant cache at Butter Point. Campbell's party – especially Browning – had been saved by just such a depot; Scott's party had perished for lack of it. It was as if they were propitiating the gods on behalf of future expeditions.

On 26 January they gained the open waters of the Ross Sea, but still they were held to the coast by the desire to fill in a bit more of the jigsaw; they attempted to chart the area around the Balleny Islands, but were driven onwards by thick weather and heavy pack. 'This last season the ice conditions appeared to be the worst on record as far as the exterior ice was concerned,' reiterated Pennell. The last vivid memory of Antarctica for most came on 2 February, when they were threatened by an encircling dock of icebergs, one six miles long. Teddy Evans manoeuvred the ship out of this floating trap with great skill. Then the temperate world greeted them in the form of rainfall – their first for years – accompanied still by hurricane winds. On 7 February the sun came out, and two days later the New Zealand coast hove into view.

By today's standards their return to civilisation was spectacularly low-key. Atkinson, Pennell and Crean crept ashore incognito at the little port of Oamaru on the east coast of South Island and cabled the expedition's media sponsor, Central News, with an exclusive update. Then *Terra Nova* hung about offshore to give the agency time to broadcast its coup to the waiting world.

Evans and Pennell described their arrival at Lyttelton: 'With flags at half-mast we steamed into port and were berthed alongside the Harbour Board shed by Captain Thorpe, the harbour-master. Thousands came to meet us and quietly notified their sympathy, and for many days afterwards we received messages of condolence from all parts of the world.' These

---

* In his diary, Evans was more explicit about his feelings: 'Campbell's simple narrative I read aloud to Bruce from Campbell's diary. It was a tale of altruism and grit, so simply told, full of disappointments and privations, all of which they accepted with fortitude and never a complaint. I had to stop reading it as it brought tears to my eyes and made my voice thick – ditto old Bruce.'

dignified commiserations gave no indication of the paroxysm of grief that was to engulf Britain and the Empire as the publicity machines of church and state took over. By the time the expedition members had made their various ways home, the ossification of Scott as supreme national hero was already under way, brilliantly choreographed by him from his deathbed.

On 27 February Teddy Evans assumed command of the expedition, appointing Campbell, Pennell, Bruce, Atkinson and the treasurer Secretary Francis Drake as the winding-up committee. Pennell sailed *Terra Nova* home to Britain, leaving on 13 March, with Levick the only officer of the shore party on board. On 11 April they rounded Cape Horn in a gale; thereafter the voyage, from Rio via the Azores to the Scilly Isles, passed in a haze of good weather. They docked at Cardiff on 14 June 1913, exactly three years after they had left her.

In London, receiving the news courtesy of Central News, a regular meeting of the Royal Geographical Society on 10 February – at which a paper was due to be read on the Balkan Peninsula – had been hurriedly adapted for the Vice-President, Douglas Freshfield, to announce 'the sudden and stunning blow which has come in contradiction of all our confident hopes and anticipations'. In a low-key but deeply felt address, he had continued:

> Tonight it is too soon to realise what we have lost, to tell the praises of these brave men, to move notes of condolence. Such formal expressions of our deep regret and our heartfelt sympathy must be left to a later day, when we can speak with greater knowledge. Captain Scott lives in all our minds, and will live in our memories, as the ideal of the English sailor of our age . . . Nor do his companions deserve less honour. They were all equal in their daring, their fortitude, and their deaths. Of their accomplished work we shall hear hereafter; for the moment we can only think of the price that has been paid for it.

The news had unleashed a blizzard of newspaper and magazine articles, public statements and international expressions of condolence. A memorial service, hastily scheduled for 14 February at St Paul's Cathedral, had attracted a crowd of some 10,000 people. King George V had been present, together with representatives of foreign powers, government ministers, scores of the great and the good, plus Ponting, who had learned the news in Switzerland from a cable thoughtfully sent to him there by Central News.

By July 1913 all the surviving expedition members were in London, and on the 26th they gathered at the expedition's old headquarters in Victoria Street prior to the awards ceremony at Buckingham Palace. King George pinned onto the lapels of civilian suits and the breasts of naval uniforms a

23. The officers of Scott's Last Expedition assembled at Buckingham Palace to receive their silver Polar Medals; the ratings were given a bronze version. The mood of grief which swept Britain led to the downplaying of the Northern Party's remarkable survival before the deaths of Scott and his companions were subsumed in their turn by the horrors of the First World War.

silver Polar Medal for each officer and a bronze equivalent for each rating. To Crean and Lashly came the Albert Medal (now the George Cross) for their bravery in saving the life of Teddy Evans. The Royal Geographical Society, who had taken over the stage-management of the whole Scott show, came up with its own silver medal 'For Polar Exploration' for the officers and scientists. The five dead men were awarded the King's Medal and the RGS Polar Medal, and £74,000 (some £3½ million today) was raised by public donation.

The Lord Mayor of London had set up a Mansion House appeal, into which all monies collected were consolidated. The sum raised was sufficient to clear the expedition's outstanding debts (some £30,000) and to finance the publication of a complete record of the expedition's scientific findings to the tune of £17,500, with a similar sum going to permanent memorials. The expedition itself remained at the forefront of the public eye until the start of the First World War and beyond.

The two-volume history of the expedition was published as *Scott's Last Expedition* by Smith Elder in 1913, edited by Leonard Huxley. The first volume consisted of Scott's own graphic account, drawn directly from his own journals; meticulous and well-written, it is a remarkable literary achievement. The second volume, less successful as a concept and patchy in interest, is a multiple-author series of reports contributed by surviving members of the expedition – Cherry-Garrard as the sole survivor of the

Cape Crozier journey, Victor Campbell as leader of the Northern Party, the scientists on their particular fields of endeavour, and Harry Pennell as ship's captain.

The two volumes, intended to satisfy public demand, were produced at break-neck speed and lavishly illustrated with watercolours by Wilson and photographs by Ponting, Levick and others. The print run numbered 1,500 copies, priced at three guineas a set. The first edition sold out immediately; surprisingly it was never reprinted.

There remained the mammoth task of publishing the detailed scientific reports. Two separate bodies were involved. The specially constituted Publication Committee consisted of Major Leonard Darwin of the Royal Geographical Society, Sir Archibald Geikie of the Royal Society and the newly promoted Surgeon-Commander Edward Atkinson as senior expedition member; Colonel Lyons was made Honorary Editor. These four were responsible for publishing the extensive records kept and measurements taken by the scientific members of the team. Meteorology was entrusted to Dr George Simpson, gravity to Charles Wright, glaciology jointly to Wright and Priestley (this report became a classic tool for future scientists), physiography (four volumes) to Griffith Taylor, Priestley, Wright and Debenham, and auroras to Wright. The Trustees of the British Museum undertook the task of producing same of the other bound volumes – eight on zoology, two on geology and one on botany. The complete publishing programme, unbeknownst to most of those who financed it, was to stretch over fifty years.

Other accounts and memorials followed. Priestley's story of the Northern Party was published in 1914, Kathleen Scott's bronze sculpture of her husband was erected in Waterloo Place, and one of Wilson in sledging gear in Cheltenham; a plaque to Bowers was unveiled in Greenhithe, and a stained-glass window to Scott in Binton church near Stratford-upon-Avon. Ponting delivered his 'beautiful series of films and lantern slides' in London for ten indefatigable months until the outbreak of war.

In May 1914, Ponting was summoned again to Buckingham Palace, this time to show his kinematograph to the King and Queen and an array of royal and distinguished guests. 'His Majesty King George expressed to me the hope that it might be possible for every British boy to see the pictures – as the story of the Scott Expedition could not be known too widely among the youth of the nation, for it would help to promote the spirit of adventure that had made the Empire.' Many of those anonymous boys were followed to the Front by Ponting's photographs: he gave the army sets of his films, which he estimated were shown to over 100,000 officers and men.

For the individuals who had taken part, the expedition was soon relegated to the background of their lives. The officers and ratings were reclaimed by the navy or merchant marine, the scientists by their universities or research departments. Gran became an aviation pioneer (he was the first person to fly across the North Sea, in July 1914) and joined the Norwegian Flying Corps during the First World War.* Two of the civilians were still in its thrall – Ponting's career hinged for many years on his photographic work among the ice floes, and for Cherry-Garrard the expedition remained the high (and low) point of his long and frequently unhappy life.

Three sailors were also unable to shake off Antarctica, and immediately applied to join Shackleton's 1914 expedition. Able Seaman McLeod, a lowly member of the *Terra Nova* crew, became a fireman aboard *Endurance*, and achieved a strange kind of distinction when he succeeded in reviving Worsley, who had lapsed into a coma during the journey to Elephant Island, by a couple of well-aimed kicks to the back of his head. Tom Crean, in an uncanny repeat of his heroic walk to Cape Evans to save Teddy Evans, was one of those chosen by Shackleton to walk across South Georgia to Stromness in their desperate bid to bring help to the men trapped on Elephant Island. *Terra Nova*'s tough, squeaky-voiced bo'sun could not stay away either: 'The smell of the ice was as the breath of life to Alf Cheetham's nostrils,' wrote Ponting.

These three had to endure a double dose of suffering, for after their return from Shackleton's expedition they were pitchforked into the maritime hell of the First World War. Cheetham, having survived no fewer than three Antarctic ordeals – aboard *Discovery*, *Terra Nova* and *Endurance* – was torpedoed and drowned at the Battle of Jutland. Another *Terra Nova* casualty of the war was Rennick, so highly regarded by Teddy Evans and all the ship's crew. Saddest of all was Pennell, appointed Commander after the expedition; his certain prospects of a fine career were snuffed out at Jutland.

Atkinson, the doctor who had shown unexpected reserves of character and courage in Antarctica, revealed their depth and strength by his war record. He served aboard HMS *Vincent* at Gallipoli and in France, was awarded the DSO and three times mentioned in dispatches. His finest hour came in 1918 aboard HMS *Glatton*, when he continued to tend the injured in spite of being severely injured himself, a display of gallantry which earned him the Albert Medal. He received further injuries in France, and eventually lost an eye. In 1920 he won the rarely awarded Chadwick Gold Medal and Prize for his special work in promoting health in the navy. He died aged just forty-six in 1928.

In his light-hearted description of life aboard *Terra Nova*, Frank Debenham threw into sharp relief the metamorphosis of the wardroom

---

* After the war he returned to Norway and took charge of the unsuccessful attempt to locate Amundsen after his aeroplane had disappeared in the Arctic.

from a tangle of wrestling youths into a party of dignified and successful Establishment men. Thus the stocky little man who had come down the companion shouting, 'Hello girls, what's doing?' became in later life Lord Evans of the Broke, an admiral and a peer of the realm, 'while somewhere in the struggling heap were Charles Wright, later to be Director of the Admiralty Research Department, Raymond Priestley, now Vice-Chancellor of Birmingham University, and George Simpson, who became Director of the Meteorological Office'. Debenham himself ended up as Cambridge University's first Professor of Geography, while the gregarious Griff Taylor, who would certainly have featured in the tussle if he had been aboard at the time, went on to become Professor of Geography at the universities of Chicago and Toronto.

The lives and careers of the six men of the Northern Party were stamped with the expedition's hallmark of growth through hardship. Dickason and Browning were on active service during the war. Abbott, who had suffered a nervous breakdown on the journey home, was hospitalised for a period in Southampton, and as Levick had feared, was forced to leave the navy on account of his disabled hand. He joined the RAF, but in November 1926 died from pneumonia after losing his helmet and goggles on a flying trip. Priestley's harsh comment was: 'P.O. Abbott ... had no memory ... he was to lose his life through an illness that stemmed directly from this particular – not fault, but weakness.'

Victor Campbell, promoted Commodore on the Emergency List, had a 'good war' at Gallipoli (where he gained a DSO), in the Dover Patrol and in Russia; from 1919 to 1922 he commanded ships in the Atlantic Fleet. Having retired once at thirty-five, he did so again at forty-eight: in 1923 he found a new home, a new wife and new fishing grounds in Newfoundland. He died in 1956.

Raymond Priestley, who declared that Campbell's extreme shyness 'forced me into prominence as historian and public relations officer of the [Northern] party and eventually made me something of a specialist in polar lore', made good this newly released assertiveness to climb the academic ladder. During the First World War he worked in wireless and signalling; after it he accumulated a variety of fellowships and other rewards and appointments – Vice-Chancellor of Melbourne and Birmingham universities, a knight of the realm and President of the Royal Geographical Society. His most lasting memorial is as co-founder with Frank Debenham in 1926 of the Scott Polar Research Institute in Cambridge. Priestley had even closer ties with two other members of the expedition – Charles Wright married his sister Edith, and Griffith Taylor his other sister Doris. He himself found romance in New Zealand, marrying Phyllis Boyd in 1915, and died in 1972.

Murray Levick's career took an unexpected series of twists, as might be expected from a man who brought chewing the mental cud to a fine art. He, like Campbell and Atkinson, found himself in Gallipoli during the war, becoming Fleet Surgeon in 1916. In 1918 he married Audrey Beeton, daughter of Sir Mayson Beeton. For several years thereafter he pursued his naval career, and, harking back to his athletic youth, helped to found the Royal Naval Rugby Union, but his interests later became focused on two quite different things. The first was helping children to find a meaning and purpose in life, and to this end he established the British Schools Exploring Society in 1932. This was essentially an early version of Col. John Blashford-Snell's Operations Drake and Raleigh, and Levick himself led many expeditions to then-unknown parts of the world. He also served on the council of two associations devoted to furthering the physical training of youth. His second preoccupation was with physical rehabilitation after illness or injury, and in that capacity he worked in several hospitals and sat on committees of public bodies. He leaned more and more towards the ideals of service and self-fulfilment that Scott himself espoused. He remained actively involved with the British Schools Exploring Society to the end of his life, with a hiatus during the Second World War when he worked for the naval intelligence service (Scott would have been amazed). He was also concerned with the training of commandos, and – in much the same spirit as his earlier enthusiasm for bizarre experiments – was in on a scheme to wall up two men in the Rock of Gibraltar for up to seven years in the case of the colony falling into enemy hands. In 1942 the Royal Geographical Society awarded him its Beck Grant for services to exploration.

Levick died in Budleigh Salterton, Devon, in 1956, aged seventy-nine. The little seaside town has remained virtually unchanged ever since; a period-piece Agatha Christie thriller was filmed effortlessly on location there for that very reason. He did not live in one of the villas rising in terraces behind the town, but he would feel perfectly at home there now. He could be the elderly man progressing, stately as a galleon, up the narrow street flanked by small shops and thronged with gossiping acquaintances, making for the cliffside golf course overlooking the Channel. Or he might be spotted setting off in his dinghy for an hour or two of mackerel fishing, inspecting his crab and lobster pots off the pebble beach, or prawning among the seaweed-covered rocks beneath the red cliffs of Sandy Bay. Raleigh's birthplace is some three miles away; a blue plaque at Budleigh Salterton commemorates the fact that Sir John Everett Millais painted his *Boyhood of Raleigh* while living in The Octagon facing out to sea. It is a fitting spot for an ordinary but remarkable naval man to have ended his days.

25. Departure from Inexpressible Island.

26. Arrival at Cape Evans

4. The Northern Party at Cape Adare. Standing, left to right: PO George Abbott, Able Seaman Harry Dickason, PO Frank Browning; seated, left to right: Raymond Priestley (geologist), Lt Victor Campbell, Dr Murray Levick.

# Epilogue

Three Antarctic conversation pieces.

In the first, six men are gathered in front of a wooden hut. The focus is on the three gleaming figures on the left. Standing to attention, Abbott is the Adonis in a white jacket, more cruise-liner steward than serving seaman. Priestley and Campbell sit relaxed, educated, polished and self-confident. The three on the right, shadowy and darker-clad, are hunched together. At the rear Dickason and Browning seem diminished; in front Levick squints at the camera, simian and tight-lipped. The lower orders stand behind, the officers command the foreground.

Compare this traditional grouping with the second photograph, where the six have just emerged into the fresh air like the prisoners in Beethoven's *Fidelio*, bearded, blackened and blubber-stained. They are survivors. Abbott remains broad-shouldered and self-confident. Campbell, neat-bearded and dainty-footed, is noticeably less scruffy than the rest. Dickason is ever the rude mechanical, and the lean and gangling Priestley wears his rags like an academic gown donned in a hurry. Levick is still as wide as a barn door; the thin and other-worldly Browning hovers like a grimy and unkempt Angel of the Annunciation at the edge of the company. Officers and men are interleaved – the traditional order has broken down.

In the third portrait the ranks are again divided, left and right. All have aged – tidied up, they look more vulnerable than before. Dickason's beard is white: he could be his own father, and Abbott has lost his startling good looks. Only Browning and Priestley loll comfortably, Browning's grin exuding the sheer joy of being alive. It is the turn of Campbell to appear wizen-faced and shrunken. Levick stands confidently upright, staring directly at the camera.

Three stages in a journey. The men's outer shells, thanks largely to Levick, have been preserved 'fat and fit' to journey's end. It is the evolution of their psyches and personalities that has been brutally telescoped into a couple of years. They have already undergone the hardening and ageing process to which the soldiers of the Great War are soon to be subjected.

There are two famous photographs of Wilson, Bowers and Cherry-Garrard taken before and after their Cape Crozier journey. Ponting wrote then: 'Their looks haunted me for days. Once before, I had seen similar expressions on men's faces – when some half-starved Russian prisoners . . . were being taken to Japan.' But the 'worst journey in the world' took just over a month. The Northern Party's Calvary lasted for nine months. The difference between the two sets of photographs and the two kinds of experience is that the one depicts suffering, the other endurance.

# An Antarctic Gazetteer

The first officially backed British expedition to Antarctica was Captain Cook's in 1772-75. Thereafter, as whaling trips and voyages of exploration multiplied during the nineteenth century, distinctive geographical features were named by successive expedition leaders. At first the adoption of names was a casual, *ad hoc* affair, as landmarks were pencilled into diaries, charts and maps as territorial markers and *aides-mémoire*. In Britain this somewhat haphazard procedure was not put on an official basis until 1945, when the Antarctic Place Names Committee was set up and ten years later placed under the umbrella of the Foreign Office (now the Foreign and Commonwealth Office). The Committee meets twice yearly and includes representatives of the Royal Geographical Society, the British Antarctic Survey and the Scott Polar Research Institute. Interestingly, however, the mix of names – patriotic, judicious and idiosyncratic – remains much the same today as during the time of Cook and Ross.

The system has always been both stratified and flexible, the names sometimes grand and sometimes humdrum. 'First-order' features such as whole regions, coasts, seas, plateaux, mountain ranges and major glaciers are dedicated, then as now, to polar heroes or major public figures: King Edward VII Land, Ross Sea, Drygalski Ice Tongue. 'Second-order' features – peninsulas, large bays, prominent peaks and capes – fall to slightly less prestigious polar explorers or scientists, or those more peripheral to the expedition in question: Mount Melbourne, Cape Adare. 'Third-order' features include hills, rocks, points and coves, and are consigned to the minor players: Evans Coves, Smith Inlet. In the early days there was always room for an expedition sponsor: Sir George Newnes (a Beaverbrook or Rupert Murdoch of his day) was rewarded with a glacier and his wife with a bay. Shackleton's sponsor, Sir William Beardmore, was likewise awarded a glacier. In addition there are inanimate names. These might commemorate organisations (Admiralty Mountains), events personal to a particular expedition (Relay Bay, Butter Point), or ships (Mt Erebus, Terra Nova Bay).

The Ross Sea area falls under the aegis of the New Zealand Antarctic Place Names Committee, although in the heroic age of polar exploration the British regarded it as their own and named most of the features they espied. The names in the list which follows are principally those laid down as a result of Captain Sir James Clark Ross's 1839-43 expedition aboard HMS *Erebus* and HMS *Terror*, Carsten Borchgrevink's *Southern Cross* expedition of 1898-1900, Captain R.F. Scott's *Discovery* expedition of 1901-4, Sir Ernest Shackleton's *Nimrod* expedition of 1907-9, and Scott's last expedition aboard *Terra Nova* in 1910-1913. Most of the names would have been chosen by the expedition leader, although there was some leeway. For example, Dr Edward Wilson recorded in his diary on 7 September 1904, as the *Discovery* expedition drew to a close: 'Captain spoke of many things to us. One was about the names of new bits of land, and I asked that "Cambridge" should be given to something as there are two Cambridge men on the expedition. He agreed to mention it and told me my name was being given to "Cape I", the fine southernmost cape we ran against on the southern journey.'

The result is a hagiography as evocative to polar enthusiasts as the daily shipping forecast is to its many devotees. The chunk of Antarctica which is the setting for this book yields a roll-call of names representing not only many of the best known characters in polar exploration but also some eminent (and sometimes forgottten) figures in seventy years of British history.

| | |
|---|---|
| Adam, Mount | See Admiralty Mountains. |
| Adare, Cape | Prominent cape with perpendicular cliff 1,000 feet high, on extreme E point of Robertson Bay. Discovered and named by Ross for his friend and supporter Viscount Adare MP. |
| Admiralty Mountains | Mountain range extending for 145 miles along N and NE coast of Victoria Land, with peaks above 10,000 feet in height and including Mts Sabine, Minto and Adam. Named by Ross for three Lords Commissioners of Admiralty. |
| Balloon Bight | Indentation (no longer present) in Bay of Whales where experimental balloon ascent was made by Scott on *Discovery* expedition. |
| Barrow, Cape | NW extremity of Robertson Bay. Named by Ross for Sir John Barrow, Secretary of the Admiralty and founder of the Royal Geographical Society. |
| Beardmore Glacier | Valley glacier over 100 miles long descending from polar plateau to Ross Ice Shelf. Discovered by *Nimrod* expedition and named for Sir William Beardmore, Scottish industrialist and expedition patron. |
| Bergs, Bay of (Berg Bay) | Natural harbour indenting front of Ross Ice Shelf N of Roosevelt Island. Named by *Nimrod* expedition for number of bergs observed there. |
| Bernacchi, Cape | Low rocky promontory forming N entrance point to New Harbour, Victoria Land. Discovered by *Southern Cross* expedition and named for Louis Bernacchi, its physicist. |
| Bird, Cape | Precipitous cape at N extremity of Ross Island. Discovered by Ross and named for Lt Edward Bird of *Erebus*. |
| Biscoe Bay | Wide bay beneath Alexandra Mountains in King Edward |

|                      | VII Land at E end of Ross Ice Shelf. Named by *Discovery* expedition for John Biscoe, British Antarctic explorer. |
| --- | --- |
| Boomerang Glacier | Glacier about 1 mile wide at its mouth flowing southwards from slopes of Mt Dickason. Named (possibly by Priestley) on account of its shape. |
| Butter Point | Glacier terminal giving access to Ferrar Glacier and high Antarctic plateau. Name derived from tin of butter depoted there by Scott on *Discovery* expedition. |
| Campbell Glacier | Glacier about 60 miles long, flowing S from W slopes of Mt Melbourne and discharging into Terra Nova Bay. Originally named Melbourne Glacier for British Prime Minister and subsequently renamed for Lt Victor Campbell, leader of *Terra Nova* Northern Party. |
| Colbeck, Cape | Ice-covered cape forming NW extremity of Edward VII Peninsula, Marie Byrd Land. Discovered by *Discovery* expedition and named for Lt William Colbeck, captain of relief ship *Morning* and previously magnetician on *Southern Cross* expedition. |
| Corner Glacier | Steep glacier about 1 mile wide descending from W slope of Mt Dickason. Named by *Terra Nova* Northern Party for its location at corner of Nansen Ice Sheet. |
| Coulman Island | Small ice-covered island about 18 miles long and 1 mile wide in western Ross Sea. Discovered by Ross and named for Thomas Coulman, father of Ross's fiancée. |
| Crozier, Cape | Cape at E extremity of McMurdo Sound, E of Mt Terror on Ross Island. Named by Ross for captain of *Terror*. |
| Drygalski Ice Tongue | Ice tongue about 30 miles long flowing into Ross Sea, fed by David and Larsen Glaciers. Discovered by *Discovery* expedition and named for Dr Erich von Drygalski, contemporary German explorer. |
| Dugdale Glacier | Glacier about 25 miles long descending from Admiralty Mountains into Robertson Bay, where it merges with Murray Glacier NW of Duke of York Island. Named by *Southern Cross* expedition for Frank Dugdale, expedition patron. |
| Duke of York Island | Mountainous, ice-free island 22 miles long near S end of Robertson Bay. First charted by *Southern Cross* expedition and named by them. |
| Dunlop Island | Small island about $\frac{1}{2}$ mile wide lying off Wilson Piedmont Glacier of Victoria Land. Charted by *Nimrod* expedition and named for H.J.L. Dunlop, ship's chief engineer. |
| Erebus, Mount | 12,450-foot peak NE of Cape Evans forming summit of |

Ross Island. Antarctica's major active volcano. Named by Ross for one of his two ships.

Evans Cove(s)

Three small coves on E side of Inexpressible Island. First charted by *Nimrod* expedition and presumably named for F.P. Evans, ship's captain.

Evans, Cape

Rocky cape on W side of Ross Island. Discovered by *Discovery* expedition and originally named The Skuary. Renamed for Lt Edward Evans, second-in-command of *Terra Nova* expedition.

Ferrar Glacier

Glacier 35 miles long flowing from plateau of Victoria Land W of Royal Society Range to New Harbour in McMurdo Sound. Discovered by *Discovery* expedition and named for Hartley T. Ferrar, expedition geologist.

Geikie Inlet

Extensive inlet lying on S edge of Drygalski Ice Tongue. Discovered by *Discovery* expedition and named for Sir Archibald Geikie, Scottish geologist and President of Royal Society.

Glacier Tongue (Erebus Glacier Tongue)

Terminal of one of main glaciers fringing Ross Island, extending into McMurdo Sound. First seen on *Discovery* expedition, it had disappeared by 1912.

Granite Harbour

Bay about 11 miles wide marking seaward end of deep valley between Cape Archer and Cape Roberts and backed by high mountains. Discovered by *Discovery* expedition and named for granite boulders found onshore.

Hut Point

Small promontory NW of Cape Armitage on S end of Ross Island. Discovered and named by *Discovery* expedition, which built stores hut there. Later used as advance base by *Nimrod* and *Terra Nova* expeditions. Hut preserved today by New Zealand government as historic monument.

Inexpressible Island

Island about 7 miles long forming W shore of Evans Cove in Terra Nova Bay at outer edge of Nansen Ice Sheet. Named by *Terra Nova* Northern Party to convey their opinion of it.

King Edward VII Land (Edward VII Peninsula)

Peninsula extending NW from Marie Byrd Land into Ross Sea between Sulzberger Bay and NE corner of Ross Ice Shelf. Named by *Discovery* expedition for British monarch.

Koettlitz Glacier

Large glacier at SW corner of McMurdo Sound, parallel to Ferrar Glacier. Named by *Discovery* expedition for Reginald Koettlitz, its chief of scientific staff.

Lady Newnes Bay

Bay about 60 miles long in western Ross Sea, W of Coulman Island on E coast of Victoria Land. Named by

*Southern Cross* expedition for wife of Sir George Newnes Bt, the expedition's benefactor.

| | |
|---|---|
| Larsen, Mount | 5,117–foot peak at S side of mouth of Reeves Glacier, opposite Terra Nova Bay. Discovered on *Discovery* expedition, and named for Capt. C.A. Larsen, Norwegian explorer and captain of whaler *Jason* on 1892–93 expedition. |
| McMurdo Sound | Stretch of water about 40 miles long and wide, bounded on W by Victoria Land and on E by Ross Island. Named by Ross for Archibald McMurdo, first lieutenant of *Terror*. |
| Melbourne Glacier | See Campbell Glacier. |
| Melbourne, Mount | Conspicuous volcanic cone 8,950 feet high between Wood Bay and Terra Nova Bay. Discovered by Ross and named for Prime Minister, Lord Melbourne. |
| Minto, Mount | See Admiralty Mountains. |
| Murray Glacier | Glacier about 20 miles long draining seawards from Admiralty Mountains on W side of Robertson Bay. Named by *Southern Cross* expedition for Sir John Murray, naturalist on *Challenger* expedition of 1872–76. |
| Nansen, Mount | 8,988-foot peak opposite Terra Nova Bay. Discovered on *Discovery* expedition and named for contemporary Norwegian Arctic explorer Fridtjof Nansen. |
| Nordenskjöld Ice Tongue | Glacier tongue about 5 miles wide extending E from Mawson Glacier into Ross Sea. Named by *Discovery* expedition for Dr Otto Nordenskjöld, contemporary Swedish geographer and Antarctic explorer. |
| North, Cape | Large snow-capped bluff on W side of Nielsen Fjord on N coast of Victoria Land. Presumed to be the one observed by Ross, and given this name. |
| Penelope Point | Promontory on W side of Robertson Bay. Named by *Terra Nova* Northern Party for nickname given to Lt Harry Pennell, captain of *Terra Nova*. |
| Priestley Glacier | Glacier about 60 miles long, originating at edge of Victoria Land plateau and draining SE to enter N end of Nansen Ice Sheet. Named by *Terra Nova* Northern Party for geologist Raymond Priestley. |
| Reeves Glacier | Broad glacier descending between Mt Larsen and present-day Eisenhower Range to merge with Nansen Ice Sheet. Discovered by *Nimrod* expedition and probably named for William Reeves, New Zealand politician and Agent-General for New Zealand, 1896–1909. |
| Relay Bay | Arm of Robertson Bay bounded on one side by Penelope |

|  | Point. First visited by *Terra Nova* Northern Party, and named by them after having to relay sledges owing to heavy pressure ridges encountered there. |
|---|---|
| Relief Inlet | Narrow inlet N of Drygalski Ice Tongue at SW corner of Terra Nova Bay, first reached on *Nimrod* expedition by Professor T. Edgeworth David's South Magnetic Pole Party and named by them for emotion engendered by delayed rescue. |
| Ridley Beach | Triangular shingle bank built up by deposits trapped by projecting Cape Adare. Used by *Southern Cross* expedition and named by Carsten Borchgrevink for his mother, claimed to be descendant of Marian martyr Bishop Ridley. |
| Robertson Bay | Bay about 23 miles wide and 25 miles long between Cape Adare and Cape Barrow. Named by Ross for John Robertson, surgeon on *Terror*. |
| Roberts, Cape | Cape at S side of entrance to Granite Harbour. Discovered by Professor T. Edgeworth David's South Magnetic Pole Party on *Nimrod* expedition and named for William Roberts, assistant zoologist and expedition cook. |
| Ross Ice Shelf | Vast ice shelf occupying entire S part of Ross Sea embayment and ending at its seaward edge in cliff edge about 400 miles long. Named Great Ice Barrier by Ross and Ross Ice Barrier by *Nimrod* expedition. |
| Ross Island | Entirely volcanic island on E side of McMurdo Sound extending 43 miles from Cape Bird on N to Cape Armitage on S, and similar distance from Cape Royds on W to Cape Crozier on E. Discovered by Ross and named for him by *Discovery* expedition. |
| Royds, Cape | Cape forming W extremity of Ross Island, facing McMurdo Sound. Named for Lt Charles Royds, meteorologist with *Discovery* expedition, and subsequently site of *Nimrod* expedition's base. |
| Sabine, Mount | See Admiralty Mountains. |
| Sir George Newnes Glacier (Newnes Glacier) | Steep valley glacier flowing into S side of Robertson Bay. Named for sponsor of *Southern Cross* expedition. |
| Smith Inlet | Bay 4 miles wide at NW corner of Robertson Bay. Named by Ross for Alexander J. Smith, mate of *Erebus*. |
| Taylor Glacier | Glacier about 35 miles long flowing from Victoria Land plateau SW of McMurdo Sound. Discovered by *Discovery* expedition and thought by them to be part of Ferrar Glacier. Renamed by Scott for T. Griffith Taylor, geologist with *Terra Nova* expedition after his discovery that these were two adjacent glaciers. |

| | |
|---|---|
| Terror, Mount | Extinct 10,595-foot volcano on Ross Island E of Mt Erebus. Named by Ross for one of his two ships. |
| Tripp Island | Ice-covered island in centre of Tripp Bay, 2 miles offshore. Discovered by *Nimrod* expedition and named for Leonard Tripp of New Zealand, friend and supporter of Shackleton. |
| Victoria Land | Mainly ice-covered plateau lying on W side of Ross Sea bounded by mountain range 50–100 miles wide and rising to elevations of about 14,750 feet. Discovered and named by Ross for British Queen. |
| Warning Glacier | Glacier on W side of Adare peninsular discharging into Robertson Bay. Named by *Southern Cross* expedition because snowcloud sweeping over glacier heralded southerly gales at Cape Adare. |
| Whales, Bay of | Natural harbour indenting front of Ross Ice Shelf N of Roosevelt Island. Named by *Nimrod* expedition because of number of whales observed there. |
| Wood Bay | Large bay lying between Cape Johnson and Cape Washington. Discovered by Ross and named for Lt James Wood of *Erebus*. |

# Acknowledgements

The idea for this book came from Richard Kossow, who generously allowed me to quote from unpublished manuscripts and to reproduce photographs in his collection. It was Peter King who set the whole project going and shared with me his knowledge of Antarctic heroes, which encompasses both Scott and Shackleton.

Thereafter, the Scott Polar Research Institute (SPRI) proved, as always, an invaluable source of reference and scholarship – my sincere thanks go to Robert Headland, and especially to Shirley Sawtell for being endlessly courteous and immediately responsive. I am grateful for permission to quote from expedition diaries and letters housed there, and also to reproduce photographs from the Institute's remarkable photographic archive, thanks to assistance by Lucy Martin. A chance conversation with John Reid set me off on a useful line of enquiry.

The voices of the six members of the Northern Party speak loudly and clearly in this book. Four of these – Levick, Abbott, Browning and Dickason – do so publicly for the first time. Three of Levick's handwritten diaries are held by the SPRI, and a further diary by him was made available to me by the Neil Silverman Collection. My thanks go to Mr Silverman and to Nick Lambourn of Christie's, who kindly arranged for this to happen. The television producer Louise Panton put me in touch with George Abbott's niece, Mrs Ann Evans, and his great-niece Sue O'Doherty, who lent me a copy of his expedition diary. The diaries of Browning and Dickason are both lodged with the SPRI, as are those of Raymond Priestley, parts of which were quoted in his book *Antarctic Adventure*, published by C. Hurst and Co. in 1914. I am also grateful to David Walton and Bluntisham Books for permission to quote from *The Wicked Mate: The Antarctic Diary of Victor Campbell*, and to the Memorial University of Newfoundland, who hold Campbell's personal archive.

Mrs Angela Mathias and Hugh Turner were most generous in allowing me to quote from Apsley Cherry-Garrard's *The Worst Journey in the World*, without reference to which no book on Antarctica can hope to be complete. Sara Wheeler's splendid biography, *Cherry* (published by Jonathan Cape in 2002), gave me valuable insights, and she kindly tied up one particular loose end for me. I am grateful also to the following publishers for permission to reproduce certain passages: Bluntisham Books for *The Quiet Land: The Antarctic Diaries of Frank Debenham* and *With Scott: The Silver Lining* by Griffith Taylor; Heinemann for *Antarctic Penguins* by Murray Levick; HarperCollins for *South with Scott* by Admiral Sir Edward Evans and *The Lord of the*

*Rings* by J.R.R. Tolkien; Weidenfeld & Nicolson for *Scott of the Antarctic* by Elspeth Huxley and *Scott and Amundsen* by Roland Huntford; Ohio State University Press for *Silas: The Antarctic Diaries of Charles S. Wright*; the National Maritime Museum for *The Norwegian with Scott – Tryggve Gran's Antarctic Diary*; Yale University Press for *The Coldest March* by Susan Solomon; John Murray for *The Life of Sir Clements Markham* by Admiral Sir Albert H. Markham, *In the Antarctic* by Frank Debenham and *The South Pole: An Account of the Norwegian Antarctic Expedition in the 'Fram', 1910-1912* by Roald Amundsen; Gerald Duckworth and Co for *The Great White South* by Herbert Ponting; Faber & Faber for *Waiting for Godot* by Samuel Beckett; the Royal Geographical Society for passages from issues of *The Geographical Journal*; and the Scott Polar Research Institute for items from *The Polar Record*, *The South Polar Times* and *The Adélie Mail*. The picture of the officers of Scott's Last Expedition assembled at Buckingham Palace is reproduced by permission of the Illustrated London News Picture Library.

The staffs of several libraries – the London Library, the Bodleian, Oxford Central, the Wellcome Institute, the Royal Pharmaceutical Society and the National Maritime Museum in Greenwich – have given me much help. The Nasjonalbiblioteket in Oslo have allowed me to quote from the diaries of Amundsen and Gjertsen, and the Norsk Sjøfartsmuseum that of Nilsen. I am indebted to Anne C. Kjelling, Head Librarian of the Norwegian Nobel Institute, for facilitating this and for translating diary entries into impeccable English.

Other people have given me the benefit of their specialist knowledge. Harold King, former librarian of the SPRI, helped with knotty problems of topography and nomenclature and allowed me to reproduce as part of a gazetteer of place names some of his notes on various Antarctic features from *The Wicked Mate*, of which he was the editor. I am grateful also to Fenella Leigh of the UK Antarctic Place Names Committee and Caroline Burgess of the Permanent Committee on Geographical Names. Dr Geoffrey Hattersley-Smith shed light with enthusiasm and authority on many aspects of Antarctica. Eddie Parkinson elucidated some nautical mysteries, and Alastair Fothergill of the BBC Natural History Unit some ornithological ones. Neil Hyslop drew the map detailing the Northern Party's peregrinations, and Angie Hipkin supplied the index.

At Pimlico, Will Sulkin provided support, encouragement and leeway, Jörg Hensgen tempered justice with mercy, and Poppy Hampson fielded every tiresome query and request with exemplary patience and efficiency. Eugenie Todd was an admirable and percipient copy editor. It goes without saying that friends and family, who have borne the brunt of this book, have my greatest thanks, especially Tom, Janie and my father, who supported me in every possible way throughout. My neighbours Neil and Anita Owen have given me both practical and moral support. Anybody I have neglected to acknowledge by name, you know who you are and how grateful I am.

# Index